PURIFYING THE LAND
OF THE PURE

PURIFYING THE LAND OF THE PURE

A HISTORY OF PAKISTAN'S
RELIGIOUS MINORITIES

FARAHNAZ ISPAHANI

OXFORD
UNIVERSITY PRESS

OXFORD
UNIVERSITY PRESS

Oxford University Press is a department of the University of Oxford. It furthers
the University's objective of excellence in research, scholarship, and education
by publishing worldwide. Oxford is a registered trade mark of Oxford University
Press in the UK and certain other countries.

Published in the United States of America by Oxford University Press
198 Madison Avenue, New York, NY 10016, United States of America.

© Oxford University Press 2017

Library of Congress Cataloging-in-Publication Data
Names: Ispahani, Farahnaz, author.
Title: Purifying the land of the pure : a history of Pakistan's religious
minorities / Farahnaz Ispahani.
Description: New York, NY : Oxford University Press, 2017.
Identifiers: LCCN 2016030376| ISBN 9780190621650 (hardcover : alk. paper) |
ISBN 9780190621674 (epub)
Subjects: LCSH: Religious minorities—Pakistan. | Pakistan—Politics and
government—1971–1988. | Pakistan—Politics and government—1988–
Classification: LCC BL2035.5.R45 I87 2017 | DDC 305.6095491—dc23
LC record available at https://lccn.loc.gov/2016030376

1 3 5 7 9 8 6 4 2

Printed by Sheridan Books, Inc., United States of America

CONTENTS

Introduction

ON MARCH 27, 2016, several Pakistani Christian families gathered at a park in Lahore to celebrate Easter Sunday when a suicide bomber detonated ten kilograms of explosives and metal ball bearings between two children's rides. The attack, claimed by Jamaat-ul-Ahrar, an offshoot of the Pakistani Taliban, killed seventy-three people, including twenty-nine children. Of these children, the youngest was merely two years old and the oldest was sixteen.[1]

A Jamaat-ul-Ahrar spokesperson, Ehsanullah Ehsan, announced that his Islamist militant group had targeted Christians as a message to Prime Minister Nawaz Sharif that they had entered Lahore—the prime minister's hometown.[2] The terrorists wanted the government to halt military operations against their safe havens in Pakistan's remote tribal areas bordering Afghanistan.

The Easter Sunday attack had been preceded a year earlier by twin suicide bombings at churches in Lahore's Youhanabad area, which killed at least fifteen people and sparked violent protests across the city by the Christian minority. That terrorists chose to target religious minorities, including their children, to caution the government reflected the vulnerability of Pakistan's already embattled religious minorities.

Pakistan, a country created in the name of Islam, has witnessed some of the worst persecution and discrimination of religious minorities in a world that is increasingly becoming unsafe for minorities. The Human Rights Watch World Report 2016 cited examples of religion-based violations of human rights from several countries, including those in

Europe and North America that are otherwise known for defending the Universal Declaration of Human Rights. "In Europe and the United States, a polarizing us-versus-them rhetoric has moved from the political fringe to the mainstream," Human Rights Watch warned. In its view, "Blatant Islamophobia and shameless demonizing of refugees" appear to have become "the currency of an increasingly assertive politics of intolerance."[3]

Religious freedom, and the right of religious minorities to live in peace, is being threatened by communal majoritarianism, which has been at the heart of Pakistan's policies over the years. This trend reflects the majority's insistence that the religious minorities practice their faith and culture within limits prescribed by the majority. It contravenes the United Nations Universal Declaration of Human Rights, which proclaimed in 1948 that "everyone has the right to freedom of thought, conscience and religion; this right includes freedom to change his religion or belief, and freedom, either alone or in community with others and in public or private, to manifest his religion or belief in teaching, practice, worship and observance."[4] That declaration represented the aspirations of a world that had just gone through the horrors of World War II and did not want further conflict on religious and ideological grounds.

Now, however, terrorist organizations acting in the name of faith are destroying religious diversity in significant parts of the Middle East, Sub-Saharan Africa, and Asia. The atrocities perpetrated by the Islamic State in Iraq and Syria (ISIS) are widely known. These include mass executions and forced conversions alongside the kidnapping, enslavement, and rape of thousands of non-Muslim women and children.

A United Nations human rights report in March 2015 noted that ISIS had "committed genocide, war crimes and crimes against humanity in its attacks against ethnic and religious groups in the country."[5] Other factions involved in the Syrian civil war have fared no better. The regime of Bashar al-Assad is accused of targeting Sunni Muslims while Jabhat al-Nusra conducted targeted executions of religious leaders, including seven Druze clerics in Dara Province and a Jesuit priest in Homs.

Regimes, such as those in Saudi Arabia and Sudan, continue to inflict harsh punishments for "apostasy" and "blasphemy." In Iran hundreds of Bahais, Christians, Sufi Muslims, Yarsanis, and Shia Muslims are in prison for professing a doctrine not approved of by the clerical regime. Religious conflict has often driven the politics of Lebanon whereas the Christian Copts in Egypt have come under attack by religious extremists.

Boko Haram has targeted non-Muslims in northern Nigeria, Cameroon, Chad, and Niger, forcibly kidnapping, converting, enslaving, and selling young women and girls. In one such incident on April 14, 2014, Boko Haram kidnapped more than two hundred mostly Christian girls from Chibok, Borno State, sold them into slavery, and forcibly converted them to their version of Islam,[6] which many mainstream Muslims find offensive.

The lack of tolerance in parts of the Muslim world has been accompanied by a resurgence of hate groups in western countries. A rise in anti-Semitic attacks has been reported across Europe, especially France and Germany, resulting in assaults on institutions, as well as desecration of monuments and cemeteries.[7] Although western nations have constitutional and legal mechanisms in place to restrain and even punish perpetrators of religiously motivated attacks, it is not always easy to shut down "hate speech" amidst controversies over freedom of expression.

India, the world's largest democracy, also faces the dilemma of having a secular constitution but a religiously divided public. Sectarian and communal hysteria, aroused to secure votes for Hindu nationalist political groups, is proving difficult to contain after elections. Having taken pride in their country's secular character for decades, Indians are now having to deal with incidents such as extremist Hindus attacking (and in some cases killing) Muslims and Christians over eating beef. Hindus deem the cow sacred but few believe its protection should involve violating the sanctity of human life.

Religious minorities in Russia and Central Asia—ruled by ostensibly secular authoritarian regimes—also face threats. For example, in eastern Ukraine, Russian-backed separatists kidnapped, tortured, and threatened Protestants, Catholics, and Jews. Russia's extremism law is open to abuse by allowing prosecution for "inciting religious discord even in the absence of any threat or act of violence."[8] Merely professing beliefs different to those sanctioned by the state could land an individual in a Russian prison. In the Central Asian republics, former communist apparatchiks continue to suppress all public manifestations of religion.

Burma is also prominent among other major violators of the idea of religious freedom. It refuses to protect the rights of its religious minorities, especially the Rohingya Muslims and Christians. Policies in place in Burma impede land ownership by Muslims in most parts of the country. Radical Buddhist monks have incited violence against the Rohingya Muslims through sermons widely circulated in print media and via videos as well as the Internet.[9] In Sri Lanka, mosques and churches have been attacked by Buddhist mobs and local law enforcement authorities are often complicit.

The Chinese constitution states that all citizens "enjoy freedom of religious belief" but that is not true in practice. The Chinese government officially recognizes only five religions: Buddhism, Catholicism, Daoism, Islam, and Protestantism. Still, Beijing has cracked down on Christians, Buddhists, and especially Tibetan Buddhists and Uighur Muslims. The Chinese government has consistently cracked down on Christianity in China but now even state-sanctioned Christian churches are being targeted. China's Uighur Muslims continue to face discrimination and suppression, with Xinjiang Province banning the practice of religion in government buildings and even wearing the veil in public. Tibetan Buddhist monasteries continue to be targeted for being associated with separatism and pro-independence activities.[10]

North Korea is another state that does not allow freedom of religion. State-sanctioned Christian churches maintain a token presence in Pyongyang, and North Koreans who live near the Chinese border practice their faiths furtively. Stories of Christian missionaries being detained and tortured for antistate religious acts are not uncommon.[11]

This shrinking space for religious diversity all over the world provides the context for understanding the situation in Pakistan, a Muslim-majority country that is often in the news for violence stemming from religious causes. Pakistan was carved out of British India as a homeland for the subcontinent's Muslims—a majority enclave designed to protect against minority status in an undivided India. It started out as a modern state led by secular individuals but has gradually descended into endless religious arguments and sectarian violence. Pakistan's history, particularly the history of its treatment of religious minorities, is a cautionary tale about how politicizing religion can lead to unintended consequences.

When Pakistan was created on August 14, 1947, the azan that day was issued five times on loudspeakers by Shias, Sunnis, and Ahmadis in the new country's capital, Karachi. That call to prayer was echoed outside of mosques too, for Karachi was home to a religiously diverse community. Its architecture reflected this: along with mosques of various Muslim denominations, there were Catholic and Protestant churches, a Jewish synagogue, and Parsi (Zoroastrian) fire temples, as well as Jain and Hindu temples devoted to various deities where worshippers congregated for prayers according to their own religions. Religious holidays were observed openly and often across communities.

Sixty-seven years later, Karachi is no longer the capital. The country's federal government now conducts its business from a purpose-built capital, Islamabad, whose very name suggests an intrinsic relationship between Pakistan and Islam. Karachi's synagogue was demolished in July 1988—reportedly on the direct orders of General Zia, Pakistan's military dictator at the time—to make way for a shopping mall. Karachi's last professed Jew, an eighty-eight-year-old woman, died in 2006. Most of its churches have shut down, and the few that remain have a dwindling number of worshippers. Many Pakistani Christians have immigrated to North America or Australia. Most Jain and Hindu temples have either been destroyed or taken over by squatters or landgrabbers and property developers. The Parsi population has also declined, though its temples still exist. Walls along the road from the Karachi airport to the city are painted with graffiti declaring Shias to be *kuffar* (unbelievers). Shia and non-Muslim families often have armed security guards, if they can afford them, or avoid calling attention to themselves.

The Muslim call to prayer no longer sounds from Ahmadi places of worship. The community has been declared non-Muslim through an amendment to the Pakistani constitution. Ahmadis are forbidden from describing themselves as Muslims, from using the term "mosque" for their places of worship, and from issuing the azan before prayers. Furthermore, Ahmadis risk a stiff jail sentence for violating ordinances that forbid them from any act that might identify them as followers of Islam.

To say that Pakistan's religious minorities are under attack is a self-evident truth. According to the independent Human Rights Commission of Pakistan (HRCP), "pervasive intolerance [is] widely tolerated" in the country, and the "religious and sectarian minorities [pay] the price for that with their blood."[12] The commission's director, I. A. Rehman, asserts that "Pakistan continues to offer evidence of its lack of respect for the rights of religious minorities." He attributes this to "the virus of intolerance" that he maintains "has infested the Pakistani people's minds." Human rights advocates like Rehman demand "visible action to end abuse of minorities' rights" instead of the "half-truths and subterfuge in defending the State" that they feel have been consistently employed by Pakistan officials over the years.[13]

Pakistani laws, especially ones that deal with blasphemy, deny or interfere with the practice of minority faiths. Religious minorities are targets of legal as well as social discrimination. Most significantly, in recent years, Pakistan has witnessed some of the worst organized violence against religious minorities since Partition. Over an eighteen-month period covering 2012 and part of 2013, at least two hundred incidents of sectarian violence were reported; these incidents led to more than seven hundred deaths and 1100 seriously wounded.

Many of those targeted for violence during this period were Shia Muslim citizens, who are deemed part of Pakistan's Muslim majority under its constitution and laws. During the same year-and-a-half period in 2012–2013, Shias were subject to seventy-seven attacks, including suicide terrorist bombings during Shia religious observances. However, fifty-four lethal attacks were also perpetrated against Ahmadis, thirty-seven against Christians, sixteen against Hindus, and three against Sikhs. Attackers of religious minorities are seldom prosecuted—and, if they are, the courts almost invariably set them free. Members of the majority community, the Sunnis, who dare to question state policies about religious exclusion are just as vulnerable to extremist violence.

Many of Pakistan's regressive religious laws were introduced under the brutal military dictatorship of General Muhammad Zia-ul-Haq, who ruled from 1977 to 1988. He got the parliament to approve various clauses to the penal code, which collectively came to be known as the blasphemy laws. They were often used against Hindus and Christians. The Ahmadis were separately targeted by the anti-Ahmadi ordinances. Systematic sectarian violence against Shias also started under Zia. Further, he armed and trained extremist Sunni Islamist militias ostensibly for geopolitical reasons: to wage guerrilla campaigns against the Soviet occupation of Afghanistan and to secure Kashmir for Pakistan. Nurtured by the intelligence agencies, these militias have been responsible for many terrorist attacks on minorities since. But while Zia can be credited with taking zealotry to new heights through his policy of "Islamization," the trend of religious immoderation can be traced to the earliest days of Pakistan's emergence as an independent state.

This book seeks to analyze Pakistan's policies toward its religious minority populations—Muslim as well as non-Muslim—since Independence in 1947. Having been created as a homeland for South Asia's Muslims, Pakistan's purpose was to protect the subcontinent's largest religious minority. But soon after Independence, some religious and political leaders declared the objective of Pakistan's creation to be the setting up of an Islamic state. Much of the prejudice against religious minorities can be traced to the effort by Islamist radicals to make Pakistan "purer" in what they conceive as Islamic terms.

Given the denominational differences among various groups of Muslims, this concept of an Islamic state has led to unending debate over the role of religion in the life of Pakistanis. Pakistan's name is an acronym, coined well before the country was established, derived from the first letters of its component provinces and regions (Punjab, Afghania, Kashmir, Sindh, and Balochistan). But the word "Pakistan" also means "Land of the Pure" in Urdu, a meaning embraced by Islamist activists since the country's founding. Their drive to "purify" Pakistan has become a quest of imposing religious conformity, which in turn requires exclusion and marginalization of people believing in religions or practices other than those of the "purifiers."

When Pakistan was founded in 1947, its secular founding fathers did not speak of an Islamic state. Muhammad Ali Jinnah, recognized as Pakistan's Quaid-e-Azam (Great Leader), clearly declared that non-Muslims would be equal citizens in the new country. Reflecting his secular views, Jinnah—himself a Shia—nominated a Hindu, several Shias, and an Ahmadi to Pakistan's first cabinet. Now, non-Muslim representation at the cabinet level is limited to symbolic appointments, while Shias face smear campaigns from Sunni Muslims that declare them non-Muslims. And the Ahmadis—who were some of Jinnah's most ardent supporters in his quest for a Muslim homeland on the subcontinent—are completely unrepresented; they live as virtual outcasts within modern Pakistan.

In his famous speech of August 11, 1947, Jinnah had stated that, in order to make Pakistan "happy and prosperous," every person living in the country, "no matter what is his color, caste or creed, [should be] first, second and last a citizen of this State with equal rights, privileges, and obligations." His speech advanced the case for a secular, albeit Muslim-majority, Pakistan: "I cannot emphasize it too much. We should begin to work in that spirit and in course of time all these angularities of the majority and minority communities, the Hindu community and the Muslim community . . . will vanish."

Jinnah also declared,

> You are free; you are free to go to your temples, you are free to go to your mosques or to any other place of worship in this State of Pakistan. You may belong to any religion or caste or creed—that has nothing to do with the business of the State. . . . We are starting in the days where there is no discrimination, no distinction between one community and another, no discrimination between one caste or creed and another. We are starting with this fundamental principle that we are all citizens and equal citizens of one State. . . . Now I think we should keep that in front of us as our ideal and you will find that in course of time Hindus would cease to be Hindus and Muslims would cease to be Muslims, not in the religious sense, because that is the personal faith of each individual, but in the political sense as citizens of the State.[14]

The vision outlined by Pakistan's founder remains unfulfilled. Indeed, it appears further from realization than at any time since this hopeful declaration of religious pluralism was made.

At the time of Partition in 1947, almost 23 percent of Pakistan's population (which then included Bangladesh) comprised non-Muslim citizens. The proportion of non-Muslims has since fallen to approximately 3 percent.

Furthermore, the distinctions among Muslim denominations have become far more accentuated over the years. Muslim groups such as the Shias, who account for approximately 20–25 percent of Pakistan's Muslim population, are often targeted by violent extremists. Ahmadis, barely 1 percent of the Muslim population, have been declared non-Muslim by the writ of the state. Non-Muslim minorities such as Christians, Hindus, and Sikhs have been the victims of suicide-bomb attacks on their neighborhoods, and their community members have converted to Islam against their will. Houses of worship of non-Muslims as well as of Muslim minority sects have been attacked and bombed while filled with worshippers.

Pakistan has descended to its current state of religious intolerance through a series of political decisions made by Jinnah's successors. The descent began in 1949 with the Constituent Assembly declaring the objective of Pakistan's constitution to be the creation of an Islamic state. It reached a nadir with the "Islamization" drive under General Zia during the 1980s. Now, the country is dealing with armed militias and terrorist groups—many of which were sponsored by the state under the Zia regime and in the civil and military governments since—each intent on imposing its version of Islam by violent means.

Pakistan's most prominent human rights activist, Asma Jahangir, warns that the worst is yet to come. "Past experience has shown that the Islamists gain space when civilian authority weakens," she pointed out in an article a few years ago. "The proliferation of arms and official sanction for jihad have made militant groups a frightening challenge for the government. Pakistan's future remains uncertain and its will to fight against rising religious intolerance is waning."[15]

The purpose of examining Pakistan's embrace of religious extremism is not revealed merely in the recognition of the country's ill treatment of its religious minorities. In the context of a Muslim world composed of a youthful population of somewhere around 1.4 billion, it is equally critical to note the actions of state-sponsored organizations or extremist groups against religious minorities in all Muslim countries. Attacks on religious minorities occur in several Muslim-majority nations, from Egypt to Indonesia, just as they do in Pakistan. But because Pakistan is the first country to declare itself an Islamic republic in modern times, the study of Pakistan's handling of its minorities can be a helpful guide in understanding and anticipating the threats that can and will arise wherever Islamist militancy is on the ascendant.

I

Demography, State, and Religion

IN MAY 1950, PAKISTAN's law minister, Jogendar Nath Mandal, confidentially told an Indian reporter that most Hindus in the new country's eastern wing felt they had no place in Pakistan and were determined to leave. "I have asked them to wait for a few weeks more and that I too am prepared to accompany them to India," he said, the only Hindu member of Pakistan's federal cabinet. "It is only a matter of time before the last Hindu reaches India from East Bengal." He lamented that "every Muslim feels that there should be no Hindus left inside Pakistan," and pointed out that after driving out the Hindus, Pakistan will not be able to live in peace with India.[1]

Mandal had been appointed to Pakistan's first cabinet in 1947 by the country's founder, Muhammad Ali Jinnah, who, through the appointment, sought to signal Pakistan's commitment to religious pluralism. Pakistan was not even three years old when its law minister voiced the fear that extremist Muslims would not allow religious diversity. Eventually, Mandal left Pakistan and moved to India, around the same time that many prominent Muslims who had initially stayed behind in India chose to move to Pakistan. Over time, Mandal's dire prediction about Pakistan's religious minorities proved correct. The proportion of non-Muslims in Pakistan dwindled in subsequent years, and with that, Pakistan moved further toward being an exclusivist Muslim state.

The 1947 Partition of British India into two states—Muslim-majority Pakistan and Hindu-majority India—did not envisage large-scale transfers of population to reduce the number of adherents of the minority religion in each state. India was to continue to be home to a large number of Muslims, while non-Muslims were to be almost a quarter of Pakistan's population. But even after the tragic ethnic cleansing and mass migrations that immediately followed Partition, debates over the role of religion in national identity and matters of state have had an adverse impact both on the demographics and the status of religious minorities in the subcontinent, especially in Pakistan.

As the prospect of democratic rule dawned in the latter part of the nineteenth century, the national politics of the subcontinent began to acquire a preoccupation with religious identity. When the British imperial rulers conducted the first decennial census in 1872 and subsequently introduced elected local governments, the rift between the religious majority and minority in India widened. Various religious communities now became aware of their respective numbers; the size, growth, and status of different religious communities became a matter of public debate. Muslim politicians started publicly worrying about the prospect of their community as a permanent minority in a predominantly Hindu India ruled by the Christian British.

In 1906, Sir Aga Khan III, worldwide spiritual leader of the Ismaili Shia Muslim community, led a delegation of prominent Muslims to the Viceroy of India, the Earl of Minto, asking for the reservation of seats in local councils for Muslims, to protect them as a minority in the upcoming elections. This request was acceded to three years later, with an amendment to the Indian Councils Acts of 1861 and 1892. The Morley-Minto reforms—named after the Liberal Secretary of State for India, John Morley, and the Viceroy—made political participation of native Indians in governance conditional upon the formation of separate electorates for Muslims.

Muslim and Hindu politicians would now seek votes only from their coreligionists, without having to garner support from adherents of other religions. This accentuated religious political identities instead of merely helping to protect the rights of minorities. Untrammelled by the democratic imperative to appeal to constituents of the Hindu majority as well as the Muslim minority—which would have inevitably moderated interreligious differences—the candidates were free to pursue an extremist communal agenda. The American journalist Louis Fischer described the separate electorates as "an institution whose mischief was incalculable, for it made religious differences the decisive factor in every political contest. The central political problem in India was to bridge the gulf between Hindus and Moslems; this widened it."[2]

The formation of separate Muslim electorates in colonial India may now be seen as a watershed event for the politics of the subcontinent. It bolstered the notion of self-determination for the region's Muslims and furthered a perception that there was a need for a separate Muslim state, which was to manifest in the creation of Pakistan less than a half century later. In short, the political bifurcation of the subcontinent along religious lines began with the Morley-Minto reforms.

At any rate, communal consciousness and fear of subjugation in the later colonial years was not limited to the religious minority. Some Hindus also raised the specter of Hindus being subsumed by a Muslim population that was rising at an increased rate between censuses. In a pamphlet disseminated in 1909 entitled "Hindus: A Dying Race"— whose premise now appears almost comically farcical—U. N. Mukherji expressed the worry that Hindus would be swallowed up by conversions to Islam and Christianity within 420 years. He based his projections on demographic trends in the 1881, 1891, and 1901 population censuses.[3] The prospect of demographic decline spurred calls for "reconversion" of India's Muslims and Christians to Hinduism and became a core element of subsequent Hindu communalism.

Driven by fear of decline or elimination of their religion, some Hindus launched the Shuddhi Movement. The term refers to purification rituals in worship but was used to refer to "reconversions" to Hinduism. By 1923, Swami Shraddhanand, a self-proclaimed Hindu reformist, had founded the Bharatiya Hindu Shuddhi Mahasabha (Indian Hindu Purification Council). Muslim religious leaders responded by creating the Tableegh (Spreading the Message) Movement, and several religious organizations emerged that both spoke of Islamic exceptionalism and denigrated Hindus and their religion.

In the 1920s, religion became a powder keg in the politics of the subcontinent. Hindu communalists demanded a ban on the slaughter of cows, which were deemed sacred by Hindus but were part of the Christian and Muslim diet. Gaurakshini Sabhas (cow-protection leagues) were set up in parts of the subcontinent. Religious riots were sometimes started by Muslims slaughtering cows, considered sacred by Hindus, in the vicinity of temples, or by Hindus throwing pigs, deemed impure by Muslims, into mosques.

The proliferation of communal violence and the coalescence of religious identities occurred almost in parallel with the rise of the Indian national movement that demanded home rule and ultimately independence from the British. Around the same time that Indians started agitating against colonial dominance, Hindu–Muslim riots became a feature of the Indian political scene, often sparked by attacks on religious processions or disputes over the location of mosques and temples. In the five-year period of 1923 to 1928, 112 riots or communal disorders were recorded by British officials, resulting in 450 lives lost and 5,000 injured.[4]

On August 16, 1932, British Prime Minister Ramsay Macdonald announced separate electorates for all minority communities in India—Muslims, Sikhs, Indian Christians, Anglo-Indians, and Europeans—before holding elections for provincial governments. The depressed classes among Hindus—the "untouchables" or "dalits," referred to as scheduled castes and scheduled tribes in the Indian constitution—were also assigned a number of seats in the legislature to be filled by election from special constituencies in which only voters belonging to those classes could vote. After lengthy negotiations, India's popular nationalist leader, Mohandas Karamchand Gandhi, reached an agreement with leaders of lower-caste Hindus to have a single Hindu electorate, with reserved seats for untouchables within it.

When elections were held for relatively autonomous provincial governments across India in the winter of 1936–1937, the Indian National Congress led by Gandhi formed the government in most key provinces. It had successfully mobilized a mass movement against British rule, though it tended, at times, to ignore or deemphasize the religious conflicts that were playing out in several regions. The Congress routinely attributed religious conflicts to British *agents provocateurs* but still courted the votes and support of the religion-based groups (such as the Hindu Mahasabha and the Majlis-e-Ahrar-e-Islam) that were involved in the emerging Hindu–Muslim divide. From the point of view of the All-India Muslim League led by Muhammad Ali Jinnah, the Congress was dominated by Hindus and could not be trusted with protecting the rights of Muslims.

The Muslim League demanded in 1940 an independent status for "areas in which Muslims are numerically in a majority, as in the north-western and eastern zones of India," which later became the foundation for the demand for Pakistan. Five provinces of British India had Muslim majorities: Sindh, Balochistan, Northwest Frontier Province (now renamed Khyber-Pakhtunkhwa), Punjab in the northwest, and Bengal in the east.

The first three of these were overwhelmingly Muslim (from 71 percent in Sindh to 97 percent in Balochistan), but in 1941 their total population, including that of attached princely states and tribal agencies, was only 10.8 million. Punjab, with 28.4 million people, and Bengal, with 55.02 million, were to be Pakistan's numerical heartland. But Muslims in Punjab were only 57.1 percent of the total, and in Bengal, 54.7 percent.[5] If Pakistan were created exactly as demanded, containing the whole of the Muslim-majority provinces, more than 40 percent of its population would have been non-Muslim.

The British dealt with this quandary in 1947 by partitioning the provinces of Punjab and Bengal, giving Muslim-majority districts of each province to Pakistan while leaving non-Muslim-majority districts in India. According to the 1941 census, there were 94.5 million Muslims and 270.2 million Hindus in the subcontinent. The Muslims comprised 24.3 percent of the total population of undivided India, and the Hindus, 69.5 percent. The high concentration of Muslims in two clusters in the northwest and northeast of the subcontinent made Pakistan possible. These clusters of districts also contained 20.2 million non-Muslims, representing more than one-fourth of their total population.[6] But 40 percent of all Muslims (38 million) lived outside these two clusters of Muslim-dominated districts.

Thus, Pakistan could not be home to all of India's Muslims, and it would have a large non-Muslim minority left within its borders after Independence. Conversely, India would remain home to a substantial proportion of Muslims on the subcontinent. Thus, inherent in the idea of a Muslim-majority Pakistan being partitioned off from Hindu-majority India was a responsibility for both countries to protect and respect their respective religious minorities. Demographic realities required pragmatism and tolerance; but sentiments unleashed by the religion-based Partition caused large-scale riots and pogroms.

Migrations forced by widespread violence impacted both the demographic composition of minorities as well as attitudes toward them in both new dominions.

Violence involving Muslims, Sikhs, and Hindus began soon after the announcement of Partition in June 1947 and continued even after Independence for Pakistan and India in August. But there is a dearth of precise figures about the number of those killed or displaced in "one of the largest and quickest mass migrations in history." It is estimated that some six million Muslims entered Pakistan and about five million non-Muslims left it. Approximately one million persons are believed to have died in the process, from starvation, exhaustion, disease, or violence.[7]

In Punjab, the violence resulted in almost complete ethnic cleansing. Very few Hindus and Sikhs were left in the western districts of the province that became part of Pakistan, whereas the number of Muslims in the eastern districts that stayed in India was reduced from 34 percent of the population to less than 2.5 percent. In his book *The Punjab: Bloodied, Partitioned and Cleansed*, Ishtiaq Ahmed cites claims by both Muslims and Sikhs about parallel plans to systematically drive out the other community from their respective parts of the divided province. Ahmed bases his research on declassified British reports from the time and first-person accounts. "The idea of a Sikh plan to drive all Muslims out of East Punjab has been mentioned by many individuals who were directly involved in the events of that period," writes Ahmed. He quotes the late Harkishan Singh Surjeet, a Sikh leader of the Communist Party of India (Marxist), as saying,

The communal attacks on the minorities were definitely planned. I know more about the persons involved in the eastern wing because I was there. I saw those dreadful acts with my own eyes. In that conspiracy the Maharaja of Patiala was involved. The idea was that if the Muslims were driven out the Sikhs could form their own state in eastern Punjab.[8]

Be that as it may, information collated by a Sikh religious organization, the Shiromani Gurdwara Prabandhak Committee (SGPC), in a 453-page book, *Muslim League Attack on Sikhs and Hindus in the Punjab 1947*, indicates "that the main Muslim communal party, the Muslim

League, wanted the whole of Punjab and therefore planned the expulsion by all means of Sikhs and Hindus from the areas that were assigned to Pakistan."[9] Justice G. D. Khosla, formerly of the Punjab High Court, traced the history of Hindu–Muslim tension and mutual suspicion to at least the beginning of the twentieth century. He insisted that the events of 1947 had deep historical and religious roots. Justice Khosla claimed that the Muslim League, its leaders and cadres, initiated the riots in western Punjab that continued as a one-sided affair until mid-August.[10]

In the years preceding Partition, British officials had noted deterioration in communal relations between Hindus and Sikhs on the one hand and Muslims on the other. In his fortnightly report to the British government on October 27, 1945, the governor of Punjab, Sir Bertrand Glancy, spoke of

> Muslim League supporters in the Ambala division declaring that Pakistan would soon be a reality, that the only laws that would prevail in a short time would be the Muslim laws of sharia [Islamic law] and that non-Muslims would have to bring their complaints to the mosques for settlement.[11]

During the election campaign, Glancy complained in his report of December 27, 1945, that the Muslim League members were "increasing their efforts to appeal to the bigotry of the electors." According to him, Pirs (elders) and Maulvis (Islamic scholars) had been

> enlisted in large numbers to tour the province and denounce all who oppose the League as infidels. Copies of the Holy Quran are carried around as an emblem peculiar to the Muslim League. [Punjab Muslim League leader] Firoz [Noon] and others preach that every vote given to the League is a vote cast in favor of the Holy Prophet; they provide a grim augury of the future peace of India and they are certainly not easy for the Unionists to counter.[12]

In yet another report, dated February 2, 1946, the governor said that

> The ML [Muslim League] orators are becoming increasingly fanatical in their speeches. Maulvis and Pirs and students travel all round

the province and preach that those who fail to vote for the League candidates will cease to be Muslims, their marriages will no longer be valid and they will be entirely excommunicated. It is not easy to foresee what the results of the elections will be. But there seems little doubt the Muslim League, thanks to the ruthless methods by which they have pursued their campaign of "Islam in danger" will considerably increase the number of their seats.[13]

In his next report on February 28, 1946, Glancy reproduced a translation from an Urdu poster circulated by a Muslim League candidate from Jhelum Tehsil, written by Abbas Ali Shah, the local prayer leader. It painted the election as "the battle of righteousness and falsehood," asked Muslims to "choose between *din* (religion) and *dunya* (worldly possessions)," and implored Muslim voters to vote for the Muslim League candidate "for the sake of your religion."[14]

After the Muslim League had won the majority of the Muslim seats, the Punjab Home Secretary, A. A. MacDonald, informed His Majesty's Government on September 14, 1946, that there was "an increasing threat of 'jihad'" and "more response to religious exhortation." According to MacDonald's contemporary report,

> Along with organized, open propaganda, quieter persuasion is taking place and it has been reported that deliberate attempts are being made to affect men on leave from the Army. It has also come to notice that in certain rural areas the message is being passed from mouth to mouth that the Hindus are in power, the Muslims have been betrayed, that Islam is in danger and that Muslims must fight. The result of all this is an increase in Muslim determination and disregard of consequences.[15]

The Muslim League attempted to negotiate with Sikh leaders to keep Punjab intact as a province while being part of Pakistan. These negotiations broke down in March 1947, after which the Sikh leader Master Tara Singh "unsheathed his ceremonial *kirpan* (sword) which he waived in the air" to declare that the Sikhs would die before conceding Pakistan.[16] Singh later told a gathering of Hindus and Sikhs, "Our motherland is calling for blood and we shall satiate the thirst of our mother with blood." He invoked the history of Sikh conflict with the Mughals and claimed, "We crushed Mughalistan and we shall trample Pakistan." It was an unequivocal call to arms:

> The world has always been ruled by minorities. The Muslims snatched the kingdom from Hindus, and Sikhs grabbed it out of the hands of the Muslims and the Sikhs ruled over the Muslims with their might and the Sikhs shall even now rule them. We shall rule them and shall get the government fighting. I have sounded the bugle, finish the Muslim League.[17]

The demographic profile of major cities in Punjab reflected a mix of Muslims, Hindus, and Sikhs that put large clusters of each group next to the other. According to the 1941 census, Lahore—which was to be part of Pakistan and where Tara Singh "sounded his bugle"—had a population of 671,659, of which Muslims were 64.5 percent, Hindus 28 percent, Sikhs 5 percent, and others 2.5 percent. Lahore district's population stood at 1,695,375, with Muslims at 61 percent, Hindus 17 percent, Sikhs 18 percent, and others 4 percent. Soon after Tara Singh's provocative speech, Hindu and Sikh students marched in the city and clashed with police. Muslims attacked shops owned by Hindus, and thirty-seven Hindus and Sikhs died in the ensuing rioting.[18] Soon, police officers also ended up siding with their respective communities. When non-Muslims resisted the looting and burning of their shops,

> a Muslim sub-inspector with a police party arrived on the scene and opened fire. A Hindu youth who tried to stop the sub-inspector was shot dead by him. Consequently tension and anxiety increased on all sides. Schools were closed down and children were kept at home by parents.[19]

Amritsar was the next city to burn after the breakdown of the Sikh leaders' dialogue with the Muslim League. The city, with a population of 390,930, was to be part of India. Its population breakdown was 47 percent Muslims, 36.8 percent Hindus, and 15 percent Sikhs.

Amritsar district, with a population of 1,413,876, comprised 46.5 percent Muslims, 15.3 percent Hindus, and 36.1 percent Sikhs. The city became a battleground for "armed Muslim and Hindu–Sikh gangs," with members of each community pouring in from nearby villages. In Multan, a city of 142,768, of which 57 percent were Muslims, 39.41 percent Hindus, and 1.87 percent other, "it was mainly Muslims who attacked Hindus and Sikhs. The attacks were confined to the city. The loss of life and property inflicted on Hindus was considerable. There were very few Sikhs in the city."[20]

In Rawalpindi, where Muslims comprised 43.79 percent of the city's 185,042 inhabitants, alongside 33.72 percent Hindus and 17.32 percent Sikhs, riots involved Muslims from outside the city. Rawalpindi district, with a population of 785,231, was 80 percent Muslim and "the situation outside the city was almost entirely in favor of the Muslims." The city's Hindus and Sikhs might have managed to avoid fights with their neighbors, but they had to contend with strangers imbued with religious fervor. On March 9, 1947, a train was stopped at the Taxila railway station by an armed group of Muslims, who killed twenty-two Hindus and Sikhs. Soon there were assaults on Sikhs and Hindus in the villages of Rawalpindi, Campbellpur (Attock), and Jhelum districts.[21] By August, when the Partition was finalized, a cycle of retaliation had started, with Sikhs and Hindus attacking Muslims in east Punjab and Muslims on the offensive in the western part of the province.

The violence displaced some twelve million people in the divided Punjab alone and some twenty million in the subcontinent as a whole.[22] Some displaced persons moved back and forth for a while before settling down in one of the two countries. But by 1949, the non-Muslim population of Pakistan had been significantly diluted. The estimated percentage of Muslims in the areas constituting Pakistan rose from 77 percent in 1941 to 83 percent in 1949.[23]

Jinnah, Pakistan's founder, understood the need for tolerance toward religious minorities in both India and Pakistan. Partition had left more Muslims in India in absolute numbers than non-Muslims in Pakistan. But in terms of proportions, Pakistan still had a higher percentage of non-Muslims within its borders than the percentage of Muslims in India.

Soon after his designation as the governor-general of Pakistan, but a month before he took office, Jinnah declared that he would ensure that the minorities were "fully safeguarded" in Pakistan. "Their religion, their faith, their belief, their life and property and their culture would have full protection," he said of the minorities, adding the now somewhat vain hope that "relations between Pakistan and India would be friendly and cordial."

Although Pakistan's founder insisted that he did "not know what a theocratic state means,"[24] some future Pakistani leaders—such as Chaudhry Khaliq-uz-Zaman (leader of the Muslim League in the United Province [UP]) and Khan Abdul Qayyum Khan in the Northwest Frontier Province—were already talking about Pakistan as the "land of the pure" and were laying the foundation for permanent conflict between Muslim Pakistan and Hindu India. Jinnah's vision of religious tolerance was also coming under attack in the towns and villages where Partition riots and organized attacks on rival religious communities were taking place.

Time magazine described the events in both parts of Punjab as "competitive massacre."[25] Its correspondent, Robert Neville, reported after flying over the Punjab that

> the number of smoking villages that can be counted from Ambala up to Lahore must be at least 150. Here and there can be seen a big town like Sialkot and Gujranwala, where charred black districts tell the story that here the property of one entire community was wiped out.

The Muslim population in the Punjab city of Amritsar, which went to India, plummeted from 49 percent of the total on the eve of Partition to just 0.52 percent by the time of the next census in 1951. About 40 percent of the city's houses were burned down. In Lahore, which went to Pakistan, six thousand houses were destroyed and its Hindu and Sikh inhabitants—who constituted over a third of the population—departed for India.[26]

Neville reported Muslim refugees telling him "how Sikhs stripped and paraded Muslim women through the streets, raped them and then killed them." According to him, "British correspondents reported having seen dead, naked women lying about villages of the Amritsar district," most of the victims being Muslim. But he also noted that "at Lahore's Central Station, Sikh and Hindu refugees from North or West Punjab were mobbed on the platform, often stabbed to death and their few belongings looted." In one district on the Pakistani side, Neville wrote, "So many Sikhs and Hindus were murdered and their bodies thrown into the canal that the canal actually had a pinkish color for a day after."[27] Other reports confirmed that all communities engaged in rape and murder of others.

Neutral outsiders realized that no single community could alone be blamed for the Partition mayhem. "When passions are aroused there is always danger that facts will be forgotten or distorted," warned the *New York Times* in an editorial on the savagery. It divided the blame for the violence equally among the Hindus (primarily the Congress), the Muslims (especially the Muslim League), the Sikhs, and the British.[28] But the Muslim League newspaper *Dawn* insisted on blaming only the Hindus and the Congress, creating a national narrative that to this day projects Muslims and Pakistanis as victims of bloodshed during Partition and absolves them of any responsibility for, at the very least, failing to protect non-Muslims.

"If the Hindus of Sind are alarmed merely because the Muslims are going to exercise the democratic right of the majority to rule, is that fear justified?" *Dawn* asked in one of a series of editorials titled "Letters to Mr. Gandhi." The newspaper described Gandhi as the leader of the Hindus and not as the father of an independent secular India, as Indians considered him. The newspaper's editors argued that the Congress and Gandhi were "encouraging disruptive and rebellious elements"[29] in Pakistan to virtually undo Partition, even though they had agreed to the fact of the division.

The notion that non-Muslims remaining in Pakistan after Partition were potential fifth columnists for a Hindu-Indian plan to reintegrate Pakistan into India became a major preoccupation of Pakistani leaders, apart from Jinnah. Pakistan's first prime minister, Liaquat Ali Khan (known commonly by his first name alone), invoked the notion right after Partition; it was popularized in *Dawn*'s editorials and amplified by Urdu newspapers such as *Nawai Waqt* and thereafter became a recurring motif for other Muslim League leaders.

Attributing antistate motives to Pakistan's non-Muslims became a major contributing factor in the subsequent adverse treatment of non-Muslim minorities in Pakistan. As Pakistan increasingly defined itself as an Islamic state, the hard-line theologians' view that non-Muslims could not be faithful to an Islamic state gained currency. As early as March 1948, Cabinet ministers voiced concern in the Constituent Assembly about the possible sympathy of Pakistan's non-Muslims for India. Many years later, Muslim-minority sects were also accused of extraterritorial loyalties: the Ahmadis were described as agents of the British and the Shias as acting at Iran's behest. A similar process of questioning the loyalty of Muslims to the Indian state appears to have taken place across the border.

Despite the Islamists' rhetoric, the minorities still nursed hope in the early days that Pakistan would emerge as an inclusive democracy. Within months of Independence, non-Muslim parliamentarians criticized Liaquat for describing Pakistan as a Muslim state, resulting in public affirmation by the prime minister of their equal rights. He explained that he "meant no offence or harm" to non-Muslims. "When I say it is a Muslim state," Liaquat declared,

> it means a state where the brotherhood of Islam will prevail, where there is no minority or majority and where human dignity and human equality will prevail. Therefore I assure them that as far as the people of Pakistan are concerned they will have equal rights, equal opportunities and equal obligations.[30]

At the same time, the prime minister insisted that Pakistan was a "laboratory" for Islamic governance and said that the non-Muslims had to "cooperate" in the experiment. This did not reassure the minorities' representatives, who "played their unhappy part with dignity, always affirming their loyalty to the State in making their complaints" about mistreatment by the majority.[31]

In contrast to Liaquat, Jinnah was a firm supporter of secular governance who recoiled from suggestions of creating a theocratic state. As Quaid-e-Azam, he enjoyed undisputed primacy among India's Muslims and in Pakistan after Partition. During the Muslim League's campaign for Pakistani independence, some of the party's officials went beyond invoking Islam as a unifying factor for the Muslim-majoritarian state that Jinnah sought. Jinnah came into conflict with the league's honorary treasurer, Amir Ahmed Khan, the raja of Mahmudabad, who engaged in "advocacy of an Islamic state." According to the raja, Jinnah "thoroughly disapproved of my ideas and dissuaded me from expressing them publicly from the League's platform lest the people might be led to believe that Jinnah shared my view and that he was asking me to convey such ideas to the public."[32]

Jinnah continued to speak of a nonconfessional future for Pakistan after agreement in June 1947 on the plan for Partition. He took care to define the future course of Pakistan as a secular, Muslim-majority nation. In an interview with Reuters in New Delhi several days before Partition, Jinnah spoke of a modern democratic state, with sovereignty vested in the people and "the members of the new nation having equal rights of citizenship regardless of their religion, caste or creed."[33]

At a press conference in New Delhi on July 14, 1947, Jinnah repeated his insistence. "Minorities, to whichever community they may belong, will be safeguarded," he declared. Further,

> Their religion or faith or belief will be secure. There will be no interference of any kind with their freedom of worship. They will have their protection with regard to their religion, faith, their life, their culture. They will be, in all respects, the citizens of Pakistan without any distinction of caste or creed.[34]

But the most comprehensive statement of Jinnah's vision for the country he founded was outlined in a speech to the Constituent Assembly of Pakistan on August 11, 1947, three days before his inauguration as governor-general of the new country.

Jinnah explained that Pakistan had been created as a solution to the constitutional problem posed by a permanent majority (Hindus organized under the All India Congress) and a permanent minority (Muslims organized under the All-India Muslim League). It was not intended to be an Islamic state nor was Partition aimed at creating permanent hostility between Hindus and Muslims. Jinnah chose his words carefully when explaining Pakistan's raison d'être:

I know there are people who do not quite agree with the division of India and the partition of the Punjab and Bengal.... One can quite understand the feeling that exists between the two communities wherever one community is in majority and the other is in minority. But ... a division had to take place.... Any idea of a united India could never have worked, and in my judgment it would have led us to terrific disaster.... All the same, in this division it was impossible to avoid the question of minorities being in one dominion or the other. Now that was unavoidable. There is no other solution. Now what shall we do? Now, if we want to make this great State of Pakistan happy and prosperous, we should wholly and solely concentrate on the well-being of the people, and especially of the masses and the poor. If you will work in cooperation, forgetting the past, burying the hatchet, you are bound to succeed. If you change your past and work together in a spirit that every one of you, no matter to what community he belongs, no matter what relations he had with you in the past, no matter what is his colour, caste, or creed, is first, second, and last a citizen of this State with equal rights, privileges, and obligations, there will be no end to the progress you will make.[35]

Pakistan was not to be a confessional state, Jinnah elaborated. Partition itself was a response to the politics of the time, not the beginning of a permanent religious conflict. He hoped that "in course of time all these angularities of the majority and minority communities, the Hindu community and the Muslim community ... will vanish." In Jinnah's view, religious divisions had been "the biggest hindrance in the way of India to attain freedom and Independence" and India could have driven the British out earlier if it was not for religious rivalries. In his words,

No power can hold another nation, and specially a nation of 400 million souls, in subjection; nobody could have conquered you, and even if it had happened, nobody could have continued its hold on you for any length of time, but for this.[36]

The creation of a Muslim-majority Pakistan and a Hindu-majority Hindustan, Jinnah suggested, made Independence for all of India possible. The reference to four hundred million souls—the population of undivided India at the time—indicated that Jinnah saw the creation of Pakistan as a means to the end of gaining the subcontinent's independence from foreign rule. "We must learn a lesson" from the religious discord that had led to Partition, he concluded.

Then, Jinnah made the clearest possible pronouncement of his conception of a secular and religiously inclusive Pakistan. "You are free; you are free to go to your temples, you are free to go to your mosques or to any other place or worship in this State of Pakistan," he said, further clarifying: "You may belong to any religion or caste or creed—that has nothing to do with the business of the State."

By way of explanation, Jinnah cited the history of religious conflict in England after the Reformation when conditions "were much worse than those prevailing in India today." He recalled that the Roman Catholics and the Protestants persecuted each other. "Even now there are some states in existence where there are discriminations made and bars imposed against a particular class," he observed. Jinnah thanked God that "we are not starting in those days. We are starting in the days where there is no discrimination, no distinction between one community and another, no discrimination between one caste or creed and another." Emphasizing that India's partition would not represent degeneration into an era of religious strife, Jinnah said, "We are starting with this fundamental principle: that we are all citizens, and equal citizens, of one State."

Jinnah further invoked British history by pointing out that

> the people of England in [the] course of time had to face the realities of the situation, and had to discharge the responsibilities and burdens placed upon them by the government of their country; and they went through that fire step by step. Today, you might say with justice that Roman Catholics and Protestants do not exist; what exists now is that every man is a citizen, an equal citizen of Great Britain, and they are all members of the nation.

He expressed the hope that the Indian subcontinent would go through a similar process:

Now I think we should keep that in front of us as our ideal, and you will find that in [the] course of time Hindus would cease to be Hindus, and Muslims would cease to be Muslims, not in the religious sense, because that is the personal faith of each individual, but in the political sense as citizens of the State.[37]

This unambiguous statement suggested that Pakistan would be no different from other pluralist democracies, except for the fact that its population would create a Muslim majority. Jinnah had chosen a Hindu, Jogendar Nath Mandal, as the country's first law minister to affirm that secular lawyers and not theologians would run Pakistan's legal system. But many of his followers could not comprehend this nuanced conception of a secular Muslim majority state.

Jinnah's address to the Constituent Assembly was seen by an influential faction of Muslim League leaders as "an abandonment of the two-nation theory" on which Partition was based. This faction, led by Liaquat Ali Khan, was backed by Finance Minister Ghulam Muhammad, a civil servant, who—along with the head of the new country's civil service, Chaudhry Muhammad Ali—tried to suppress the publication of Jinnah's speech by the media.[38]

Jinnah, himself a Shia, also rejected calls by clerics to declare certain sects, which considered themselves Muslim, as being beyond the pale of Islam. While the Majlis-e-Ahrar-e-Islam described the Ahmadiyya as unbelievers (or kafirs), the Muslim League actively courted the Ahmadis' votes. At a public event in Srinagar, Jinnah declared that he could not call someone who deemed themselves Muslim a non-Muslim. He personally complained to the British Viceroy about the reluctance of Punjab government officials to register the votes of Ahmadis in their headquarters at Qadian on the register of Muslim voters for the 1946 election.[39] After Independence, he appointed Sir Zafrulla Khan, a prominent Ahmadi, as Pakistan's first foreign minister.

The Quaid-e-Azam was frail and seriously ill by the time Pakistan came into being. He died thirteen months after his pronouncement that the ideal of the new state would be for Hindus to cease to be Hindus and Muslims to cease to be Muslims in the political sense.

Even during his final days, while he was severely ill, those who had risen to positions of power in the new Pakistan government ignored Jinnah's call for religion to be kept out of the business of the state. The Muslim League had recruited thousands of new members during its campaign for Pakistan, especially the 1945–1946 elections. Many of these new members had divergent views and were united only by concern about the future of Islam and Muslims in India. Pakistan's fledgling government included these disparate elements, as well as bureaucrats and British-era functionaries. While some officials truly considered Pakistan "a laboratory for applying Islamic ideals" in the modern world—a phrase Jinnah had used during the campaign for Pakistan—others thought of binding the country's disparate ethnicities with the glue of religious sentiment as a practical matter of statecraft.

During the chaos of Partition, the Muslim League media on the Pakistan side ran detailed accounts of attacks on Muslims in India, fueling further attacks on Hindus and Sikhs in Pakistan. Government officials spoke of protecting Pakistan's minorities but linked it to similar protection being accorded to Muslims in India. Cabinet ministers were now describing Pakistan as a citadel of Islam that was under attack from Hindu India. Hindus in Pakistan were seen not as Pakistan's equal citizens, as Jinnah had proposed, but as hostages from a country with which Pakistan was virtually at war.

Liaquat, a westernized man closely associated with Jinnah, led the way in creating a national narrative for Pakistan that perpetuated the sense of Islamic victimhood. In addition to the British colonizers, Hindus were projected as the victimizers of Muslims, who had been able to save themselves only partly by creating an independent Pakistan. Liaquat also embraced Islamic clerics, many of whom had earlier opposed the creation of Pakistan on the grounds that, according to Jinnah's pronouncements, it was not to be an Islamic state. Discussions about how to transform Pakistan into an Islamic state thus started almost immediately after Independence.

In a speech soon after Independence, Liaquat described Pakistan as a response to the "British Policy to destroy [the] Muslim economy in order to render the Muslims incapable of what might be termed a come-back. . . . While the ground was being cut from under the feet of Muslims, economically and politically, Hindus were being given every possible encouragement." Thus, any success the Hindus achieved was attributable to British patronage, while the Muslims had to struggle for "self-respect and dignity," and Pakistan was the result of that struggle. Even the loss of Muslim lives in the carnage of Partition was not the result of violence that involved all sides; it represented "the massive sacrifice of Muslims" for their goal of attaining Pakistan.

Liaquat described Pakistan as "a moral sheet anchor" for Muslims in India. He hoped to ensure the security of India's Muslims "by according honorable treatment and equal political and civic rights to the Hindu minority in Pakistan." But good treatment of Hindus in Pakistan was not to be unconditional. It depended on India's attitude toward Pakistan and was linked to diplomatic and political issues between the two new countries.[40]

"India must abandon the idea that being larger she can bounce and bully Pakistan into doing what she wants her to do," the prime minister asserted.

> It is as much in our interest to have an economically proud and prosperous neighbor as it is in the interest of India to have a strong Pakistan. It must not be forgotten by those who rule the destiny of India today that Pakistan is the custodian of the two invasion gateways of the sub-continent.[41]

Liaquat's choice of words, acknowledging that the land upon which the new Pakistani state stood was inextricably linked to earlier Muslim invasions of South Asia, reflected the militarism that was soon to sweep over the new dominion. Pakistan had inherited one-third of British India's military, and Liaquat's government devoted 75 percent of Pakistan's first budget to pay for its maintenance. As the largest and most organized institution in a young country that was already at war with India over Kashmir, the army began asserting itself in political matters right from the earliest days.

Pakistan's soldiers were projected to the world as being part of a "martial race"; the country was described as the successor to the Muslim conquerors and invaders who had ruled India for almost eight centuries before the arrival of the British. This emphasis on the martial origins of Islam in the subcontinent, in a narrative that was historically questionable, had two consequences. First, it framed relations between India and Pakistan as the continuation of a centuries-old conflict between Muslims and Hindus. Second, it increased the vulnerability of non-Muslims—particularly Hindus—to Islamist extremists, who had already declared the purification of Pakistan as a land of Islam as the ultimate objective.

Finance Minister Ghulam Muhammad, who later became governor-general, had begun questioning the rationale for restricting religion to the personal sphere even in Jinnah's lifetime. His closest ally in this endeavor was Chaudhry Muhammad Ali, the head of the civil service then and, later, prime minister. It was Ali who had ordered the suppression of Jinnah's speech of August 11, 1947. Both Ghulam Muhammad and Ali had served in the British Indian civil service and both hailed from Punjab, as did many of the most powerful men in Pakistan after Jinnah's death.

In a public statement in January 1948, barely five months after Jinnah had spoken about religion having nothing to do with the business of the state, the finance minister insisted that Pakistan should be established on purely Islamic concepts. "There are so-called progressives who suspect 'theocratic motives' when Muslims seek to derive inspiration for the regulation of the affairs of their government and society from Islamic principles," he said. In a direct swipe at Jinnah, he questioned those who "insist that religion must remain a man's 'personal affair'" and argued that it was an "error" to consider "Islam as a religion in the same sense as other religions."

According to Ghulam Muhammad, the Quran provided "guidance in respect of every sphere of man's activity, spiritual and temporal. . . . The administration of a country, the making of laws, etc. are only aspects of collective human activity and they are as much governed by the teachings of Islam as is an individual human being's personal conduct."[42]

With their public statements and political machinations, Pakistan's early leaders adroitly steered the country away from the Quaid-e-Azam's secular vision. Jinnah's address before the Constituent Assembly on August 11, 1947, was meant as a comprehensive statement of the principles for Pakistan's future constitution. But at the behest of politicians with opposing views it was suppressed: its secular principles were kept from public discourse, and discussion of Pakistan as an Islamic state thus began. With this began the denial of minorities' rights, along with the official denial of atrocities committed against them. Within the first few months of Independence, non-Muslim members of Pakistan's first Constituent Assembly, in particular, expressed concern about what they described as the mass expulsion of Hindus from Pakistan. In a debate in the Assembly in March 1948, Raj Kumar Chakravarty questioned the government's claim that Hindus were voluntarily leaving East Pakistan and going to India.

"Certainly the people are not leaving their homes and hearths, the lands of their forefathers where they have lived for generations, for the mere fun of it," Chakravarty said. He continued:

> The fact is that there is a sense of insecurity in the minds of the people of the minority community. There is a want of confidence in the government of Eastern Pakistan.... I say with all sense of responsibility that I possess that there is no doubt peace but it is the peace of the grave that exists with regard to the minority communities in East Bengal.[43]

The official strategy even before Chakravarty's complaints was to hint that Pakistan's Hindus were trying to undermine the new state by leaving Pakistan. *Dawn*, which carried Jinnah's name as its founder on the masthead, wrote,

> Hindu hostility to Pakistan has manifested itself in the flight of capital and the shifting of business headquarters from Karachi and Lahore to cities in Hindustan. Behind this ill-advised and hasty act on the part of Hindu capitalists lies the deep-seated suspicions and fear engendered by unscrupulous anti-Pakistan propagandists that the Pakistan government would either freeze or expropriate all private monies in banks and other assets.[44]

In other editorials, *Dawn* had suggested that Hindus sought to avenge centuries of Muslim rule over the subcontinent by converting Muslims in India to Hinduism. "Hundreds of thousands" of Muslims, it wrote, "were forcibly converted to Hinduism almost simultaneously with the attainment of Independence by the Hindus after a thousand years of slavery."[45]

The assertion was, as is often the case with propaganda, based on inexactitude and exaggeration. While Muslim kingdoms dominated most of North India since the eleventh century, Hindus had maintained their own kingdoms in parts of the subcontinent. The depiction of Hindus as an enslaved monolithic society that had not governed itself for a millennium, and were now keen to avenge their past subjugation, flew in the face of historic truth. Furthermore, rape, kidnapping, and forced conversion had been perpetrated against countless members of each community throughout Punjab in the frenzy of Partition. To suggest that only Hindus had forced Muslims to convert was a deliberate falsehood propagated in the effort to arouse Muslim passions within Pakistan.

Liaquat tried to balance his new commitment to an Islamic state with promises of equal rights for all citizens. Addressing Chakravarty and other non-Muslim parliamentarians who spoke up about atrocities against Hindus, he said, "When I say it is a Muslim State it means a State where the brotherhood of Islam will prevail." He added that Pakistan would be a state "where there is no minority or majority and where human dignity and human equality will prevail." According to the prime minister,

> It is our State as well as yours. You will have the same freedom as we will have; you will have the same rights as we will have; and I do expect the same cooperation and support from the non-Muslims who have chosen to stay on here in Pakistan which Pakistan would expect from us.

But he also added, "When I talk of principles of Islam, I mean the principle of equality, justice and brotherhood of mankind. That is Islam and that is what the Muslim State will stand for."[46]

Huseyn Shaheed Suhrawardy, a former premier of Bengal, became the most prominent Muslim to openly disagree with what he saw as efforts to make Pakistan an exclusive Muslim state under the influence of clerical leaders. He concerned himself with the "fundamental aspect of the foundations of Pakistan," which, he argued, "has two branches: one is the goodwill of the people and of the citizens of Pakistan within the State, and the other is the mutual relationship between the dominion of Pakistan and the sister dominion, the Indian Union."[47]

Pakistan, according to Suhrawardy, needed its Muslim and non-Muslim citizens to live in harmony and India–Pakistan relations had to be friendly. He recalled a statement by Mahatma Gandhi that "if the Indian Union eliminates Muslims from within its fold and forms a Hindu State, Hinduism will be destroyed in the Indian Union and if Pakistan eliminates non-Muslims from its fold and forms a Muslim state, Islam will be destroyed in Pakistan." He noted assurances about "toleration, equality [and] brotherhood" given by Jinnah and various government ministers but asked "whether apart from these high sounding sentiments of yours you are doing anything for the purpose of capturing the confidence of the minorities within Pakistan; whether in spite of these high sounding sentiments you are not establishing in effect a communal state within Pakistan."

In words that seem prophetic with hindsight, Suhrawardy said he felt that the Pakistan government's tendency was in the direction of a communal state. "Do not blame the authorities of the Indian Union that they sent their missionaries here amongst the masses and are asking them to leave your territories for nefarious purposes," he insisted.

In Suhrawardy's view, the Muslim League government was not making non-Muslims, especially Hindus, feel safe within Pakistan and questioned the government's claims to the contrary. "Why are the Hindus running away from Sindh [if] they were safe and sound, where they had established business on colossal scales and which they made their homes?" he asked, pointing to the deep cultural ties of Sindhi Hindus to Sindh. According to Suhrawardy, the rhetoric of an Islamic state was responsible for causing insecurity among non-Muslims. "The Pakistan State, if it is to be maintained, must be maintained by the goodwill of Pakistanis of all people, Muslims or non-Muslims whom you consider to be your nationals," he stressed. The minorities could not depend "merely on the goodwill of the Muslims or on their authority or their strength."[48]

Suhrawardy was the first Pakistani public figure to state that, after Independence, Pakistan no longer needed the rhetoric that had been deployed to mobilize Muslims for the creation of Pakistan. Addressing Muslim League leaders, he said,

> You are raising the cry—which was raised at the time and I was party to it and I think it was justified in those days because we did not have Pakistan and India but for which there is no justification at the present moment—that the rights of Muslims were in danger.[49]

"Now you are raising the cry of Pakistan in danger for the purpose of arousing Muslim sentiments and binding them together in order to maintain you in power," Suhrawardy said further. He asked that Pakistani leaders "be fair not merely to your own people whom you will destroy" but also to the minorities, adding that

> a state which will be founded on sentiments, namely that of Islam in danger or of Pakistan in danger, a state which will be held together by raising the bogey of attacks and which you keep together by keeping up a constant friction between yourself and your sister dominion— that state will be full of alarms and excursions.

According to Suhrawardy, a religion-based state that did not protect its minorities would be one in which "there will be no commerce, no business and no trade." With remarkable prescience, the Bengali leader warned that "those lawless elements that may be turned today against non-Muslims will be turned later on, once those fratricidal tendencies have been aroused, against the Muslim gentry." As time went on, Pakistan's religious parties ferociously attacked Pakistan's elites for their un-Islamic lifestyle while demanding greater Islamization of laws and social practices. Each round of Islamization was followed by demands for an even greater role for religion in public life. The anger that had been unleashed originally against non-Muslims became an instrument for theologians and clerics to challenge the class of Muslim politicians, civil servants, and military officers who had hoped to use Islam for political ends without having to concede their own authority.

Suhrawardy wanted Pakistan's Muslim leaders "to open your mind, your heart, your bosom and take within your fold the non-Muslim minority here that is seeking for expression."[50] But this call for a secular Pakistan was not heeded. By the time of Jinnah's death in September

1948, the unhealthy nexus between Islamist politicians and extremist groups emboldened by their patronage—or at least their tacit approval—was already evident. Officials insisted that as many as a quarter of a million Muslims had been forcibly converted to Hinduism or Sikhism in India. Bringing them back into Islam was described as an official objective.[51] Hard-line Islamic groups used the reports of the forcible conversion of Muslims to justify a similar use of force against Hindus and Sikhs, if for no other purpose than to create a "balance" in the treatment of minorities between India and Pakistan.

From December 1948, the Constituent Assembly had to deal with various proposals for Islamizing Pakistan. Nazir Ahmed Khan, a Muslim League member from Punjab, demanded the creation of a separate ministry for the collection of zakat, the Islamic obligation of charity. He also proposed that religious endowments (auqaf), shrines, and mosques should also be handed over to the ministry. Nazir insisted that the government's involvement in religion "would never apply to the personal religion or belief or customs or temples or places of worship of the Hindus or of any other minority in Pakistan."[52]

The proposal was supported by the government. Sir Firoz Khan Noon, a government minister, argued that

> in England if the state religion is Christianity, it does not mean that England ceases to be a democratic state. Similarly, if the state religion in other countries like Iran, Afghanistan or Egypt is Islam, it does not mean that these countries cease to be democracies ... if any of our laws are going to be modeled for the Muslims on Islamic lines, the minorities should have no objection because under the Islamic law and under the Holy Quran greater safeguards are given to minorities.[53]

But the religious legislation alarmed Pakistan's non-Muslims. Even before these latest calls for Islamization, Raj Kumar Chakravarty had asked in February 1948 "whether Pakistan is going to be a secular democratic state or a theocratic state?" He had cautioned against the state being involved in matters of religion, saying a secular state should not make different rules for Hindus and Muslims. "If Pakistan is going to be a theocratic state," he explained, "it will be the government of a religious community by that religious community and for that religious community."[54]

Non-Muslim politicians, and secular Muslim leaders like Suhrawardy, had also opposed the Muslim League's decision to maintain separate communal electorates after Independence. Communal electorates, they argued, might have made sense under colonial rule and to ensure adequate representation of minorities. Now, an independent state that proclaimed the equality of all its citizens did not need to divide them electorally on the basis of religion. But Pakistan was on the slippery slope of conceding ground to clerics seeking greater influence in political decision making: this could only lead to further Islamization, greater divisions on the basis of religion, and the further undermining of the equality of its religious-minority citizens.

Although many Islamic clerics and theologians participated in the campaign to demand Pakistan's transformation into an Islamic state, the blueprint for a step-by-step transition was offered by Abul Ala Maududi, founder of the Jamaat-e-Islami (JI), the South Asian analogue of the Arab Muslim Brotherhood. Maududi, joined by Mufti Shabbir Ahmad Usmani, a cleric elected to the Constituent Assembly on the Muslim League platform, called for the future constitution of Pakistan to be based on the underlying assumption that sovereignty rested with Allah and that the state's function was solely to administer the country in accordance with God's will. Both Islamic scholars also insisted that only the ulema (those trained in Islamic theology) could interpret the laws of Allah.

In March 1949, Prime Minister Liaquat Ali Khan moved in the Constituent Assembly what came to be known as the "Objectives Resolution": a declaration of the goals of the new state that would form the basis of its future constitution and laws. The resolution described a vision for Pakistan diametrically opposed to the secular one Jinnah had offered in his August 11, 1947, speech.

"The Objectives Resolution accepted the premise that 'sovereignty over the entire universe belongs to God Almighty alone' and that the State of Pakistan would exercise authority 'within the limit prescribed by Him.'"[55] The resolution declared that "Muslims shall be enabled to order their lives in the individual and collective spheres in accord with the teachings and requirements of Islam as set out in the Holy Quran and the Sunna" and "adequate provision shall be made to safeguard the legitimate interests of minorities and backward and depressed classes."

The net effect of the Objectives Resolution was to define the state in Islamic terms, opening the door for further legislation based on the interpretation of Islam by a parliamentary majority. In the ensuing decades, however, democracy in Pakistan became intermittent, leaving the authority of inferring the Quran and Sunnah (practices of the Prophet Muhammad) for long intervals in the hands of military dictators.

Liaquat, an Oxford-educated and thoroughly westernized landowner not known for personal religiosity, may have seen the Objectives Resolution as a political masterstroke. By securing approval of the resolution from the Constituent Assembly, he had placated clerics who would otherwise have been an irritant for his government. Introducing the resolution, Liaquat said that "Pakistan was founded because Muslims of this subcontinent wanted to build up their lives in accordance with the teachings and traditions of Islam."[56] He described his resolution "as the most important occasion in the life of this country, next in importance only to the achievement of Independence."

After the passing of the Objectives Resolution, Liaquat did not announce plans for further Islamic legislation, which suggested that he intended to continue the structure of government inherited from the British. Some officials who served in senior positions in Pakistan's first government have argued that the resolution was intended to placate clerics and Islamists only in the most cosmetic sense.[57] But non-Muslim members of the Constituent Assembly saw the dangers of tying state policy to "the teachings and requirements of Islam." They realized that the resolution would open debate about what Islam's teachings really were, with some of the interpretations being detrimental to modern ideas of equal citizenship for Muslims and non-Muslims.

Bhupendra Kumar Dutta, a Hindu politician from East Bengal, warned against the likelihood of internecine battles among Muslims, as well as discrimination against non-Muslims. Politics, he pointed out, came within the sphere of reason, while religion fell within the sphere of faith. Intermingling religion and politics runs the risk of subjecting religion to the type of criticism common to politics, which would be presented as sacrilegious.[58]

In some ways, Dutta anticipated Pakistan's blasphemy laws that came almost four decades later. He also cautioned that tying Islam and politics would weaken reason and curb criticism as far as state policies were concerned. Given the current state of debate and discussion in Pakistan, wherein religion is invoked to discredit scientists, economists, and politicians alike, Dutta's warnings were impressively farsighted.

Liaquat and his westernized colleagues thought they had given Islamists what they wanted. But for Maududi and his fellow Islamists, the Objectives Resolution marked the beginning of a process of cleansing non-Muslim influences from the Pakistani state and society. In one of his writings, Maududi had argued that non-Muslim culture had a negative impact on Muslim life. "It destroys its inner vitality, blurs its vision, befogs its critical faculties, breeds inferiority complexes, and gradually but assuredly saps all the springs of culture and sounds its death-knell," he wrote. He argued that "the Holy Prophet has positively and forcefully forbidden the Muslims to assume the culture and mode of life of the non-Muslims."[59]

In his speech in the Constituent Assembly on the Objectives Resolution, Maulana Shabbir Ahmad Usmani had made a similar argument. He had said that since an Islamic state was an ideological state, "people who do not subscribe to those ideas may have a place in the administrative machinery of the State but they cannot be entrusted with the responsibility of framing the general policy of the State or dealing with matters vital to its safety and integrity."[60] The obvious corollary of Usmani's proposition was that discrimination against non-Muslims in state services was inevitable and justified.

The clerics' view seemed to be that Islam had set up a wall between believers and unbelievers and, as Khalid bin Sayeed put it, "the overall impression is that a community of believers is surrounded by a hostile world and that the latter will not leave Muslims alone unless they are converted or overcome."[61]

In 1950, soon after the adoption of the Objectives Resolution, thirty-one Muslim clerics led by Maududi issued a twenty-two-point plan for implementing sharia (Islamic law; lit. "pathway to be followed") in the country. The ulema insisted that the state would be run only under Islamic laws and would be headed by a Muslim male as its president. Included in the twenty-two points was the notion that the freedom of non-Muslim citizens would be subject to "prescribed boundaries and law," a clear reference to the dhimmi (lit. "protected person") tradition that allowed non-Muslims to live within an Islamic state on condition of paying jizya (a poll tax). The Islamists thus made it clear that they did not aspire to modern notions of equal citizenship regardless of religion. For them, the most non-Muslims in Pakistan could expect were the protections traditionally afforded to dhimmis and that too only on the sufferance of the majority. The battle for Pakistan's Islamization had just begun.

The adoption of the Objectives Resolution caused much consternation among Pakistan's non-Muslims. The government was most concerned by the prospect of international criticism at a time when Liaquat was also trying to secure US military support and projecting Pakistan as a staunch western ally. Nevertheless, and regardless of his motives for passing the Objectives Resolution in the first place, the prime minister—or, indeed, any cabinet minister—could not as much as hint publicly that the resolution was only a political ploy and that Pakistan would remain secular. To do so would have negated the Islamic sentiment that the resolution had generated, amid much fanfare, and provoked a dangerous political backlash.

Consequently, the task of placating Pakistan's non-Muslims and explaining that Pakistan would not impose sharia or further roll back the rights of its already embattled minorities fell to Pakistan's high commissioner (ambassador) to India, Mohammad Ismail. "Pakistan is a secular democratic state," Ismail declared in an interview ahead of the debate over the Objectives Resolution in the Constituent Assembly. "Secular democracy implies equality of opportunity and justice for all. Pakistan does not recognize any distinctions on the basis of religion." He did not rule out the possibility of sharia rule in Pakistan but explained that whenever there was talk of the law of sharia, its application was meant only for Muslims. "No one ever dreamed of applying the sharia to non-Muslims. That would be monstrous," he explained.[62]

This did not reassure the millions of non-Muslims who had already crossed over from Pakistan to India. Some Muslims who had migrated to Pakistan from India also returned. The uncertainty over citizenship caused by interdominion movement of populations necessitated a framework for regulating that movement. Eventually, Pakistan and India signed an agreement in April 1950 to guarantee the protection of their respective religious minorities and pave the way for refugees to return to dispose of their properties if they chose citizenship of the other dominion. The Liaquat-Nehru Pact, or Delhi Pact, as it became known, stated:

> The Governments of India and Pakistan solemnly agree that each shall ensure, to the minorities throughout its territory, complete equality of citizenship, irrespective of religion, a full sense of security in respect of life, culture, property and personal honor, freedom of movement within each country and freedom of occupation, speech and worship, subject to law and morality. Members of the minorities shall have equal opportunity with members of the majority community to participate in the public life of their country, to hold political or other office and to serve in their country's civil and armed forces. Both Governments declare these rights to be fundamental and undertake to enforce them effectively. The prime minister of India has drawn attention to the fact that these rights are guaranteed to all minorities in India by its Constitution. The prime minister of Pakistan has pointed out that similar provision exists in the Objectives Resolution adopted by the Constituent Assembly of Pakistan. It is the policy of both Governments that the enjoyment of these democratic rights shall be assured to all their nationals without distinction. Both governments wish to emphasize that the allegiance and loyalty of the minorities is to the State of which they are citizens, and that it is to the Government of their own State that they should look for the redress of their grievances.[63]

Although commissions were set up under this agreement to facilitate the return of Muslim refugees to India and Hindus to Pakistan, they were unable to stanch the flow of Hindu refugees from Pakistan. Soon after the signing of the Liaquat-Nehru agreement, one million more Hindus left East Pakistan for West Bengal.

2

Ideological State

ON OCTOBER 11, 1947, less than two months after Partition, Ahmed Said Khan, the nawab of Chhatari, wrote with alarm to his friend Liaquat Ali Khan, prime minister of Pakistan, "in the interest of Muslims of the minority provinces." The nawab was a prominent Muslim from Uttar Pradesh (then known as United Provinces), had held senior positions in politics and government, and had also been part of the Muslim League. His letter to Liaquat, who was also from a Muslim-minority province, was meant to warn against declaring "an Islamic government" in Pakistan, as it might create difficulties for the large number of Muslims who stayed on in India.

Nawab Chhatari was moved to write to Liaquat after reading a statement by the premier of Pakistan's Sindh Province, Ayub Khuhro, declaring his government as Islamic. "If they are going to form theocratic governments in Pakistan there will be every justification for Hindus to form a Hindu Raj in the rest of India," observed the nawab. He requested that either Liaquat or Jinnah announce clearly "that formation of Governments in Pakistan will be on a secular basis and not on a religious basis." Nawab Chhatari also asked for

a declaration about the protection and rights of minorities in Pakistan; and an expression of disappointment and regret at what happened in Western and Eastern Punjab with an assurance of protection and fair treatment to those who had left their homes and property if they come back to Western Punjab; so that on the basis of reciprocity Muslims in minority provinces may hope to receive the same protection.[1]

While pronouncements about the protection of minorities in Pakistan were made by both Jinnah and Liaquat, as well as other Pakistani officials, Nawab Chhatari's other proposals were not even seriously considered. Opening the possibility of return to non-Muslims who had left Pakistan would have eroded the numerical consolidation that had resulted from the unfortunate Partition riots. Moreover, Liaquat was unwilling to offer unequivocal assurances about Pakistan being a secular state, because that could benefit secular allies of the Congress at the expense of the Muslim League.

The fact of the matter is that Pakistan was not a territorial nation in the traditional sense. Its leaders had to explain its raison d'être, and most found it convenient to do so in religious terms. Once Liaquat Ali Khan was assassinated in October 1951, even the hope of successfully balancing the demands of modernity with calls for an Islamic state diminished. The country was plunged into a power struggle pitting regional politicians against either bureaucrats or generals, with each side invoking religion to enhance its standing and credibility.

Liaquat was succeeded by Khawaja Nazimuddin, a conservative Bengali Muslim League leader who had served as governor-general after Jinnah's death. Ghulam Muhammad took over as governor-general. The prime minister and the governor-general differed on several issues, which culminated in Ghulam Muhammad dismissing Nazimuddin within two months of his taking office. In a series of political maneuvers, which in hindsight can be seen to have indelibly shaped the political landscape of the country, Ghulam Muhammad secured a greater share of power for civil servants and military officers at the expense of elected politicians.

Ghulam Mohammad's closest allies were the army chief General Ayub Khan and Defence Secretary Major-General Iskander Mirza. It was this alliance with the military that allowed him to dismiss Nazimuddin's elected government in April 1953 and to further subvert democratic norms by dissolving the Constituent Assembly in the following year. With his actions, *Time* magazine in its November 8,

1954, edition stated, "Bloodlessly, Pakistan has changed from an unstable, pro-Western democracy to a more stable, pro-Western military dictatorship."[2]

The governor-general's seizure of power with military support was the earliest incarnation of Pakistan's national security establishment. It foreshadowed a number of dictatorships in the succeeding decades. The bloodless coup was facilitated by the authoritarian and martial tenor of the fledgling country, where minorities were either exiled or cowed into silence, and religious exclusivism had delivered more power to extremists.

The incessant power struggles of these early years of nationhood had significant implications for the debate about the role of religion in the running of the state. India had written and implemented a constitution in 1949, less than two years after Independence. It also held general elections in 1951. Pakistan, on the other hand, remained bogged down by ideological debates and political divisions that prevented the writing of a constitution for almost nine years. The absence of a constitution meant that religious minorities lived through the toleration of the majority rather than by protections guaranteed by the rule of law.

Pakistan's post-Partition demographics greatly influenced its politics. The Bengali-speaking eastern wing of the country comprised the majority of its population, even though the capital and the center of power remained in West Pakistan. The viciousness of the Partition riots had made West Pakistan religiously more homogeneous, making the non-Muslim population negligible in absolute numbers. West Pakistani leaders could afford to ignore the minorities and focus on courting the Muslim majority, often with appeals to religious sentiment. In East Pakistan, Bengali Hindus constituted roughly 20 percent of the populace. They were generally better educated, more affluent, and more actively engaged in politics than their Muslim counterparts.

East Pakistan, though, was virtually unrepresented in the higher echelons of Pakistan's civil services and military. Its leadership comprised primarily politicians and intellectuals, who shared bonds of language and culture with Bengali Hindus. They demanded a secular constitution and sought to assert their power through democratic elections. The West Pakistani civil servants, in alliance with Muslim League politicians from Punjab, sought to contain the Bengali majority by insisting on separate electorates, even after Independence, and by defining Pakistani nationhood narrowly—in religious terms.

The dominant view of the West Pakistani elite was that Bengali Hindus were well-organized, formidable opponents, a threat to be contended with. When a coalition of Bengali political parties defeated the Muslim League in regional elections—the first polls in the eastern wing after Independence—the result was seen by West Pakistani rulers as a danger to the idea of Pakistan. "Their economic power is great," wrote a Punjabi scholar, describing the influence of Hindus in East Pakistan, adding that "they sometimes exploit to their advantage provincial and cultural feelings of the Muslims."[3] The demand for a secular Pakistan was now seen as amounting to empowerment of the Bengalis, particularly the Hindus, leading to a clamoring in West Pakistan for clear adherence to Pakistan's Islamic ideology.

Foreigners saw the debates over Pakistan's ideological direction as a "controversy between the mullahs and the progressives" and assumed that "most civil servants and officers of the defense forces" were opposed to obscurantist ideas.[4] But the reality was more complex. F. M. Innes, a former British civil servant who stayed on as a commentator on affairs of the new country, wrote, "It is common ground that Pakistan, in terms of population the largest Muslim country in the world, is to be an Islamic State, but no two persons agree on what precisely this means."[5] In effect, the demand for Islamic law served as an excuse for putting off elections, delaying constitution writing, and keeping the Bengali majority from exercising authority.

Had the Ghulam Muhammad–led national security establishment been serious about "the spread of education and the march of progress," as they claimed, they would have honored the mandate of the East Pakistan–based secular political parties. The religious leaders seeking Islamization had no electoral mandate, whereas the secular parties did. But the appeasement of religious groups served a useful purpose in putting off democracy and defining an anti-Indian Pakistani national identity. The national security establishment, whose overriding objective was consolidating the new state, viewed the beleaguered religious minorities—which bore the brunt of intermittent outbreaks of violence and other kinds of discrimination—as merely collateral damage.

By 1953, the resentment against Hindus was supplanted by antagonism toward the Ahmadiyya sect, also referred to pejoratively as "Qadianis" or "Mirzais." Members of the Punjab-based sect deemed themselves Muslim, but their belief in a nineteenth-century prophet or messiah, Mirza Ghulam Ahmad, led to their excommunication by clerics of other Muslim sects. The Ahmadis had actively supported Jinnah and the demand for Pakistan and one of the sect's members, Sir Zafrulla Khan, served as Pakistan's first foreign minister.

The issue of whether members of the Ahmadiyya community were Muslims and should or should not be allowed to join the Muslim League had been discussed as early as 1944. At that time, Jinnah had said that the Ahmadis "would be entitled to such privileges as are enjoyed by members of other various sects of Muslims."[6] But after Independence, a coalition of clerics led by the orthodox Sunni ulema of the Deoband school demanded that the Ahmadis be declared non-Muslims under the law and the sect's adherents be removed from senior government positions.

According to political scientist Lawrence Ziring, an American foreign policy expert on Pakistan, Jinnah "was not one to yield to the complaints of the orthodox leaders." Quaid-e-Azam had refused to accept demands to dismiss Zafrulla Khan, "always noting that he was the best person to serve Pakistan's foreign policy needs."[7] Similarly, many Ahmadis also served as officers in the Pakistan army and were promoted on merit without regard to their religion. The anti-Ahmadi campaign also targeted them. In 1948, an Ahmadi army officer was murdered in Quetta near the site of an anti-Ahmadi rally. The community demanded protection, "but these demands only added more fuel for those building the fire against the minority community."[8]

By 1953, police intelligence in Punjab Province reported "intensification of the campaign against the Ahmadis" and warned the government of the likelihood of a collapse in law and order. The provincial government ignored all such intelligence reports, as did the federal government. In spite of the horrors of religious slaughter that the Punjab had witnessed during Partition, the government did not seem eager to avoid further violence.

The demands of the anti-Ahmadi agitators were unusual for a modern, democratic state. Not only was the state being asked to decide who was or was not part of a specific religion, it was being called upon to officially discriminate against members of a religious sect. The anti-Ahmadiyya campaign called itself the Tehrik-e-Tahaffuz-e-Khatm-e-Nabbuwat (Movement for the Protection of the Finality of the Prophet). Its appeal to mainstream Sunni Muslims was emotive. The believers had to defend the Prophet Muhammad's status as the final prophet of God and this could only be done by legislation declaring Ahmadis non-Muslims and by restricting their role in government.

The problems with conceding these demands were manifold. At the most fundamental level, it would set the dangerous precedent of involving the state in determining which sects were acceptably Muslim. Once the Ahmadis were officially declared non-Muslim in 1974, a new campaign started with the intent to subject the Shias to similar proscriptions. That the protestors resorted to violence against a minority religious sect pointed to the likelihood that such campaigns might become the norm—a fear that has since been realized in the form of sectarian terrorism. With the anti-Ahmadiyya protests, Pakistan had moved from purging non-Muslims to an extended period of bitter fighting over who may be deemed Muslim, which has lasted to the present day.

Khawaja Nazimuddin, Pakistan's prime minister at the time of the outbreak of anti-Ahmadi riots in Punjab Province in February 1953, was a pious Muslim. While his sympathies were thought to be with the Islamists, he felt that as head of government he was "duty bound to defend public order." Nazimuddin was "caught between his personal convictions and official responsibility,"[9] and his hesitation to act resulted in the loss of many lives. The politician's dithering response to the pogrom in 1953—as many as two thousand Ahmadis were murdered by rioting mobs before order was restored—foreshadowed the response of Pakistani leaders in later years to religion-motivated violence.

Instead of taking a stand against religious intolerance, officials such as Mumtaz Daulatana, chief minister of the Punjab during the anti-Ahmadi riots, thought only about the political disadvantage they might incur if they took any action. Instead of protecting Ahmadis, Daulatana tried unsuccessfully to direct the protests against the federal government.[10] Daulatana argued that grievances against the Ahmadis reflected popular religious sentiment, thus inexcusably abrogating the rule of law.

The Punjab riots began on February 27, 1953, "spearheaded by the fundamentalists but assisted by a wide array of the Punjab public, drawn from both the educated as well as the illiterate classes."[11] Nazimuddin, a Bengali, lacked a popular base in West Pakistan and his party had just lost an election in his own home base. He now feared losing yet another constituency: the Islamists.

After initially vacillating, Nazimuddin rejected the demands of the anti-Ahmadiyya movement and imposed martial law in Punjab. He banned many of the religious parties involved in the riots and arrested hundreds of perpetrators. The prime minister, though, had "not acted until the rioters had destroyed much of the province's vital infrastructure."[12] The devastation during the riots was clearly well organized and planned. According to the account by Pakistan-based American journalist Herbert Feldman, "In Lahore, parties of men roamed the streets, forcing shopkeepers to close and intimidating others who tried to hold out. Violence developed so rapidly and in so alarming a manner during the ensuing days that the situation passed out of police control."[13]

Feldman also reports that "members of the Ahmadiyya community were attacked, their property destroyed and some lives lost." Police were also butchered while trying to save Ahmadi lives. "The telephone system, the railways and electrical distribution equipment were damaged and by 6 March it seemed as if Lahore might fall totally into the hands of the mob, and the Army's assistance was requested," writes Feldman. As a result, martial law was declared in Lahore. Military courts were set up and the city was placed under military control that lasted for two months.

The army was able to quell the violence, but not without resistance from the anti-Ahmadi agitators. Several religious leaders were arrested and put on trial. Influential figures like Maulana Maududi, head of the Jamaat-e-Islami, were tried before military courts and sentenced to death, though no death sentence was carried out. The governor-general commuted the sentences to imprisonment for life. The Jamaat-e-Islami organized protests, including mobilization of support in other Muslim capitals with help from the Arab Muslim Brotherhood, to demand the release of Maududi and other arrested clerics. All of them were released after relatively brief periods in jail.

The anti-Ahmadiyya protests anticipated the more brutal treatment decades later of non-Muslims and heterodox sects within the fold of Islam who did not accept the beliefs and practices of the Sunni majority. When addressing public gatherings, religious leaders described Foreign Minister Zafrulla Khan as an apostate and a traitor and justified the killing of Ahmadis. There were reports that "enraged individuals would leave these meetings in such a state of fury that they would search out Ahmadis and kill them."[14] The federal and Punjab provincial Muslim League governments did nothing to nip the anti-Ahmadiyya campaign in the bud when it started. About 377 Muslim League leaders from all over West Punjab actually supported the movement.[15]

The clerics had turned the role of minorities in Pakistan into a wedge issue. As Iranian-American academic Vali Nasr explains, the Shias and Ahmadis as well as the Barelvi (non-orthodox) Sunnis "had been far more involved in the Pakistan movement than the [orthodox] Deobandis." Many of the Muslim League's early leaders, including Jinnah, had been Shias while the Ahmadis "were prominent among Muslim League supporters and the bureaucracy that founded the new State." The orthodox clerics, on the other hand, had been allied to the Congress and opposed the idea of Pakistan. They used the minority issue to shift the focus away from their opposition to Pakistan's creation and onto the "Islamicity" of the state and its leaders.[16]

The orthodox Sunni Deobandi clergy as well as Maududi's Jamaat-e-Islami were thus propelled to the forefront of Pakistan's politics by their much-vaunted concern for the Islamic purity of the state. But they attained their power at the expense of Pakistan's religious minorities, who were henceforth subject to constant harassment and periodic massacres. The Islamists' recurring agitations, with occasional support from the national security establishment, consequently destabilized the country, making it a garrison or jihadi state. Pakistan remains a state besieged from within and enervated by the very factions that profess the most fervent patriotism.

In the wake of the anti-Ahmadi riots in Punjab, there was some official recognition of the quandary that governments in Pakistan faced in trying to appease Islamist demands inasmuch as the diversity of belief among the country's Muslim clerics was seemingly irreconcilable.

A judicial inquiry commission convened in July 1953 examined not just the events culminating in the anti-Ahmadi pogrom of that year but also the state of religious intolerance in Pakistan. Comprising Supreme Court Justice Mohammed Munir and Punjab High Court Justice Muhammad Rustam Kayani, the two-member commission (known as the Munir commission) produced a 387-page report after exhaustive hearings, which concluded early in 1954. The commission interviewed almost all leading clerics and found that they often considered each other's beliefs incompatible with Islam. And although all Islamists wanted Pakistan to become an Islamic state, their visions of such a state differed significantly. They seemed to agree only on their contempt for and opposition to non-Muslims. Moreover, their definitions of "non-Muslim" often extended to members of other Islamic sects with whom they had doctrinal differences.

The Munir commission held 117 sittings of which 92 were devoted to the hearing and recording of statements of various parties. Its record consists of 3,600 pages of written statements and 2,700 pages of evidence. It formally exhibited 339 documents and went through a large number of books, pamphlets, journals, and newspapers. The commission also received a large number of letters, "each extending to several pages and a few to even more than a hundred pages."[17] After such painstaking research, the judges on the commission wrote a comprehensive report that pointed out the problems Pakistan faced by allowing religion to become part of the business of the state.

"It has been repeatedly said before us that implicit in the demand for Pakistan was the demand for an Islamic state," the commission said in its report. "Some speeches of important leaders who were striving for Pakistan undoubtedly lend themselves to this construction." But its members added that "no one who has given serious thought to the introduction of a religious State in Pakistan has failed to notice the tremendous difficulties with which any such scheme must be confronted." The commission pointed out that before Partition "even Maulana Abul Ala Maududi of Jamaat-i-Islami was of the view that the form of Government in the new Muslim State, if it ever came into existence, could only be secular."

The Munir commission confronted the religious scholars that testified before it with Jinnah's post-Independence speech about religion having nothing to do with the business of the state and asked if Islam should not be merely a matter of personal faith for the individual. The commission pointed out that Jinnah conceived of Pakistani citizenship with "equal rights, privileges and obligations, irrespective of color, caste, creed or community." They asked the ulema whether this conception of a state was acceptable to them and "every one of them replied in an unhesitating negative."[18] The Jamaat-e-Islami's Maulana Amin Ahsan Islahi testified that "a state based on this idea is the creature of the devil." In the mullahs' conception, Pakistan could not be pluralist and tolerant as well as an Islamic ideological state at the same time.

The clerics claimed before the commission that Jinnah's understanding of a modern national state "became obsolete with the passing of the Objectives Resolution on 12 March 1949," even though they described the resolution as "nothing but a hoax" because "its provisions, particularly those relating to fundamental rights, are directly opposed to the principles of an Islamic state."

Just as Jinnah and supporters of his secular ideals and their Islamist compatriots were divided over what form of government the fledgling state needed, for the ensuing six decades, Pakistanis have remained divided between those who would like the state to be nonconfessional and those who feel that it needs further Islamization. Several generations later, the conundrum remains, only now it is this: which version of Islam should the state adopt in becoming Islamic?

The Munir commission went into great detail while discussing the multiple interpretations of Islam and pointed out the difficulty of securing consensus over what form of Islam could be imposed as the basis of law in a modern country. "According to the Shias all Sunnis are kafirs," said the commission's report, "and Ahl-i-Quran; namely, persons who consider hadith to be unreliable and therefore not binding, are unanimously kafirs and so are all independent thinkers." The net result of all this, according to the jurists on the commission, was that

neither Shias nor Sunnis nor Deobandis nor Ahl-i-Hadith nor Barelvis are Muslims and any change from one view to the other must be accompanied in an Islamic state with the penalty of death if the government of the State is in the hands of the party which considers the other party to be *kafirs*.[19]

The intense disagreement among the mullahs over who was a Muslim meant that it was virtually impossible to adopt their doctrinal differences into law without creating endless divisions within society. Defining who is or is not a Muslim would best be left outside the realm of the law and the constitution. According to the Munir commission,

> It does not require much imagination to judge the consequences of this doctrine when it is remembered that no two *ulema* have agreed before us as to the definition of a Muslim. If the constituents of each of the definitions given by the *ulema* are given effect to, and subjected to the rule of "combination and permutation" and the form of charge in the Inquisition's sentence on Galileo is adopted *mutatis mutandis* as a model, the grounds on which a person may be indicted for apostasy will be too numerous to count.[20]

One of the most noteworthy findings of the Munir commission related to the Islamist leaders' attitude toward non-Muslims. The basis for the demand of removal of Foreign Minister Zafrulla Khan and other Ahmadis occupying key positions in government was that Ahmadis were non-Muslims and as dhimmis (protected subjects) in an Islamic state they were ineligible for appointment to higher offices. "This aspect of the [ulema's] demands has directly raised a question about the position of non-Muslims in Pakistan if we are to have an Islamic Constitution," observed the commission. It pointed out:

> According to the leading *ulema*, the position of non-Muslims in the Islamic State of Pakistan will be that of *dhimmis* and they will not be full citizens of Pakistan because they will not have the same rights as Muslims. They will have no voice in the making of the law, no right to administer the law and no right to hold public offices.[21]

Several clerics who appeared before the commission stated that position, contradicting the high-sounding language of the Objectives Resolution about equal rights for non-Muslims. The rub, clearly, was in the Objectives Resolution's qualifying language about non-Muslim rights being subject to Islamic law. From the ulema's perspective, Islamic law simply did not have the same view of equality for non-Muslims as modern conceptions of human rights.

Maulana Abul Hasanat, Sayyid Muhammad Ahmad Qadri, Maulana Ahmad Ali, Mian Tufail Muhammad, and Maulana Abdul Hamid Badayuni were among the clerics and Islamist leaders who admitted before Justice Munir and his colleagues that non-Muslims could not have the same rights as Muslims. Each one of them repeated the ortho- dox position that non-Muslims could not have any say in lawmaking, could not be involved in administering the law, and did not have the right to hold public offices, except when allowed by Muslims.

The commission noted the confusion of Maulana Abdul Hamid Badayuni, a Sunni Barelvi scholar who had been an early supporter of Jinnah, about the Quaid-e-Azam's conception of Pakistan. Badayuni was asked whether he believed in "only one Pakistan nation, consisting of Muslims and non-Muslims, having equal civic rights, without any distinction of race, religion or creed and that religion would be merely a private affair of the individual." He replied,

> I accept the principle that all communities, whether Muslims or non-Muslims, should have, according to their population, proper representation in the administration of the State and legislation, except that non-Muslims cannot be taken in the army or the judiciary or be appointed as ministers or to other posts involving the reposing of confidence.[22]

When Badayuni, who was seen as a moderate Islamist, was asked whether non-Muslims in Pakistan would be treated as dhimmis, he replied, "By dhimmis are meant non-Muslim people of lands which have been conquered by an Islamic state, and the word is not applicable to non-Muslim minorities already living in an Islamic state. Such minorities are called *mu'ahids*, i.e., those people with whom some agreement has been made." Upon further questioning, Badayuni conceded that there was "no such agreement with such communities" in Pakistan that allowed non-Muslims to be deemed mu'ahids.

The Munir commission observed that "according to the evidence of this learned divine, the non-Muslims of Pakistan will neither be citizens nor will they have the status of *dhimmis* or of *mu'ahids*." The clerics also unanimously advocated imposition of the death penalty for apostasy and denied to non-Muslims the right to preach their religion. According to the commission's report, "The prohibition against public preaching of any non-Muslim religion must logically follow from the proposition that apostasy will be punished with death and that any attack on, or danger to, Islam will be treated as treason and punished in the same way as apostasy."[23] It is important to note that the stringent antiblasphemy laws that were passed in the 1980s derived from the 1950s debate about apostasy; the issue continues to live on in the twenty-first century.

When asked whether they were bothered by the prospect of mistreatment of Muslims in countries where they lived as minorities, the ulema were surprisingly callous in their responses. Ataullah Shah Bukhari said that it was not possible for a Muslim to be a faithful citizen of a non-Muslim government. Others, including Maulana Abul Hasanat and Maulana Maududi, said that they would have no objection to Muslims in India being subjected to Hindu law or Muslims in non-Muslim countries in general being discriminated against. Most of the ulema seemed to believe that Pakistan was somehow the reincarnation of the seventh-century caliphate and that other countries should be viewed as the caliphs (khalifa) looked upon non-Muslim empires of the time.

The judges on the commission had difficulty reconciling the clerics' aspirations of seeking to resurrect the seventh century, and they pointed out the difficulties of using the early Islamic caliphate as the prototype for a modern state. "During the Islamic Republic, the head of the State, the khalifa, was chosen by a system of election, which was wholly different from the present system of election based on adult or any other form of popular suffrage," they explained. Fourteen centuries ago, the oath of allegiance (bayah) rendered to the caliph possessed a sacramental virtue and after being chosen by consensus, he became the source of all channels of legitimate government. The caliph alone then was competent to rule, though he could delegate his powers to deputies and seek advice from "men of outstanding piety and learning, called Majlis-i-Shura or Ahl-ul-Hall-i-wal-Aqd."

The commission pointed out that the principal feature of this system was to exclude unbelievers from the Majlis-i-Shura and "the power which had vested in the *khalifa* could not be delegated to the *kuffar*."

The khalifa was the real head of the state; all power was vested in him and not bound by a constitution that conferred equal rights of citizenship in the modern sense. "He could not appoint non-Muslims to important posts, and could give them no place either in the interpretation or the administration of the law, the making of the law by them, as already pointed out, being a legal impossibility," observed Justice Munir and his fellow judges.[24] They implied that the caliphate was easily maintained in the earliest period of Islam, when there were no sects among Muslims, and the distinction between Muslim and non-Muslim was clear.

In the modern era, the Islamists' dream of recreating a system similar to the caliphate required devising some machinery by which the distinction between a Muslim and a non-Muslim could be determined and its consequences enforced. The Munir commission asked most of the leading ulema to give their definition of a Muslim, given the fundamental importance of the question of whether a person is or is not a Muslim. Moreover, if the religious scholars of various sects believed the Ahmadis to be kafirs, they should conceivably have been quite clear about the definition of a Muslim. In its report, however, the commission listed the various definitions of Muslim offered by the ulema and concluded that "considerable confusion exists in the minds of our *ulema* on such a simple matter."

The Munir commission's conclusion on the issue of the definition of "Muslim" was as follows:

> Keeping in view the several definitions given by the *ulema*, need we make any comment except that no two learned divines are agreed on this fundamental. If we attempt our own definition as each learned divine has done and that definition differs from that given by all others, we unanimously go out of the fold of Islam. And if we adopt the definition given by any one of the *ulema*, we remain Muslims according to the view of that *alim* [scholar] but *kafirs* according to the definition of everyone else.[25]

The findings of the Munir commission went far beyond explaining the anti-Ahmadi riots in Punjab in 1953. They highlighted the bankruptcy of obscurantist beliefs and the troubles that lay ahead for Pakistan if it continued to pursue the objective of becoming an Islamic ideological state. The mullahs who wished to impose Islamic rule in Pakistan lacked clarity about what that actually meant, but their zealous advocacy could create endless strife. Furthermore, the clerics' bleak vision was decidedly hateful and exclusive in relation to non-Muslims. It also did not offer tolerance for pluralism in the interpretation of Islam.

The government had every reason to advance a clear secular vision with the backing of the electorate: East Pakistan had voted for secular parties, and in West Pakistan too, the Munir commission report had laid out any number of grounds that could be used to advocate such a course. But the national security establishment preferred to align with West Pakistani Muslim League politicians in persisting with the notion of an Islamic state.

In 1956, when the second Constituent Assembly was finally able to arrive at some sort of consensus, it named Pakistan "the Islamic Republic of Pakistan" and included the Objectives Resolution as the preamble to the constitution.[26] Part 3 of the new constitution laid down several "Directive Principles of State Policy," which included Islamic provisions such as "steps shall be taken to enable the Muslims of Pakistan individually and collectively to order their lives in accordance with the Holy Quran and Sunna" and "to promote unity and the observance of Islamic moral standards." The Pakistani state was now committed to securing "the proper organization of *zakat, wakfs* [religious endowments] and mosques," to "prevent the consumption of alcoholic liquor," and to "eliminate *riba* [usury or interest] as early as possible."

The 1956 Pakistan constitution barred non-Muslims from holding the office of head of state. As if that were not enough, part 12 of the constitution was titled "Islamic Provisions." It included Article 197, which said that "the president shall set up an organization for Islamic research and instruction in advanced studies to assist in the reconstruction of Muslim society on a truly Islamic basis." According to Article 198, "No law shall be enacted which is repugnant to the Injunctions of Islam as laid down in the Holy Quran and Sunna, hereinafter referred to as Injunctions of Islam, and existing law shall be brought into conformity with such Injunctions."[27]

Although Article 198 was qualified by the words "Nothing in this Article shall affect the personal laws of non-Muslim citizens, or their status as citizens, or any provision of the Constitution," it was enough for the Islamists to continue pressing for further Islamization, including limiting the rights of non-Muslims according to the various orthodox interpretations of Islam.

Huseyn Shaheed Suhrawardy, from Bengal, who served as prime minister for a brief period under the 1956 constitution, warned against the preoccupation with "segregation of our voters into religious communities" and the emphasis on Pakistan's destiny as an ideological state. This, he said, "would keep alive within Pakistan the divisive communal emotions by which the subcontinent was riven before the achievement of Independence." He proposed instead that Pakistanis start seeing Pakistan "in terms of a nation state." Suhrawardy saw "a Pakistan great enough and strong enough to encompass all of its citizens, whatever their faith, on a basis of true civic equality and by that fact made greater and stronger."[28]

That conception, like Jinnah's before it, was not embraced. The 1956 constitution was abrogated by President Iskander Mirza in little more than two years after its adoption, after Mirza—the country's first president—imposed martial law on October 7, 1958. Mirza was deposed by the army chief General Ayub Khan in a coup d'état twenty days later. Pakistan was now under the first of its several prolonged military dictatorships. Focused on national security and conflict with India, the new government was unable to move away from the paradigm of the ideological state.

Ayub ruled Pakistan for more than ten years and styled himself as a pro-western authoritarian reformer. Although his supporters compared him with Turkey's Kemal Ataturk or the Shah of Iran, the Pakistani dictator—unlike Ataturk or the Shah—shied away from embracing a secular model for his country. Part of the problem was Ayub's belief that Pakistan's continued existence as an independent state depended not on the will of its people expressed through democracy, but on a national identity forged through Islam.

General Ayub Khan saw Pakistan not as a conventional state defined by territory and a claim to the land itself, as has been the raison d'être of most nations, but as a state defined by ideology. And for Ayub, and indeed the Islamists of Pakistan, that ideology was unquestionably and exclusively Islamic. "Till the advent of Pakistan none of us was in fact a

Pakistani, for the simple reason that there was no territorial entity bearing that name," Ayub explained.

> Actually, the boundaries of Pakistan were still being drawn and re-drawn secretly in the Viceregal Lodge at New Delhi when Independence was proclaimed. So prior to 1947 our nationalism was based more on an idea than on any territorial definition. Till then, ideologically we were Muslims, territorially we happened to be Indians, and parochially we were a conglomeration of at least eleven smaller, provincial loyalties.[29]

His anxiety, Ayub insisted, was "to unite the people of Pakistan in the light of their faith and ideology." The military dictator sought to "define the ideology of Islam and to apply it to present-day conditions of life and especially the conditions of life in Pakistan." But he was not willing to let religion be a private matter or to accept the idea of equal citizenship of all Pakistanis, irrespective of their faith.[30]

General (and later Field Marshal) Ayub Khan asserted, as Liaquat had done before him, "that the sine qua non of the establishment of Pakistan as a State was to give shape and reality to Islamic ideology." In his view, Arab and other Muslim states, but not Pakistan, could embark on a territorial and secular nationalism.[31] Observers such as Professor Khalid bin Sayeed thought that Ayub "shrewdly used Islam to support the kind of authoritarian system that he [had] envisaged for Pakistan."[32] Ayub's argument was that "without centralization, unity and solidarity no system can claim to be an Islamic system." He invoked Islam's tradition of the caliphate—with one person wielding absolute authority in both religious and political matters—to support the idea of a presidential system. Arab Muslim rulers succeeding Prophet Muhammad had a council of pious advisers and Ayub argued that an Islamic state's assembly or parliament should be modeled on that rather than on modern legislatures with political parties. Ayub even referred to the advisory council set up by Muhammad's second successor, Omar bin Khattab (who ruled as the caliph in 634–644 AD) as the proper Islamic type of parliament.[33]

When Ayub arbitrarily framed a new constitution for Pakistan in 1962, he enshrined in it his views on the system of government he

proposed for the country. His only secular gesture was to initially refer
to the country as the "Republic of Pakistan," though later he reverted to
the nomenclature of "Islamic Republic of Pakistan." Like the 1956 constitution, the new basic law also included several "Islamic provisions"
and restricted the office of president to Muslims. A Council of Islamic
Ideology was assigned the task of recommending to the government
how to bring all laws "in conformity with [the] Quran and Sunna."

From the perspective of Pakistan's religious minorities, Ayub's self-
styled benevolent authoritarianism offered little relief against the tide of
intolerance that had engulfed the country since Partition. The minorities' treatment now depended on the dictator's view of each community.
Circumstances improved somewhat for Christians, whom Ayub did not
view as a threat to the state, resulting in some of their coreligionists gaining senior positions in government. The anti-Ahmadi agitation was also
contained because the field marshal chose not to exclude groups from
the fold of believers that deemed themselves Muslims. Pakistan's Hindus
bore the brunt of Ayub's particular variety of prejudice.

Ayub saw Hinduism and communism as equal threats to Pakistan.
In 1959, he wrote in the foreword of a book titled *The Ideology of
Pakistan and Its Implementation* that one of the questions of concern for
Pakistanis was "how can the offensive of Hinduism and Communism
against the ideology of Islam be combated?"[34] In his autobiography,
which was published toward the end of his regime in 1968, Ayub made
clear his low regard for Hindus and bluntly expressed his steadfast views
on why they could not be friends of Pakistan.

"It was Brahmin chauvinism and arrogance that had forced us to
seek a homeland of our own where we could order our life according to
our own thinking and faith," Ayub averred. "They wanted us to remain
as serfs, which was precisely the condition in which the Muslim minority in India lived today."[35] Ayub also felt that Muslim Bengalis "have
been and still are under considerable Hindu cultural and linguistic influence" and had "all the inhibitions of downtrodden races and have
not yet found it possible to adjust psychologically to the requirements
of the new-born freedom."[36]

The Ayub regime's anti-Hindu prejudice, coupled with the higher
percentage of Hindus in East Pakistan, meant that "the majority of
deaths inflicted in the course of Hindu–Muslim disturbances in

Pakistan . . . occurred in the eastern province."[37] When religious riots broke out in the Indian town of Jabalpur in 1961 over the alleged rape of a Hindu girl by Muslim youths, retaliatory attacks against Hindus took place in many parts of Pakistan. According to an American commentator, the Indian leaders "Jawaharlal Nehru and Jayaprakash Narayan spoke with shame and horror" about the attacks on Muslims in their country, but Pakistan's martial law administration "made no particular effort to assuage" feelings of religious ill will.[38]

In keeping with a tradition that took root soon after Independence, Pakistan's leaders and media continued to conflate the nation's tensions with the state of India with a broader struggle against Hindus, the adherents of a religion. Soon after India's annexation of the Portuguese enclave of Goa, a *Dawn* editorial expressed almost hysterical fears of Hindu irredentism: "As soon as India feels strong enough to do so she will try to wipe out Pakistan because Indians in their heart still regard the areas now forming Pakistan as basically parts of Akhand Bharat [undivided India] over which some day Hindu rule must be extended."[39]

To ensure that Pakistan's future citizens be raised to become well indoctrinated in the national ideology, the Ayub regime made social studies compulsory from grades six to ten and Islamic studies from grades six to eight in all schools. An official report proudly proclaimed, "Students of Islamic history as now presented will develop confidence in themselves and instead of looking for leadership to other Muslim countries, will try to lead others in the presentation of Islam."[40] The syllabus emphasized Islam's martial traditions, spoke of a long-standing conflict between Hindus and Muslims in the subcontinent, and drilled into students' minds the idea that Pakistan was created to be an Islamic state.

The anti-Hindu sentiment espoused in the name of Pakistan's Islamic ideology contributed substantially to the periodic migration of Bengali Hindus to India. The proportion of Hindus in East Pakistani society, which stood at an influential 20 percent of the province's population in the 1951 census, fell to just 12 percent by the time of the 1961 census.

3

Militarism and National Identity

THE ROLE OF PAKISTAN's third military dictator, General Zia-ul-Haq (who ruled from 1977 to 1988), in imposing draconian laws curtailing individual freedom and religious liberty is widely known. The promotion of religious intolerance by the military regimes of Field Marshal Ayub Khan (1958–1969) and General Yahya Khan (1969–1971), however, is often overlooked.

Ayub and Yahya characterized Hindus as "the other" and emphasized Islam as Pakistan's raison d'être. This legitimized the view that religious minorities lived in the country only at the sufferance of the Muslim majority. Instead of the modern conception of inalienable human rights, the minorities' survival and religious freedom depended on various interpretations of traditional Islamic law. The Islamization of Pakistan, therefore, was incremental. The developments under the military dictatorships of Ayub and Yahya paved the way for Zia's much harsher interpretation of Islamic law, primarily to the detriment of religious pluralism and minority rights.

In addition to their quests for a preeminent military and greater power for themselves as military's commanders, each of Pakistan's dictators seems to have been preoccupied by a desire to control national discourse. This was sometimes presented as an effort to "save" the country from disagreements among its people and forge a coherent national identity, which they felt could be done under only the banner of religion. Ayub voiced his concern that "our society is torn by a number of schisms" while Yahya often spoke of the need for everyone to fall in line for "the unity of Pakistan and the glory of Islam."

Like Zia in later years, Ayub and Yahya considered democratic political parties with regional support bases or ethnic identities as a threat to the country's integrity. All military dictators sought to create a centralized, authoritarian Pakistan, using Islam as the national rallying cry. It was perhaps unsurprising then that they also regarded religious minorities as peripheral, and possibly hostile, to their campaigns of shaping a Pakistani national identity around an Islamic ideology.

By the time Ayub assumed power in 1958, Liaquat and his successors had already built a basic national narrative for Pakistan. The Pakistani military, which had received the lion's share of government resources since the country's first budget was drawn up in 1948, vehemently embraced the notion of Pakistan as an ideological state. Explaining the genesis of Pakistan, Ayub wrote, "What worried the Muslims was not the pace of freedom (in united India) but that when freedom came they should be able to order their lives according to their own lights." According to him, "The end of British domination should not become for the Muslims the beginning of Hindu domination. They were not seeking to change masters. They knew through past experience that the Hindus would not agree to live with them on equal terms within the same political framework."[1]

Ayub's approach was "to effectively utilize Islam for national cohesion and a progressive societal outlook." Law Minister Manzur Qadir, who drafted the constitution for Ayub, said that there were "72 sects among the Muslims and as many interpretations of Quran and Sunnah." This, according to him, rendered the framing of an Islamic constitution "not only a difficult but also a dangerous exercise."[2] But while Ayub's constitution had initially settled on the title "Republic of Pakistan," he did not resist when the National Assembly voted to restore "Islamic" within the nation's official nomenclature.

Ayub pushed through an agenda of social reform in the name of a liberal interpretation of Islam and took a hard line with the ulema. Ayub described his regime's three "cherished goals" as "a strong central government, economic development and modernization of religious institutions."[3] But his effort to establish the "supremacy of Islamic modernism over and above that of the 'Mullahs' " had the unintended consequence of keeping Islam and Islamic history at the center of Pakistan's national discourse.

The centrality of Islam to Pakistani politics favored the orthodox keepers and interpreters of the faith. Ayub's efforts to advance what he deemed Islamic modernism created a backlash. Instead of arguing that religion should be a personal matter, Ayub endorsed Islamic law as defined by two unorthodox Islamic scholars, Fazlur Rahman and Ghulam Ahmed Parvez. These scholars pleaded for interpreting Islam "in consonance with modern needs." In one article, Rahman argued that the traditional ulema were "taking such an anachronistic position that Muslims are being driven away from Islam to secularism" and asked for reinterpretation of Islamic texts in keeping with contemporary requirements instead of dogmatic insistence on traditional rites and rituals.[4]

These modernists were unable to prevail against the traditionalist scholars and eventually only weakened the case for a secular Pakistan. The ulema accused the modernists of heresy and religious dissension. Parvez questioned the authenticity of Hadith (sayings attributed to the Prophet Muhammad) as the basis of Islamic law. As a member of the constitutional Council of Islamic Ideology, Rahman had argued that the modern concept of interest could not be equated with riba (usury), which is prohibited by Islam. He also offered other "bold and ingenious interpretations" of Islamic themes, including the suggestion that "drinking of alcohol was permissible, provided it did not result in intoxication."[5]

Such reinterpretation of Islamic law did not impress conservative believers, who could now be convinced once again by the ulema that "Islam was in danger"—this time from heterodoxy. The traditional clerics and organized Islamist groups argued that, once Pakistan's status as an Islamic state had been settled, the only remaining question was who should lead the country. According to the clerics, the task of interpreting Islam in an Islamic state could only be undertaken by those well versed in Islamic doctrine and theology.

Field Marshal Ayub Khan's handpicked coterie of progressive Islamic thinkers could not thwart the obscurantist tendencies of the traditionalist clerics, rendering his attempt to modernize Islamic dogma an abject failure. If anything, its net effect was to perpetuate the framing of social and political issues in Pakistan—including questions of religious freedom and human rights—in purely theological terms. And insofar as all points of reference in Islamic theological arguments related to the early history of Islam, any contemplation of Pakistan as a modern state based on shared citizenship irrespective of religious or other beliefs was circumvented. In the end, it was the orthodox religious leaders who gained in influence during his military dictatorship.

While traditionalist Islamists paradoxically grew in stature from Khan's quest for modernization, prominent Pakistanis who may otherwise have championed the country's modernization faced sanction. Secular politicians like Huseyn Shaheed Suhrawardy, and intellectuals like the poet Faiz Ahmed Faiz were targeted by Ayub's regime on the grounds that their ideas were not conducive to Pakistan's unity or ideological coherence. A triumphant Islamic orthodoxy defined the country's identity, and the notion of the separation of mosque and state had been firmly brushed aside.

In addition to defining Pakistan's national identity and pursuing economic development through external assistance, the Ayub regime also undertook a major military buildup. Ayub projected himself as a western ally against communism and secured from the United States modern fighter planes for Pakistan's air force, submarines and frigates for the navy, and artillery and tanks for the army. As soon as Pakistan's military felt confident about the quality of its weaponry being better than that of arch-adversary India, nationalism in Pakistan took on a decidedly jingoist flavor. As has often been the case in Pakistan's history, nationalist rhetoric against India obliged denigration of the Hindu religion. This was in no small measure responsible for fostering further hostility toward Pakistan's Hindu minority.

During the India–China war of 1962, Pakistan's official media called upon Ayub to take advantage of the opportunity and settle by force the Muslim country's territorial dispute over Kashmir with Hindu India. The support of western nations for India against China was condemned in an orchestrated fashion. An editorial in *Dawn*, the semi-official newspaper of the time, spoke of "the imperialist white countries" that "had once combined to subjugate through foreign zones of influence and drugging through opium," denying China and Pakistan the right to pursue their peaceful goals.[6] Indian Prime Minister Nehru was accused in another editorial of being "bent on pursuing expansionist and atavistic policies."[7]

When Ayub refused an Anglo-American proposal for a Pakistani no-war declaration, *Dawn* wrote, "Muslims do not stab their worst adversaries in their back and if they have a showdown they do it in an honorable manner" and blamed India's Hindu ethic for stabbing Pakistan in the back in the past.[8] Nehru was also accused of trying to "hold Pakistan to perpetual ransom and even undo the partition of India which the Hindus have never really accepted."[9] The official Urdu- and Bengali-language press went further in employing inflammatory language and propagandist images. India was represented in cartoons of the era as a conservatively clad Hindu of the trading class, reinforcing the view in Pakistani minds that their conflict was not with India, the state, but with Hindus, the people.

The conflation of Hindus with India meant that whenever Pakistan's relations with India entered a tense phase, Islamist extremist groups in the country targeted Hindu businesses and temples, especially in East Pakistan. Beginning with the 1962 India–China war, Pakistan's relationship with India entered a downward spiral for a decade, culminating in Pakistan's military defeat and the supplanting of East Pakistan with the nation of Bangladesh in 1971. In this period, India and Pakistan fought a full-scale war along the West Pakistan border and in Kashmir in 1965. Riots against Hindus and the burning of Hindu temples in Pakistan occurred several times during this period.

Between January and March 1964, a series of Hindu–Muslim communal riots took place on both sides of the India–Pakistan border. The riots started in Khulna (East Pakistan) and spread to Calcutta (India), then to Dacca (East Pakistan) and afterward to Jamshedpur and Rourkela, both in India. "The ostensible cause of this carnage was the indignation said to have been felt in Khulna over the theft of a precious Muslim relic in Srinagar, in Kashmir," wrote the US journalist Herbert Feldman.

This relic, a hair of the Prophet's beard, was stolen from the Hazratbal Mosque on December 26, 1963 and no doubt a great deal of publicity was given to this in Pakistan. At all events, the rioting began and during the next three months spread from place to place. An explosive situation existed partly because of the dispersal and resettlement of Hindu refugees from East Pakistan in West Bengal, Orissa, Madhya Pradesh, Andhra Pradesh and Maharashtra.[10]

Tathagata Roy, a West Bengali Hindu nationalist, recounts rather harshly the impact of the Hazratbal Mosque incident in East Pakistan. According to Roy, on January 3, 1964,

> A protest day was observed following the loss of Prophet Mohammad's hair from Hazratbal Mosque in Kashmir, India. On that day, at Daulatpur, Khulna district, Sabdul Khan made an inflammatory speech to a crowd of non-Bengali, mostly Bihari, Muslim factory workers, who immediately thereafter took out a procession, looted and set fire to Hindu houses, raped women and killed them indiscriminately without any interference from the police.[11]

The anti-Hindu attacks were followed by retaliatory attacks on Muslims in West Bengal, and then the violence escalated on the Pakistani side. Hindus reported that several factories and mills owned by non-Bengali Muslims closed their businesses on January 14 and 15 and encouraged their employees to attack Hindus in their area by supplying them "motor vehicles, iron rods, daggers, firearms, petrol cans and sprayers."[12] At least three Hindu-owned cotton mills were burned to the ground and their Hindu workers slaughtered. Rioters attacked a fair marking a Hindu festival, where violence continued until the arrival of law enforcement personnel a day later.

Lawrence Ziring points out that the ostensible theft of the Prophet Muhammad's relic from the Hazratbal shrine affected both India–Pakistan and Hindu–Muslim relations. "In Kashmir, news of the theft resulted in severe disorders and rioting soon spread to India and Pakistan," he writes.

> In the midst of mounting unrest the Jammu and Kashmir Liberation Executive called an emergency meeting in Azad Kashmir to consider the situation and its impact on Muslims all over the subcontinent. Meetings were held in Pakistan to condemn the disappearance of the

sacred relic and rumors circulated that right-wing Hindu organizations were behind the theft.

According to Ziring,

> Reports spread throughout Pakistan that Jan Sanghis and members of the Hindu Mahasabha had begun a reign of terror in Kashmir and some of India's northern states and were set on destroying Muslim life and property. At the same time riots broke out in East Pakistan, where a large Hindu minority resides. On 2 January 1964, the West Pakistan assembly unanimously passed a resolution expressing a deep sense of anger and sorrow at the theft of the holy relic and the attack perpetrated on defenseless Muslims. Similar protests emanated from the Indian legislatures, where concern was voiced for the Hindus in East Pakistan.[13]

These frictions were still simmering when Nehru died of natural causes on May 27, 1964. Anti-India hard-liners within Ayub's government persuaded him that this was the best time to exercise Pakistan's US-funded military muscle, which would be backed by the country's recently fortified Islamic identity. Pakistan first went to war with India along the Sindh border in the Rann of Kutch over a boundary dispute. Under international pressure, both countries agreed to refer the dispute to international arbitration. Pakistani media, however, presented the referral to arbitration as a victory of Pakistan's armed forces, claiming that "the Hindus" could not fight well and for that reason India had sought refuge in peacemaking.

Then, in August 1965, Pakistan sent trained infiltrators into Kashmir with the expectation of generating a populist uprising. On September 6, India launched a full-fledged attack across its border with West Pakistan, widening the war beyond Kashmir. The fact that there was no invasion of East Pakistan and India had only reacted to Pakistan's "Operation Gibraltar" in Kashmir did not deter Ayub from claiming that, as predicted, India wanted to finally undo Partition and finish off Pakistan.

The war, which ended in a stalemate seventeen days after it began, accentuated Islamic religious sentiment and aggravated anti-Hindu feelings across Pakistan. Ayub Khan described the war against India as jihad, and official propaganda used religious symbolism to bolster the nation's morale.[14]

In his declaration of war, Ayub Khan said, "The 100 million people of Pakistan whose hearts beat with the sound of 'La ilaha ill Allah, Muhammad Ur Rasool Ullah' [There is no God but God and Muhammad is His messenger] will not rest till India's guns are silenced."[15] Invoking the Muslim declaration of faith as the rallying cry for war did not take any account of Pakistan's non-Muslim minorities. Matters were made worse by the tenor of official propaganda, primarily on Radio Pakistan and in newspapers, which described Hindus as Pakistan's enemies and warned against non-Muslim conspiracies against the country.

Pakistan's state-controlled media "generated a frenzy of jihad, extolling the virtues of Pakistan's 'soldiers of Islam' who were said to have received 'divine help.'"[16] People, both soldiers and civilians, claimed seeing with their eyes "green-robed angels deflecting bombs from their targets—bridges, culverts, mosques—with a wave of the hand. Soldiers were reported shooting enemy aircraft with their .303s [rifles]."[17]

The space for secular ideas in Pakistan shrank further with the 1965 war and the state-sponsored propaganda of that era. "The war brought out a striking characteristic of Pakistan's political culture," observed Khalid bin Sayeed, writing soon after the 1965 India–Pakistan war. Bin Sayeed continued:

> There is a considerable reservoir of religious emotions that a Pakistan government can draw upon for purposes of national unity during a time of crisis. Throughout the war, *Dawn* carried verses from the Quran on its front page. On 13 September, *Dawn's* front page had the following verse: "O Prophet! Urge the believer to fight. If there be of you twenty steadfast they shall overcome two hundred and if there be of you a hundred they shall overcome a thousand of those who disbelieve, because they are a people who do not understand." Quran, Chapter 8, Verses 65–66.[18]

Casting the conflict between India and Pakistan as a conflict between "true believers" and "unbelievers" had dire consequences for Pakistani "unbelievers." Throughout the war there were widespread rumors of

Pakistan's Hindus and Christians operating as spies or facilitators for the invading army. In some instances, Muslim neighbors engaged in vigilante violence against their non-Muslim compatriots. Even after the war was over, Hindus were described in movies, television plays, and patriotic songs as enemies of Islam and Pakistan, while Christians were portrayed as instruments of western imperialists. Although no new legal discrimination was instituted against non-Muslims in this period, Pakistani society's hostility toward them now was almost as virulent as at the time of Partition.

In this civic mood of heightened xenophobia, some extremist Islamists also began to publicly insinuate that Shias and Ahmadis, both groups that were deemed Muslims for legal purposes, were also unreliable in the event of war. The Shias, it was argued, harbored sympathy for Iran while the Ahmadis were accused of being a west-sponsored conspiracy against Islam.

In January 1966, Ayub and Indian Prime Minister Lal Bahadur Shastri signed an agreement at Tashkent to end the state of war and resume bilateral relations. This provoked violent demonstrations in Lahore and other cities of West Pakistan. Ayub was accused by the demonstrators of "selling Kashmir" to "the Hindu 'babus' and 'warlords.'"[19] While Khan and his purported betrayal of Pakistan's interests were the ostensible subjects of the unrest, the property the demonstrators burned or looted mostly belonged to Hindus, Christians, and Ahmadis.

Pakistan remained unstable over the next couple of years. The 1967 Arab–Israeli war generated pro-Palestine protests, which sparked attacks on British and American government property and resulted in boycotts of businesses with alleged links to Israel or Jews. The presence of the Ahmadi community in Israel, dating back to the period of the British mandate in Palestine, was cited to advance claims about an Ahmadi–Israeli alliance. Protests against Ayub's dictatorship simmered by 1968. They were supported by all opposition political parties as well as trade unions and student groups. While the main agenda for the protestors was seeking the end of the Ayub dictatorship, religious parties such as Jamaat-e-Islami, Nizam-e-Islam, and Majlis-e-Khatm-e-Nabuwwat interposed anti-Ahmadi rhetoric to the protest and decried Ayub's attempted modernization of Islam.

Ayub resigned in March 1969, handing over power to General Yahya Khan, who imposed martial law and promised to hold multiparty elections for a new Constituent Assembly. Although all political parties in the country were allowed to contest the election, the military seemed to favor conservative parties described in the official media as "Islam-loving" parties who were expected to keep in check the influence of secular and socialist factions. As the election campaign got under way, foreign observers spoke of "a distinctly obscurantist tendency" developing in the country. According to Feldman, who lived in Pakistan at the time, "This had much to do with an unconstructive harping on Islam and during the ensuing months it seemed as if no one could talk about anything else."[20]

Perhaps in response to the extremist fervor gripping the country, a martial law regulation was passed, which pronounced a maximum penalty of seven years' rigorous imprisonment for "any person who published, or was in possession of, any book, pamphlet, etc., which was offensive to the religion of Islam."[21] This 1970 law foreshadowed the infamous blasphemy laws imposed under Zia-ul-Haq's military dictatorship a few years later. The term "offensive to Islam" was not well defined in martial law regulation 51, and attempts to define it could only have resulted in the kind of religious exclusion that later emerged during the Zia era and after. Sunni extremists could claim that the views of Shias are offensive to them, while a similar opinion could be proffered by Orthodox Muslim sects about the beliefs of the Ahmadis.

In any event, military authorities were using religious zeal to stifle free debate in the country. An officially sponsored symposium on academic freedom, for example, declared that "such freedom must be allowed but only to the extent that it did not conflict with the ideology of Pakistan."[22] The emphasis on the "ideology of Pakistan" was aimed at ensuring that the Constituent Assembly emerging from Pakistan's first general election (held twenty-three years after Independence) would not veer too far from the idea of Pakistan as cultivated by its establishment since 1947.

The greatest challenge for the establishment view of Pakistan came from the secular Awami League, led by Sheikh Mujibur Rahman. The party, which was popular in East Pakistan, wanted the future constitution of Pakistan to be truly nonconfessional and federal, with less power for the central government. The Awami League also sought closer ties with India, which was anathema to Pakistan's military. In the country's western wing, the Pakistan Peoples Party (PPP) led by Zulfikar Ali Bhutto also bothered the generals with its advocacy of social democracy and its opposition to the nation's alliance with the United States. Although Bhutto maintained a staunchly anti-India stance, he spoke of Islam as the personal religion of the majority. Significantly, he did not endorse the concept of Pakistan as an ideological state during his election campaign.

Bhutto asserted that Pakistan was "a Muslim country. It came into being because we are Muslims." But he rejected the slogan that Islam was in danger and needed to be protected by the constitution or through legislation. "How can Islam be in danger in a country where the Muslims are in majority?" Bhutto asked his audience at a public rally. "Do you feel any danger to Islam in Pakistan?" he asked rhetorically, wondering aloud if anyone had "advised" the Islamists "against offering prayers or reciting the Holy Quran or to give up their religion."

The PPP leader argued that the "progress of a nation means the betterment of the lot of the common man" and that the exploiting elites "only try to cover their exploitation behind the slogan of 'Islam in danger.'"[23] Bhutto's aspiration for secularism was more clearly articulated during his election campaign than was evident when he attained power in a divided Pakistan two years later. (The reason for his changing stance will be discussed in a later chapter.)

The Muslim League contested the 1970 elections as three different factions but its division was caused by the personality clashes among its leaders, not because of their beliefs. Each Muslim League faction called for the introduction of separate communal electorates and pronounced Islam as Pakistan's raison d'être. Several religious parties also joined the electoral fray, though the three most important were the Jamaat-e-Islami, the Jamiat Ulema Islam (comprising Sunni Deobandi clerics), and Jamiat Ulema-e-Pakistan (led by Sunni Barelvi mullahs and Sufi Pirs). The three Muslim League factions and the Islamic parties, covertly supported by an election cell in the military government's National Security Council, strived to make the election about Islam and Pakistani identity, instead of allowing people to decide on the basis of bread-and-butter issues.[24]

The campaign season began with Jamaat-e-Islami supporters disrupting an Awami League rally in Lahore, describing the party as a grouping of Indian agents and secessionists. The Awami League returned the favor by making trouble at a Jamaat-e-Islami public meeting in Dhaka. Then, in a swipe at Bhutto and the PPP, several clerics issued a fatwa against socialism, declaring its supporters as being beyond the pale of Islam. Jamaat-e-Islami and its allies marked the launch of their full-fledged election campaign as Youm-e-Shaukat-e-Islam (Glory of Islam Day). When left-leaning groups in West Pakistan organized a workers' and peasants' conference, the Islamists retorted with their own "Sunni conference" in an attempt to bolster sectarian religious sentiments.

Elections were held under joint electorates, despite the insistence of the Muslim League and religious parties on the reinstatement of separate electorates. While the vote share of the religious minorities in West Pakistan was minuscule, non-Muslim voters could influence many seats in East Pakistan, especially in a close election. Given the choice between religion-based parties and the Awami League, most minority voters in East Pakistan were inclined to choose the latter.[25] The religious parties and the three Muslim League factions highlighted this and exploited it in their propaganda, especially in West Pakistan. They accused the Awami League of representing Hindu interests and of undermining the unity and integrity of Pakistan.

The political narrative that Hindus were conspiring against Pakistan had been widely promulgated since the days of the Ayub dictatorship. Accordingly, the Yahya regime encouraged anti-Hindu rhetoric and speculation of Hindu conspiracies. These were advanced in a bestselling book about the political situation of East Pakistan, written by the journalist Altaf Hasan Qureshee. The book claimed that "influential Hindus in East Pakistan were still engaged in anti-national activities"[26] and attempted to transfer the blame for East Pakistan's economic deprivation on its Hindu population. The Hindus were accused of smuggling rice, jute, and steel from East Pakistan to India so that the Muslims would not advance economically.

Qureshee also wrote of Hindu "influence in the Bengali media," the "Hindu role in East Pakistani politics," and "economic sabotage by Hindu factory owners, managers and workers." He blamed the Hindus for creating hatred against West Pakistanis among the Bengalis and insisted that the Hindu minority was acting as a fifth column for the Indian government, which wanted to reincorporate Pakistan into an undivided India.[27] These views were largely shared by the country's elite, especially those in senior positions in Yahya's military regime.[28]

Although a large number of minority candidates, mainly Hindus and Christians, contested the election, there was little representation of religious minorities among those elected to the new Constituent Assembly. Only one Hindu was elected from the entire western wing whereas a Buddhist and a Hindu were elected from East Pakistan. The joint electorate had clearly not worked to the advantage of non-Muslims in Pakistan, though their votes swung many seats to candidates of the more secular parties.[29]

When the votes were counted after polling day on December 7, 1970, the Awami League had swept to victory in East Pakistan while the PPP emerged with the largest number of seats in the western wing. The two parties disagreed over convening the Constituent Assembly, and Awami League supporters protested in East Pakistan's streets against what they saw as denial of their electoral mandate. Yahya Khan ordered a savage military crackdown in March 1971 that led to bloody civil war and the emergence in December of an independent Bangladesh.

The 1970 election, the ensuing civil war, and the breakup of Pakistan were perhaps the most significant events in Pakistan's history since Partition. They were to greatly influence the nation's future policies relating to religion and religious minorities.

Indubitably, geography and ethnicity were compelling factors in the power struggle that precipitated East Pakistan's secession as Bangladesh. And the glaring threat to West Pakistani hegemony posed by the Awami League's decisive victory could barely have been countenanced without incident, given the authoritarian tenor of the times. Less obvious though was the fact that the east and west had sharply differing views on the role of religion in public life. It was a strong undercurrent drawing the two parts of Pakistan into direct confrontation.

Since 1947, power in Pakistan had been largely vested in West Pakistani (mainly ethnic Punjabi) politicians, generals, and civil servants, most of whom looked upon Islamic religious sentiment as the glue that would hold the country together. The spectacular victory of the Awami League, led by Sheikh Mujibur Rahman, in the 1970 elections challenged the status quo in more ways than one. Bengalis, not Punjabis, would call the shots if the national assembly was convened according to the election results. Moreover, Mujib was publicly committed to reducing the role of religion in government by advancing the causes of secularism and federalism.

The Awami League won a clear majority in the three-hundred-member Constituent Assembly by winning all but two seats in East Pakistan; but it did not win a single seat in West Pakistan. Compromise was needed between the parties (Awami League and PPP) that represented the electorate of the two wings of Pakistan, but the initial discussions between the two sides did not yield agreement. General Yahya Khan then ordered the military to suppress the ensuing mass uprising in East Pakistan, alleging inter alia that the Awami League's electoral victory was attributable to the Hindu community and "its sinister purposes."[30]

By the time of the 1970 election, several waves of immigration to India since Partition had reduced the size of East Pakistan's Hindu population to around 15 percent of the province's citizenry. The community could not, therefore, have swung the poll on its own. The Awami League did well in districts with Hindu concentration, but so did the Jamaat-e-Islami and the Muslim Leagues. Feldman's explanation was that "in these districts Muslims tended to vote for the sectarian parties because they feared Hindu ascendancy, while Hindus voted for the Awami League because they feared the sectarian parties."[31] Be that as it may, the magnitude of the Awami League victory showed that it received an overwhelming share of the Muslim vote as well.

When the Pakistan army began its military operation against Bengalis in March 1971, General Khan reportedly told his commanding general in Dhaka: "Sort them out!" Feldman reported, "In the ensuing weeks this phrase was on the lips of many an army officer, whether or not Yahya [had] actually used it."[32] The Pakistani military objective was to crush Bengali nationalism and to eradicate those who favored separation from West Pakistan or were suspected of harboring such sentiments. Countless Bengalis in the army and police had stood up against West Pakistani domination. In addition to suppressing these mutinous elements, the Pakistan army sought to eliminate "subversives, left-wing intellectuals, suspect educationists, and students; political [activists] and professionals known for separationist tendencies or other uncongenial notions; trade union leaders; and Hindus, the last named, as a class, being considered traitorous."[33]

Much has been written about the brutality of the Pakistan army in its attempt to suppress the 1971 uprising in East Pakistan. Estimates of those killed in the military operations range from a low of three hundred thousand (preferred by Pakistani officials) to a high of three million (cited by Bangladeshi officials). The Pakistan army's actions are widely described as attempted genocide, with even Pakistani generals later admitting that their orders were to secure control of territory, even if it involved elimination of large numbers of citizens.[34] But the most significant element of this tragedy in the context of understanding Pakistan's policies toward religious minorities is the Pakistan army's treatment of Bengali Hindus, who were at the time Pakistani citizens.

According to Ziring, "Pakistani troops, largely drawn from West Pakistan, were instructed to believe that in fighting the local population they were actually fighting India and a Hindu challenge to their Islamic tradition."[35] In its initial operations, the Pakistan army "focused on clearing the province of its entire Hindu population" but the large-scale violence affected Bengali Muslims in similar proportions.[36] Feldman offered the explanation that "it is probable that troops sent from West to East Pakistan were possessed by the idea that Hindus were at the bottom of all the trouble and that if they were called upon to fire on civilians it would not be on their Muslim co-religionists but on the Hindu troublemakers."[37]

The army's attitude toward Hindus was summarized by the *New York Times* reporter Sydney Schanberg, in a report from the town of Faridpur, published on June 29, 1971, titled "Hindus Are Targets of Army Terror in an East Pakistani Town." "The Pakistani Army has painted big yellow 'H's' on the Hindu shops still standing in this town to identify the property of the minority eighth of the population that it has made its special targets," Schanberg wrote.

Members of the Moslem majority—who, though not exempt from the army's terror, feel safer than the Hindus—have painted on their homes and shops such signs as "All Moslem House." The small community of Christians, mostly Baptists, have put crosses on their doors and stitched crosses in red thread on their clothes.

Schanberg continued:

> Though a number of shops, most of them belonging to Hindus, have been razed in Faridpur most of it is physically intact.... An undetermined number of Faridpur's 10,000 Hindus have been killed and others have fled across the border to predominantly Hindu India.... Some Hindus are returning to Faridpur, but it is not out of faith in a change of heart by the army but rather out of despair. They do not want to live as displaced persons in India and they feel that nowhere in East Pakistan is really safe for them so they would rather be unsafe in their own town.

The *New York Times* reporter quoted a Hindu barber as saying that he was still in hiding, but that he sneaked into Faridpur every day to do a few hours' work to earn enough to eat. "'I come into town like a thief and leave like a thief,' he said. Those Hindus who have slipped into town keep guards posted at night. 'None of us sleep very soundly,' a young carpenter said. 'The daylight gives us a little courage.'"

Schanberg also narrated the story of a seventy-year-old Hindu woman who was shot through the neck and said that "as bad as conditions were and as frightened as she was, 'this is our home—we want to stay in golden Bengal.'" According to Schanberg, on April 21, when the army rolled into Faridpur, the old woman and her eighty-four-year-old husband had sought refuge in a Hindu village, Bodidangi, about three miles away. "The next day the army hit Bodidangi and reliable reports say, as many as 300 Hindus were massacred," he reported. The old woman stumbled and fell as she tried to flee Bodidangi, she related to the reporter, and two soldiers caught her.

"She said they beat her, ripped off her jewellery, fired a shot at pointblank range into her neck and left her for dead. She and her husband had owned a piece of property on which they rented out a few flimsy huts. Only the dirt floors are left, she said," Schanberg wrote. In his opinion, "The campaign against the Hindus was—and in some cases still is—systematic. Soldiers fanned through virtually every village asking where the Hindus lived. Hindu property has been confiscated and either sold or given to 'loyal' citizens."

Many of the beneficiaries, the *New York Times* said, were Biharis,

non-Bengali Moslem migrants from India, most of whom are work-ing with the army now. The army has given weapons to large numbers of the Biharis, and it is they who have often continued the killing of Hindus in areas where the army has eased off. Hindu bank accounts are frozen. Almost no Hindu students or teachers have returned to the schools.

Publicly Yahya appealed to the Hindus to return from their hiding places and from India and assured them of an equal role in East Pakistani life. But Schanberg pointed out that

army commanders in the field in East Pakistan privately admit to a policy of stamping out Bengali culture, both Moslem and Hindu—but particularly Hindu. Although thousands of "anti-state" Bengali Moslems have been killed by the army, the Hindus became particular scapegoats as the martial law regime tried to blame Hindu India and her agents in East Pakistan for the autonomy movement.

The chilling reportage explained that in Faridpur—"and the situation was much the same throughout East Pakistan—there was no friction to speak of between Hindu and Moslem before the army came." The army had tried to drive a wedge between them, said Schanberg. He elaborated:

In April, as a public example, two Hindus were beheaded in a central square in Faridpur and their bodies were soaked in kerosene and burned. When some Hindus, trying to save their lives, begged to convert to Islam, they were shot as unworthy non-believers (in some cases, however, converts are being accepted).

The report also spoke of the army forcing "Moslems friendly to Hindus to loot and burn Hindu houses." The Muslims were ostensibly told that if they did not attack Hindus, they themselves would be killed.

"Most of the Hindu houses in the region around Faridpur—some say 90 percent—were burned as a result," Schanberg wrote.

> Still there is no sign of a hate-Hindu psychology among the Bengali Moslems. Many have taken grave risks to shelter and defend Hindus; others express shock and horror at what is happening to Hindus but confess that they are too frightened to help. Many Bengalis, in fact feel that the army has only succeeded in forging a tighter bond between Hindu and Moslem in East Pakistan.[38]

The Pakistan army's campaign of terror led to a mass evacuation from East Pakistan into India and became the basis for India's direct involvement in the situation. The exact number of persons—Muslims and Hindus—who fled across the border is often debated by Pakistanis, but no one has questioned the magnitude of the exodus. Yahya ordered a census of persons who left East Pakistan in this way and the result was a figure in the order of 2.25 million. As of June 11, 1971, some estimated 5.5 million refugees—of which 90 percent were Hindu Bengalis—had reached India.[39] The Indian government claimed a figure exceeding nine million Hindus and Muslims, and the UN High Commissioner for Refugees stated that by August 1971, 7,144,300 Pakistani refugees had entered India and that more were still crossing the border.[40]

By the beginning of December, Pakistan and India had again gone to war. As fighting began along the border of West Pakistan, Sindhi Hindus too were uprooted from villages in the Tharparkar desert, and many went across into India's Rajasthan state. But the expulsion of Hindus and the massive use of force against Bengalis did not keep Pakistan together. The Pakistan army surrendered to India in Dhaka on December 16, 1971, and East Pakistan finally became the sovereign state of Bangladesh.

In less than a quarter century, Pakistan had thus lost more than half its population and two-fifths of its territory. Nevertheless, the remaining state of Pakistan was physically contiguous and had a much smaller percentage of non-Muslims in its population, diminishing some of the basis for the nation's insecurities. This smaller, less diverse country would surely be easier to govern. Now was a chance for Pakistan to shun

extremist ideology and emerge as a more secure and less volatile country. But the loss of East Pakistan did not end the drive for Islamization.
On the contrary, Pakistan's leaders persisted in nation building through
religion, rather than embracing inclusive civic nationalism. Pakistan's
religious minorities were now more beleaguered than ever.

4

Balancing Act, 1972–1977

THE HUMILIATING DEFEAT OF the Pakistan army in the 1971 war with India, and secession of East Pakistan to become Bangladesh, made it impossible for the military to continue in power. Soon after the surrender at Dhaka, General Yahya Khan handed over power to Zulfikar Ali Bhutto, the charismatic leader of the Pakistan Peoples Party (PPP), which had won the largest number of seats in West Pakistan during the December 1970 election. Pakistan now had a representative government, contiguous territory, and—with more than 96 percent Muslims composing the citizenry—a more religiously homogeneous population. The country could make a fresh start, leaving behind the stultifying baggage of ideology and conflict that had accumulated since 1947.

Bhutto revived the morale of a demoralized nation and promised to pick up the pieces in building a new Pakistan.[1] His own inclinations and previous public pronouncements indicated his preference for a modern, secular state. Bhutto had spoken of ties between Pakistan's Muslims with "Buddhists and the Hindus among whom they have lived for almost a thousand years."[2] On the campaign trail, he had questioned the logic of the Jamaat-e-Islami's slogan "Islam in danger," saying, "How can Islam be in danger in a country where the Muslims are in majority?" According to Bhutto, real service to Islam involved "enabling the Muslims to prosper and progress."

Rejecting the ideology of religious division, Bhutto listed practical issues that needed the government's attention. "We want the children of the poor to be educated," he had said during his election campaign, adding, "We want to establish hospitals for the treatment of the poor. We want to provide housing for the common man. . . . Islam will be served only if the people of Pakistan, who are Muslims, are served. This is going to be our endeavor."[3]

But the Pakistan that Bhutto governed, first as president and then as prime minister, had been influenced, in the words of a foreign commentator, by "a distinctly obscurantist tendency" and "an unconstructive harping on Islam."[4] The Yahya regime had imposed laws that banned publications questioning the orthodox ulema's interpretation of Islam, creating an environment favorable to Islamist hard-liners. Although religious parties had fared badly in the 1970 election, they still had a strong presence in Pakistani society: the three factions of the Muslim League and the three Islamist parties, between them, had received 37 percent of the votes compared with 44 percent for Bhutto's PPP.

Furthermore, the proportion of non-Muslims in Pakistan's population had shrunk significantly with the loss of East Pakistan. When a census was conducted in 1972, none of the non-Muslim communities counted even a million members. Pakistan's total population of 62.4 million at the time included 60.4 million Muslims, 907,861 Christians, and 899,000 Hindus. The number of Buddhists was down to 4,318 while the Parsis (Zoroastrians) numbered only 9,589.[5] In the past, the larger proportion of Hindus in united Pakistan had given some voice, however limited, to non-Muslims; that would no longer be the case. Having achieved a measure of purity in relation to non-Muslims within Pakistan, Islamists were now getting ready to purify the country of unorthodox groups hitherto identified as being Muslim.

The loss of Bangladesh and the national humiliation caused by the 1971 war had, in fact, increased the influence of Islamist groups. The Jamaat-e-Islami had provided cadres to fight alongside the army in East Pakistan, creating bonds between military officers and Islamists. The people of West Pakistan had been kept in the dark about the situation in Bangladesh until the end, and when the news of defeat and surrender arrived, a shocked nation turned to religion for solace.[6] Mullahs told prayer gatherings that the division of the country was the Allah's punishment for not implementing His law in Pakistan.

As the political scientist Lawrence Ziring pointed out, "The loss of East Bengal obviated the need for a bridge between disparate communities, and centered attention on constructing a Pakistan that was more akin to Islamist doctrine and precept than that suggested by the constrained and tortured secularism of the earlier vision." The new Pakistan was also no longer anchored in South Asia and was seen as "attached to the Muslim world of the Middle Eastern states." Pakistan had been divided between nationalists and provincialists and between secularists and Islamists, and according to Ziring, the provincialists and Islamists appeared to have won their respective contests.

Disturbingly, Ziring observed that

> who was the "better" Muslim, who was more worthy to be called a Muslim, was as much at play in the Pakistan army assault on the Bengali population as was the effort to cleanse the region of its Hindu population. The soldiers from Baluchistan, Pashtunistan and the Punjab were convinced that their mission to kill Bengalis, of whatever persuasion, was a call to preserve the faith, even if doing so meant destroying Pakistan.[7]

In 1968, a study had showed that only 8 and 12 percent of Bengali university students took pride in Islam and Islamic nationalism, respectively, whereas in West Pakistan the corresponding figures were 17 and 30 percent.[8] The Islamist appeal to "national honor" and "Islamic pride" immediately after the loss of East Pakistan increased their support on college campuses, especially in the Punjab and Karachi. Within days of coming to power, Bhutto faced protests from Islamist students against potential secularization or even the recognition of Bangladesh's sovereignty.

These political realities and changes within Pakistani society prompted Bhutto to adopt a pragmatic approach to the Islamists' ideological demands. Avoiding the Islam versus secularism debates that stalled constitution making during the 1950s, Bhutto secured consensus on a draft within a year by negotiating and giving ground on the Islamic content. Rafi Raza, a member of his cabinet, pointed out that Bhutto "was conscious of the need not to appear too secular" in response to the Islamist attacks against him for being "the leader of a socialist party in an Islamic State."[9] Worried by the fatwas and religious rhetoric unleashed during the 1970 election campaign, the PPP leader had already opted for using the term "Musawaat-e-Muhammadi" (Muhammad's principle of equality) instead of "Islamic Socialism," which had earlier been the cornerstone of the PPP's election manifesto.

The 1973 constitution not only retained the Islamic provisions from earlier versions but also added new ones. Islam was declared the "State religion of Pakistan" and a promise was made to ensure that "all existing laws" conform "with the Injunctions of Islam as laid down in the Holy Quran and Sunnah." The constitution declared that "no law shall be enacted which is repugnant to such Injunctions." The preamble of the basic law spoke of enabling the Muslims "to order their lives in the individual and collective spheres in accordance with the teachings and requirements of Islam as set out in the Holy Quran and Sunnah." But it also promised that "adequate provision shall be made for the minorities freely to profess and practice their religions and develop their cultures."[10]

In addition to appealing to the Islamists with constitutional provisions, the Bhutto government also created a Ministry for Religious and Minorities Affairs, which was to undertake programs appealing to the religious sentiments of the populace. Over the next four years, the Imams of Islam's holiest shrines in Mecca and Medina were invited to tour the country in well-publicized religious ceremonies that were telecast live on state television; the printing of the Quran was standardized, and religious schools began to receive government funding. The government also provided subsidies for Hajj pilgrims. The result was that, the number of Pakistani Hajj travelers increased from a few thousand to tens of thousands annually.

Bhutto initially tried to balance these "Islamic" measures with efforts to emphasize pluralism and tolerance for religious minorities. The PPP was strongly supported by Shias, Ahmadis, Christians, and Hindus at the polls. These communities expected the party in government to protect them, and the PPP government acquitted itself well on this score in its first two years. While negotiating with India over what became the Simla Accord in 1973, Bhutto insisted that the Hindus who had fled Sindh during the 1971 war should return to their homeland.

In follow-up meetings between Indian and Pakistani officials after the accord, the return of Sindhi Hindus was given priority alongside delineation of the Line of Control in Kashmir and determining the timetable for troop withdrawals from areas occupied by each side along their international border. India and Pakistan agreed that "political leaders from Tharparkar would visit the areas of Sindh occupied by Indian forces to ensure that the Hindu inhabitants returning would be welcome to remain in or return to their homes in Pakistan in safety and dignity from camps in India."[11] Pakistan accepted a draft Indian plan for the resettlement of Hindus in Sindh, which would in earlier times have been condemned as "gross interference" in Pakistan's internal affairs.

Nonetheless, the balancing act between implementing liberal ideas and appeasing Islamist sentiment was not easy, as Bhutto discovered when he assembled scholars from all over Pakistan at a congress on Pakistan's history and culture. His idea was to redefine Pakistani nationalism away from the Islamic ideology that had prevailed since Liaquat and had intensified under Ayub and Yahya. The gathering was meant to emphasize Pakistan's identity as a Muslim homeland that did not need Islamization—the argument that Bhutto had advanced through most of his political career thus far. It ended up being dominated by those who did not want to revisit the established notion of Pakistan as an Islamic state.

At the Congress, secular scholars spoke of "geological, geographic, ethnic and historical grounds for regarding the Indus Valley and its western and northern mountain marches as a distinct national unit separate from the rest of South Asia."[12] But the view of the majority of scholars was summed up by the Pakistani historian Waheed-uz-Zaman: "The wish to see the kingdom of God established in a Muslim territory . . . was the moving idea behind the demand for Pakistan, the cornerstone of the movement, the ideology of the people and the raison d'être of the new nation-state."

Echoing the sentiment of Ayub and Yahya, Zaman said that "if we let go of the ideology of Islam, we cannot hold together as a nation by any other means." He also voiced the "dilemma" that faced Pakistanis in defining their nationalism: "If the Arabs, the Turks, the Iranians, God forbid give up Islam, the Arabs yet remain Arabs, the Turks remain Turks, the Iranians remain Iranians, but what do we remain if we give up Islam?"[13]

Soon Bhutto also adapted some of the Islamic rhetoric in defining Pakistani nationalism, especially against the assertion of ethnic identities by Punjabis, Pashtuns, Sindhis, or Baluchs. "Islam is a great unifying factor and its role has varied in different places and times," he declared in a speech. "In South Asia," Bhutto said, "Islam was a catalyst that unified the Muslims of the subcontinent. . . . Here, ever since the advent of Islam it has had a cementing role."[14]

Mubashir Hasan, then secretary-general of the PPP, wrote later that by 1974 he noted "Bhutto's tilt towards an obscurantist interpretation of Islam."[15] That year, Pakistan's constitution was amended, in a concession to Islamists, to declare members of the Ahmadi sect to be non-Muslims. Bhutto expected the measure to steal the mullahs' thunder; instead, it only encouraged them to make further demands over the next few years.

The Ahmadi controversy had resurfaced after a violent incident in May 1974 at Rabwah, the small Punjab town that served as the Ahmadiyya movement's international headquarters. Medical college students traveling on a train passing through Rabwah shouted anti-Ahmadi insults and slogans. When the students were on their return journey a few days later, a group of Ahmadis beat them up.[16] Although there were no casualties during the incident, the student wing of Jamaat-e-Islami used it to foment anti-Ahmadi protests around the country. Soon, other religious parties joined the campaign and the Majlis-e-Tahaffuz-e-Khatm-e-Nabuwwat (Society for the Protection of the Finality of the Prophet) reiterated its old demand that Ahmadis be declared non-Muslims by law. During the ensuing riots in Punjab, forty-two persons died, twenty-seven of whom were Ahmadis.[17]

Parallels were drawn immediately between the anti-Ahmadi violence of 1953 and this campaign, though clearly the 1974 protests were milder and easily contained. Orthodox religious groups in Punjab had agitated against the Ahmadis, referring to them pejoratively, at different times, as Qadianis (after the name of the religion's place of birth) since the beginning of the twentieth century. As the historian Herbert Feldman observed, "Because anti-Qadiani [Ahmadi] agitation is such inflammatory material, it has become, especially in the Punjab, a classic method of embarrassing and undermining authority."[18]

Bhutto was concerned about an escalation in sectarian violence and the likelihood of it impacting his ability to maintain influence in Punjab, Pakistan's largest province. According to Rafi Raza, the Ahmadis had supported the PPP during the 1970 election, but Bhutto had been told (most likely by the intelligence services) that they were transferring their support to the opposition leader Air Marshal Asghar Khan.[19] After the Rabwah incident, the government initially showed little tolerance for anti-Ahmadi demands. Officials were told to focus on protecting Ahmadi citizens and their property and to arrest those involved in fomenting violence. On June 3, 1974, Bhutto accused his opponents of manufacturing the controversy against Ahmadis,[20] affirming that it was not the state's business to define who was or was not a Muslim. The next day, the speaker of the National Assembly ruled out a debate on the Ahmadi issue, saying that the constitution already defined religious minorities and a redefinition, to describe as non-Muslim a sect that considered itself Muslim, was not necessary. However, ten days later, on June 13, Bhutto changed his position and declared that he would ask Parliament to debate and vote on whether Ahmadis were Muslim.

Instead of releasing pressure, the prospect of the Ahmadi issue being taken to Parliament resulted in new maneuvers by religious parties. The Jamiat Ulema Islam members of the Northwest Frontier Province (now known as Khyber-Pakhtunkhwa)—reflecting the orthodox Deobandi denomination of Sunni Islam—managed to secure support from members of secular opposition parties for a unanimous resolution that "recommended and requested the federal government to declare the Mirzais, Ahmadis or Qadianis as a minority because they do not believe in Khatm-e-Nabuwwat."[21]

For his part, Bhutto continued a balancing act of appeasing the Islamists and defending the rights of Ahmadis as citizens of Pakistan. He opposed calls for a social and business boycott of Ahmadis, "which, he said, could not be justified on human or moral grounds. He asked whether it was an Islamic act to deny a section of the citizens the necessities of life. After all, they were human beings." But he also insisted that "it [was his] foremost duty to serve Islam. Everything else comes later."[22]

In September, both houses of Pakistan's Parliament passed the second amendment to Pakistan's constitution, pronouncing Ahmadis non-Muslims.[23] The decision was welcomed, among others by Maulana Maududi, founder of the Jamaat-e-Islami, who "thanked the Almighty that collective endeavors of the people, *ulema, mashaikh* [spiritual leaders], students, political organizations and the National Assembly have at last resulted in the solution of the ninety-year-old problem that constituted a big internal threat to the Muslims and Islam." He claimed that "previous regimes in Pakistan had tried to suppress the problem" and had effectively forced Muslims to accept within their fold a group considered non-Muslim by the majority.[24]

The second amendment of the Pakistani constitution altered Article 106, Clause 3, which lists religious minority communities, to include "persons of Qadiani group or the Lahori group (who call themselves 'Ahmadis')." The Ahmadis were the only religious minority who were listed in the constitution not by the name they use but by pejoratives applied to them by their detractors. It was akin to a predominantly Protestant Christian country describing Catholics as "Papists" in its fundamental law. Moreover, a new clause that attempted to define "Muslim" was added to Article 260 of the constitution, transforming a purely religious question into a matter of law. "A person who does not believe in the absolute and unqualified finality of The Prophethood of Muhammad (Peace be upon him), the last of the Prophets," it read, "or claims to be a Prophet, in any sense of the word or of any description whatsoever, after Muhammad (Peace be upon him), or recognizes such a claimant as a Prophet or religious reformer, is not a Muslim for the purposes of the Constitution or law."[25]

Bhutto described the constitutional amendment as an expression of the "will and aspirations of the Muslims of Pakistan," but insisted that he was determined to ensure that the rights of every citizen of the country were fully protected. "There should be no ambiguity in any-one's mind that we will not tolerate any kind of vandalism or insults and brutality of any citizen of the country," he declared. In an attempt to reassure religious minorities, Bhutto said his government believed that "every citizen of the country had the right to practice his religion without any fear."[26]

As Feldman points out, Bhutto saw himself as handling a poten-tial political crisis and believed he had "sidestepped" further agitation against Ahmadis through the constitutional amendment. Addressing the National Assembly, Bhutto said, "Let us close this chapter,"[27] indi-cating that his intention was only to silence the mullahs. But in his con-gratulatory statement, Maududi also expressed the hope that Bhutto "after solving well the Qadiani issue constitutionally would take all such legal and administrative measures as were necessary."[28] This was a reference to demands of excluding Ahmadis from senior positions in the civil service and armed forces and barring them from using Islamic nomenclature. These demands were later fulfilled by draconian anti-Ahmadi ordinances imposed by Zia-ul-Haq in 1983.

But the constitutional amendment created a religious dilemma for the Ahmadis and effectively took away their freedom of religion. Their faith required them to insist that they were Muslims, albeit with some beliefs that departed from those of other Islamic denominations. The law, however, would now deem them non-Muslims. Now, if they stated Islam as their religion on government documents, as their faith dictated, they would be breaking the law.

The government made things even more complicated by requiring all applicants for passports and mandatory national identity cards to sign a declaration if they wanted to be identified as Muslims. The declaration states, "I do not recognize any person who claims to be a prophet in any sense of the word or of any description whatsoever after Muhammad (peace be upon him) or recognize such a claimant as prophet or a religious reformer as a Muslim." It goes on to say, "I consider Mirza Ghulam Ahmad Qadiani to be an imposter *nabi* [Prophet] and also consider his followers whether belonging to the Lahori or Qadiani group to be non-Muslim." This meant that no Ahmadis could get a passport or national identity card as a Muslim without denouncing their denomination's founder as an imposter. On the other hand, accepting a passport or national identity card that described them as non-Muslim also ran against the Ahmadi religion.

Publicly, the Ahmadis put on a brave face. The head of the Ahmadiyya community, Mirza Nasir Ahmad, said, "It doesn't matter what they call us. We have a living connection with our God—and he calls us Muslims." Asked what he thought was behind the move to declare Ahmadis non-Muslims, Ahmad responded, "There is only one word for it: 'Fanaticism.'" He expressed confidence that "my people" would not abandon their faith and asserted that "this current trouble has been prophesied" by Ahmadi divines. But soon after being declared non-Muslims, Ahmadi professionals started seeking asylum in Europe and North America. From their perspective, it was important to be able to travel around the world on passports that did not have a column for religion, and for which they were not required to renounce articles of their faith.

Some authors have suggested that Bhutto's decision to take the Ahmadi issue to Parliament was meant to draw attention from other challenges facing the government. According to Raza, "He felt a need to counter concern over India's nuclear bomb"[29]—a reference to India's test of a nuclear device a few days earlier. Husain Haqqani asserts that "Bhutto's tilt towards religious conservatism was connected to his economic and national security agendas." He was drawing close, especially to Saudi Arabia, "to benefit from the flow of petro-dollars, which required playing up Pakistan's Islamic identity."[30] But it is also possible that Bhutto was simply trying to negotiate his way through a maze of religious issues that had become intertwined with Pakistan's politics. In Rafi Raza's words, what Bhutto "lost sight of was the fundamental principle of whether religious issues can or should be settled in a political forum."[31]

Several legislators who voted for the second amendment later "regretted privately that this decision had to be taken by the Assembly."[32] Bhutto was also "ambivalent about its desirability and was concerned over this fusion of religion and politics." He was not an orthodox man but had ended up making a decision that had been eschewed in 1953—amid greater agitation and violence—by a far more religiously conservative prime minister, Khawaja Nazimuddin. During the 1953 anti-Ahmadi riots, the federal government had conveyed to the Punjab government that "the Ahmadis or indeed any section of the people, cannot be declared a minority against their wishes. It is not the job of the government to coerce any group into becoming a minority community."[33]

The constitutional amendment against Ahmadis did not go down well internationally. "In this pretty little Punjab town live 20,000 people who look, dress and worship like Moslems, are born, married and buried like Moslems, and who consider themselves Moslems in every respect," said an article in the *Washington Post*. "Two weeks ago Pakistan's National Assembly amended the country's constitution to declare these people and some 4 million like them throughout Pakistan 'non-Moslems.' Now the people of Rabwah, the spiritual centre of the

Ahmadi sect of the Moslem religion, are nervously waiting for the practical consequences of this drastic legal step."[34] The article also cited Ahmadi fears of being forced out of their jobs; having their mosques, schools, and libraries closed; and their lives threatened. In subsequent years, all of those fears materialized.

It was a tragedy that, instead of diminishing the difference between Muslim and non-Muslim over time, as Jinnah had envisioned, Pakistan had created a new non-Muslim minority through a constitutional amendment. It was a greater tragedy that this had happened under an otherwise progressive and pluralist government. It is not unusual in the history of most faiths for religious leaders to classify members of other denominations as not belonging within the mainstream of their faith. But the purported heresy of a sect had not been made the subject of legislation in any country in modern times.

In any case, even after this major concession to Pakistan's extreme Islamists, Bhutto's efforts to be seen by the orthodox section of society as "a proponent of Islam" did not succeed. "He had given up his earlier views that the State and religion should be kept apart," wrote Raza with hindsight, "only to find the new ground on which he chose to tread was firmly occupied by the religious parties."[35]

Despite failing to capture the following of the Islamist parties, Bhutto's PPP was widely predicted to sweep the polls in Pakistan's second parliamentary elections in March 1977. "Most of the parties composing the opposition are known for their professed dedication to Islam, which they equate with the 'ideology of Pakistan,'" explained a US-based Pakistani political scientist. "They will probably accuse the government of being untrue to the national ideology," he continued, arguing that Bhutto would defeat them as he had stolen their thunder. Listing the government's services for Islam, the scholar predicted at the end of 1976 that "Bhutto has plenty of ammunition with which to repell any Islam-related attacks the opposition may choose to launch against him."[36]

Three secular parties and the Muslim League joined five religious parties to contest the election as the Pakistan National Alliance (PNA). The ostensible purpose of the alliance was to check what opponents believed to be Bhutto's authoritarian tendencies and socialist economic policies. But the PNA's election campaign reflected Islamist sentiment from its beginning. "For forty-five days, the two political coalitions—the PPP representing the landed interests, rural poor and urban marginals and the PNA standing for the powerful middle class—fought what the *Economist* labeled as a campaign 'of whiskey, war and Islam,'" observed Shahid Javed Burki.

Rejecting Bhutto's hard-cultivated Islamic credentials, PNA orators transformed the election into an ideological confrontation between the PNA and PPP. The opposition made much of the fact that Bhutto drank alcohol, even though several PNA politicians were no teetotalers themselves. The prime minister responded by saying that he drank wine, "not people's blood." "The PNA in charging the prime minister, was defending the middle class's [religious] values," observed Burki, adding, "Bhutto's riposte was meant to remind the opposition and the electorate that he stood for the poor."[37]

Meanwhile, Pakistan's religious minorities stayed on the sidelines of the electoral battle, though they were obviously concerned about the Islamic religious zeal that was being unleashed by the PNA. If the past was any guide, religious-political campaigns always ended up turning against religious minorities, particularly the Hindus and the Ahmadis. But the PNA restrained antiminority rhetoric because it did not want to alienate the religious minorities to a point where they would vote en bloc for the PPP. Its strategists calculated that Hindus, Christians, and Ahmadis may have less enthusiasm for Bhutto and the PPP than in the past and saw no reason to fire up that enthusiasm in what they saw as a tight election.

In the end, the PPP won 155 seats in the National Assembly with 58.1 percent of the total votes cast to PNA's 36 seats with 35.4 percent of the votes. The PNA won mostly in large cities where the alliance had demonstrated most support during the campaign. Economic factors may have worked to Bhutto's advantage. The rate of inflation at 6 percent was well below the average rate of inflation of 25 percent between 1972 and 1975. Economic growth in 1976 stood at 5 percent, up from 3 percent a year earlier. The agriculture sector was growing after years of stagnation with help from heavy public investment in tube wells and subsidies for fertilizer, pesticides, and other farm inputs.[38] As one observer put it, "The PPP's majority was, in all likelihood, more padded than stolen."[39]

But Bhutto's opponents rejected outright the election results, claiming that the poll had been massively rigged. The PNA refused to accept the explanation that the PPP had won the election because of improved economic performance and quiet support from women and minorities who feared the religious laws promised by some of the opposition leaders. The party called for street protests to demand fresh elections. Once violent protests had started, the PNA changed its demand to seeking Bhutto's resignation as prime minister. The protestors later started asking for Nizam-e-Mustafa (the system of the Prophet of Islam). The religious fervor whipped up during the election campaign was now at its height.

After the government banned rallies and demonstrations on streets, the PNA started organizing its protests from mosques. Activists from religious parties deliberately confronted police and paramilitary units and several "offered" themselves for martyrdom by provoking the law enforcement officials to shoot and kill them. At least two hundred people were killed in clashes between demonstrators and security forces between March, when the election was held, and July, when martial law was finally imposed.[40] In between, Bhutto tried to placate Islamists. He prohibited the sale and use of alcoholic beverages, banned gambling, and closed bars and nightclubs, while promising to "move Pakistan toward the objective of a chaste Islamic state."[41]

But on July 5, 1977, Chief of the Army Staff General Zia-ul-Haq took over the reins of power, deposing the elected Bhutto government and declaring martial law. Zia promised that he would hold fresh elections within ninety days of his coup, and he insisted that he had only intervened to avoid further bloodshed. After initially setting a date for new elections, Zia reneged on his promise and consolidated his rule. He executed Bhutto after a disputed trial in 1979 and ruled with a heavy hand for eleven years.

Zia legitimated his dictatorship by claiming the mantle of Islamization. He promised to be guided by "the spirit of the people's struggle for Nizam-e-Mustafa"[42] from his first day in power. Some scholars have wondered whether he and Islamist leaders had been in collusion from the beginning to transform the dispute over the fairness of elections into an agitation for an Islamic system of government.[43] Even before the controversy over the election, the Jamaat-e-Islami's founder, Maududi, had declared that "only Nizam-e-Islam [Islamic system] would be acceptable in Pakistan."[44]

The end of the Bhutto government also marked the end of efforts to strike a balance between Jinnah's vision of a pluralist Pakistan and the demands of Islamists for an Islamic state. After Zia's ascent to power, Pakistan moved in a decidedly obscurantist and sectarian direction.

5

Islamization, 1977–1988

FOR THIRTY YEARS AFTER Independence, Pakistanis at least debated the role of Islam in matters of state, even as the political balance gradually shifted against secular and pluralist ideas. Once General Muhammad Zia-ul-Haq seized power through a military coup in 1977, debate was terminated and replaced by arbitrary and forced Islamization. Zia changed laws by decree, imposed draconian punishments based on medieval interpretations of Islam, silenced secular critics, and changed school curricula to pass on his bigoted worldview to the next generation.

Hard-line clerics with limited followings now preached on national television, and orthodox religious schools (*madrasas*) proliferated with state and foreign funding. Islamist militias, trained to fight the communist occupation in Afghanistan, also turned their guns on non-Muslims, Ahmadis, and Shias within Pakistan, often with a nod from Zia's officials and political allies. If the 1947 Partition virtually cleansed Pakistan of Hindus and Sikhs, Zia-ul-Haq's decade-long dictatorship marked the beginning of a period of heightened sectarian violence, in which all but the most obscurantist Muslim sects and groups were targeted.

Zia had removed Zulfikar Ali Bhutto's elected government ostensibly to hold free and fair elections in the aftermath of the controversy over the March 1977 legislative election. He had promised to hold the election under military supervision within ninety days before returning to barracks. "During the next three months my total attention will be concentrated on the holding of elections and I would not like to dissipate my energies as Chief Martial Law Administrator on anything else,"[1] he declared after the coup in July. He also insisted that he did not have any political ambitions "nor does the army want to be taken away from its profession of soldiering." But there is considerable evidence that Zia and the military intelligence service had colluded with Islamist parties to orchestrate protests against Bhutto. These parties, especially the Jamaat-e-Islami, celebrated Zia's coup by distributing sweets in the streets of major cities and outside mosques.[2]

Zia, who used the phrase "soldier of Islam" to describe himself in his very first speech, subsequently insisted that he was a pious Muslim seeking to revive Islamic law as practiced in earlier times. He praised the "spirit of Islam" that had characterized the opposition protests, adding, "It proves that Pakistan, which was created in the name of Islam, will continue to survive only if it sticks to Islam. That is why I consider the introduction of [an] Islamic system as an essential prerequisite for the country."[3]

After his consultations with leaders of all political parties a few days after seizing power, Zia insisted that "all these political parties should work for establishing an Islamic order because this country had been created in the name of Islam and will survive only by holding fast to Islam."[4] A month later Zia professed that "the key to the welfare of the common man lies in the Islamic system which was promised to him thirty seven years ago," a reference to the date when the demand for Pakistan was first voiced. "Had the Islamic system been introduced at the appropriate time," he claimed, "all the basic necessities of every citizen would have been met easily. . . . This is my faith and I have mentioned it previously that this country had not only been created in the name of Islam but could survive only in the name of Islam."[5]

By September 1977, Zia was insisting that he would only allow political parties that framed their election manifestos "in accordance with Islamic law and values" to participate in elections. He identified the safety, security, and ideology of Pakistan as the three fundamental points that must be part of every party's program. Politicians who did not conform to these "Islamic" conditions "will be out of the field as far as I am concerned," he declared. Although Pakistan's constitution provided for a Westminster-style parliamentary system, Zia said he considered the presidential form of government "most suitable" for Pakistan as it was very close to the Islamic concept of "amir."[6]

Zia's Islamic rhetoric worried secular Pakistanis as well as non-Muslim minorities. If the chief martial law administrator planned on amending the constitution to translate into reality his professed ideal of an Islamic state headed by an "amir" and run under sharia, would he also limit the minorities' rights to those of *dhimmis* in early Islam? A delegation of the National Council of Churches of Pakistan approached Zia about the "status of minorities in a truly Islamic state" only to be assured that "their rights as a minority community would be fully protected." Zia said that Islam laid down certain safeguards for rights of minorities in an Islamic state and added that these safeguards would be fully honored.[7]

Thus, within months of his military coup Zia was methodically building, on religious grounds, a structure of support to enable his indefinite rule. Zia lacked a legal or constitutional mandate and planned to exercise power with an iron hand. Two American academics observed at the time that Zia had introduced Islamic themes in all contexts. "There is talk of an Islamic cargo fleet, an Islamic science foundation and an Islamic newsprint industry and the All Pakistan Lawn Tennis Association has instituted the Millat Cup, 'the first big tennis gala of Muslim youth,' " noted the professors.[8]

Veteran Pakistan scholar Lawrence Ziring argued that, "temperamentally, but also strategically, Zia was convinced that only by emphasizing Islamic precepts and traditions, by practicing the sociopolitical values of the Muslim faith, could he expect to weather both the internal and external storms that shook his country."[9] The dictator's approach was validated internationally by endorsement from the United States, which from 1979 onward allied with Zia in using Islam as a bulwark against communism in Afghanistan. Zia's regime received military aid from the United States and drew strength from the support received from his regional Muslim neighbors, notably Turkey, Saudi Arabia, the United Arab Emirates, and Egypt.[10]

At home, forceful advocacy of an Islamic state was Zia's sole, albeit limited, source of legitimacy. His conduct was both cynical and hypocritical. But backed by military force, Zia was able to manipulate Pakistan's foundational dilemma—Muslim homeland or Islamic state—to his advantage. Pakistanis had heard the rhetoric of Islamic ideology before and were skeptical about promises of an Islamic state.

Zia carefully nurtured his image as a man of Allah, with televised attendance at prayer congregations and annual pilgrimages to Mecca. He also met regularly with clerics, many of whom were given state jobs and titles. Zia thereby assembled a protective cohort of Islamist shock troops around himself, in addition to the uniformed military that he already commanded.

From the first weeks of his martial law regime, Zia imposed laws, which he described as reforms, designed to create Nizam-e-Islam (Islamic system of government) in Pakistan. After arresting Bhutto and putting him on trial on a trumped-up murder charge, Zia invited Bhutto's opponents to join his government. Key portfolios in the cabinet, including planning as well as information and broadcasting, were allocated to the Jamaat-e-Islami, which enthusiastically joined Zia's Islamization effort.

This partly civilianized government described its "major task (after the insurance of elections)" as "the implementation of Nizam-e-Mustafa (the system of the chosen one, Muhammad), which involves the complete Islamization of the laws of economic life and of social life." Professor Eric Gustafson pointed out that "the details of the Nizam-e-Mustafa [were] left conveniently vague, since aside from obvious points like the banning of alcohol and gambling, the contents [were] bound to be controversial."[11] In addition to the problem of contending schools of Islamic law, the notion of "Islamic economics," as espoused by Jamaat-e-Islami and initially supported by Zia, was ambiguous at best and without precedent in the contemporary world.

According to Gustafson, a further difficulty in implementing Zia's Islamization plan was "the status of the minority Shia community which seems, judging by straws in the wind, to be increasingly nervous."[12] The Shias regarded "much of the current Islamization drive as an attempt by the dominant Sunnis to extend their domination." Shias objected to the imposition of a common religious curriculum, given their differences with Sunnis in religious interpretations of key aspects of Islamic history. Still, "a general Islamic tone" pervaded everything, "obviously much influenced by the president, who [had] performed both Umra and Haj [in that year]."[13]

However ridiculous most of Zia's Islamization efforts appeared to outside observers, they significantly altered the daily lives of Pakistanis.

"Government letters are now to begin with the 'Bismillah' invoking the name of Allah, the merciful and benevolent," wrote Gustafson. He added, "A State enterprise advertises for a manager 'who should be a God fearing and practicing Muslim.' Floggings are common." Television was greatly changed, with increased religious programming. An Arab observer described Zia's Islamization as "petro-Islam" because of his government's dependence on economic support from Saudi Arabia, while former Pakistan Peoples Party (PPP) stalwart Hanif Ramay said that the type of Islamic system being introduced was "nothing short of theocracy."[14]

According to the British reporter Trevor Fishlock, Zia's Islamization measures were "one of the remarkable spectacles of Asia" that helped "keep people preoccupied." Zia conflated Islamization and Pakistani nationalism. "Thus school ties and blazers, relics of British rule, [were] vanishing as boys [were] encouraged to wear *kurta* tunics and baggy *salwar* trousers," even though these modes of dress had nothing to do with Islam. Fishlock noted that Zia gave greater emphasis to Urdu language in the schools, and textbooks were being rewritten with a stronger Islamic tone. "References to Western figures are being reduced and pupils are learning more about the great men of Islam," he observed. But Fishlock could see the potential for "rift between Sunnis and Shias" and predicted that "the debate on Islamization could grow bitter."[15]

By December 1978, Zia had extended Islamization to include an official directive to arrange prayers in government offices during office hours.[16] In February 1979, he ordered a revision of educational curricula to ensure that "the ideology for which this nation had achieved Pakistan" may "permeate" the lives of people. "Our text books and courses of study have drifted us away from our orbit," he insisted. "Consequently we had to devise a new educational policy to keep us within our intellectual orbit. The basic aim of this policy is to rear a new generation wedded to the ideology of Pakistan and Islam," Zia said.[17] This decision had far-reaching consequences: it quashed the potential for critical thinking in the next generation, encouraged a false narrative of history, and introduced religious bigotry to students as an early age.

In addition to this massive rewriting of history and indoctrination of children through schoolbooks, the Zia regime also ordered a complete makeover of Pakistan's founder, Jinnah. The Quaid-e-Azam could now no longer be shown in western dress, and his official portraits hung in all schools, and government offices showed him in a formal traditional *sherwani*, garments that Jinnah wore only occasionally. Mention of Jinnah's August 11, 1947, speech that declared that religion would have nothing to do with the business of the state was banned in the media. Jinnah's biographies were unceremoniously bowdlerized—pages that spoke of his western ways were ordered to be torn out before the books were sold at bookshops. Zia and his fellow Islamists wanted to cast Jinnah in their own mold: as a religious fundamentalist with no tolerance for other faiths.

Zia's lack of tolerance for other faiths was particularly evident in his general disregard for the concerns of Pakistan's minorities. Accordingly, as his Islamization of the nation was global in its scope and almost obsessive in its thoroughness, it is hardly surprising that Zia's Pakistan would, at least partially, impose sharia. This undertaking could only have served to further marginalize the country's non-Muslims and dismay the Muslim-minority sects whose views of sharia would depart significantly from that of the Islamists.

At any rate, on February 7, 1979, marking the Prophet Muhammad's birthday, Zia amended the constitution through a military decree to change the concept of judicial review. Instead of merely judging laws in the light of the constitution, the higher courts were now given jurisdiction to establish sharia benches to determine whether a law was repugnant to Islam.[18] The regime claimed that the religious courts were meant to supplement, not replace, the conventional court system inherited from British rule. A *hudood* (lit. "limit": a class of crimes under Islamic law) decree was issued concomitantly with the decree creating the sharia courts. The intent of these decrees was to place an emphasis on Islamic codes of personal behavior.

Zia spoke of the need to foster Islamic cultural and ethical norms and criticized the prevalence of *maghribi adab* (western culture) among the people. He said that the true "soldiers of Islam" and not westernized leaders could protect the Pakistani nation. Zia promised to consolidate the Islamization process so that no subsequent government could reverse it. In his speech on the Prophet Muhammad's birthday, Zia announced establishment of "Nizam-e-Islam" in Pakistan. He identified three aspects of an Islamic system: social, economic, and legal. In his view, the reform of social-economic conditions was a long-term objective that would be reached only through a gradual process. According to Zia, the most effective path to Islamization was to "introduce certain legal reforms in order to attain socio-economic reformation." He insisted that it was for this reason that he wanted to reform the prevailing legal system in Pakistan in accordance with the Islamic sharia.

Zia issued a presidential decree providing stringent sharia punishments for four offenses that were subject to *hudood* under Sunni Islamic law: intoxication, theft, adultery, and false allegation. Non-Muslim citizens and foreigners were exempted from prohibition and were issued permits for "reasonable quantities" of alcohol for private consumption, though they were forbidden from being drunk in public. Violators of the prohibition law were to be punished with three years' rigorous imprisonment and whipping (eighty stripes). The Offences against Property (enforcement of hudood) Ordinance in 1979 specified amputation of the right hand or the left foot, with death sentence for the offenses of theft and armed robbery.

The Offence of Zina (unlawful sexual intercourse) Ordinance in 1979, sometimes referred to as the adultery ordinance, prescribed severe punishments, such as stoning to death, one hundred stripes, and rigorous imprisonment for a period of between ten and twenty-five years. The offenses covered by the ordinance included rape, abduction, and kidnapping. But clerics insisted that rapists could only be convicted on the evidence of four male adult Muslim witnesses. Further, the law subsequently became controversial because it was used to prosecute and punish rape victims; a woman's allegations of rape were routinely countered by perversely framing her statements as admissions of adultery or fornication. Of some small consolation to those accused under the Offence of Zina Ordinance were the protections against false charges of rape or adultery by the Offence of Qazaf (false allegations) Ordinance. This prescribed a punishment of eighty stripes for those making false accusations of rape or adultery.

In addition to the controversy generated by the new laws, Zia's decision to allow judicial review of laws on the grounds of their lack of conformity with Islam led to a plethora of litigation, with various groups and individuals challenging different aspects of the legal structure. A retired Supreme Court judge, Badiuzzaman Kaikaus, filed a major case that he argued himself before the sharia bench of the Lahore High Court, challenging the entire concept of representative democracy. He claimed that Islamic law only permits an amir and a *shura*, an assembly of dignitaries that is not representative in the western sense. Ironically, these themes were echoed in Zia's own sporadic comments on the need for a "new political system."[19]

Legal experts and human rights specialists realized the complexities created by parallel judicial systems. "Shariat courts rule on the sharia (the canon law) of Islam," explained a special representative of human rights advocates in her report about the Zia-era legal changes. She elaborated:

> Each sect of Islam has some rules unique to it. These differences frequently relate to the issue of the sources of Islamic law generally consisting of the Quran and the Sunnah (behavior codes).... Needless to say, in an Islamic country with many sects of Islam there could not be a uniform body of opinion in shariat courts. A shariat court of the Shi'a sect would rule different than a Sunni court on *ushr* (a Muslim tax on agricultural products). The Shias use a tax called *khums*, not *ushr*.[20]

The shariat courts established by Zia had been given authority to approve laws conforming to Islamic canon law and to invalidate laws that conflicted with Islamic canon law. This resulted in a plethora of litigation based on theological questions, which besieged the judges, delaying decisions for years. For example, some borrowers refused to pay interest on their bank loans while waiting for ruling on a petition before the shariat court seeking abolition of interest because of Islam's disapproval of usury. However, Zia had cynically retained his power of decree to deal with shariat court judgments that might interfere with his ability to govern. When Zia did not like a ruling, he overturned it or even removed the judge from office. Non-Muslim judges could not be appointed to shariat benches and non-Muslim lawyers were not allowed to represent clients before these courts.

"The most serious concern about government-empowered canon law courts with jurisdiction over state law is that freedom of religion and right to democracy and popular participation are seriously jeopardized," observed US attorney Karen Parker. She added, "A state functioning as a religion automatically persecutes those not of the official religion or sect of a religion."[21]

It was also pointed out that a state's enforcing or imposing a religion contravened the Universal Declaration of Human Rights, the Human Rights Covenants, and the Declaration on Religious Intolerance. Several of the shariat offenses, especially zina (adultery) and qazaf (false accusation of adultery), seriously impacted the human rights of women. Many of the shariat punishments violated the international human rights law prohibition on "torture, cruel, inhuman and degrading treatment or punishment."[22]

Zia also appointed a twelve-member committee of scholars, jurists, and *ulema* "to formulate recommendations about the structure of an Islamic democratic government." Pakistan, he stressed, "was created in the name of Islam and in Islam there was no provision for Western-type elections."[23] These maneuvers bought him time against those who demanded that Zia keep his promise of holding elections and handing over power to elected leaders. Although ultimately Zia did not fulfill his desire to scrap democracy altogether, he weakened the Pakistani consensus on democracy.

Further to his weakening the Pakistani people's sense of self-determination under the guise of religious piety, General Zia-ul-Haq's Islamist legislative adventure drastically impacted the lifestyles of ordinary Pakistanis. Although non-Muslims were exempted from the prohibition against alcohol, the other provisions of the law amounted to imposing a government-sanctioned Islamic lifestyle on people with different faiths. And if the sharia courts opened a pandora's box about Pakistan's constitutional and legal framework, the hudood laws exhibited tremendous potential for abuse.

According to Ziring, "Zia called upon the nation to find their need for escape and recreation in prayer, family activities and constructive social acts."[24] But non-Muslims as well as nonobservant Muslims were now at the mercy of neighbors, coworkers, and servants who could falsely implicate them in a variety of cases ranging from bawdy conduct to dressing improperly or traveling with unrelated members of the opposite sex. Public lashings under the law were carried out on numerous occasions, though, after much public clamor and international objection, the cutting off of limbs for theft was not widely applied. The rate of executions in Pakistan, though, became alarmingly high.

The creation of sharia courts and imposition of hudood laws meant that the opinion of mullahs could now have legal effects, exacerbating the struggle between concepts of modern jurisprudence and medieval notions of justice. The Muslim clergy often encountered disagreement over specific Islamic injunctions, and these disagreements led to the confusion that the Munir commission had warned about in 1953. Non-Muslims worried about being declared *dhimmis* while the revived debate about "who is a Muslim" caused concern among minority Muslim sects.

Zia often allowed religious scholars to debate various interpretations of the sharia before deciding on one, usually that which was supported by the orthodox Sunnis of the Deoband school. Among one of the earliest controversies over Islamic law under Zia related to a judgment by sharia judges giving different weight to the testimony of Muslims, non-Muslims, and Muslim women in civil and criminal proceedings. Mullahs cited Islamic texts to argue that equal weight could not be given to the evidence of a believer and a nonbeliever, while a woman's testimony in certain matters required corroboration by another woman or man. Such "Islamic" interpretations reduced the value of a woman's testimony to half that of a man's and dispensed with the concept of equal rights of citizenship before the law.

Non-Muslims' standing as citizens was reduced before the courts, and the power of their franchise was also diluted by shrewd alterations to the electoral laws. Although Zia did not hold legislative elections until 1985, he changed the Representation of the People's Act of 1976 to reintroduce separate communal electorates. Non-Muslim minorities could no longer vote along with Muslims to elect officials to local councils or provincial and federal legislatures. A fixed number of non-Muslim seats were to be allocated in each elected body and non-Muslims could vote for members only of their own religious community. This measure was designed partly to deprive less conservative parties opposed to Zia and martial law, such as the PPP, of their non-Muslim vote bank. It also diminished the political influence of non-Muslims, as their representatives in elected bodies did not carry any weight within the major political parties. The Ahmadis, who did not accept their designation as non-Muslims, refused to accept electoral representation as a minority and therefore were effectively disenfranchised.

By 1980, the Islamization process expanded to include the implementation of *zakat*, a 2.5 percent annual wealth tax that is required by Islam to be used for the relief of the poor. The Zia government imposed zakat through a compulsory levy on bank deposits. In its first year, 485 million Pakistani rupees were collected as zakat to be distributed through local committees, which would serve as a patronage network for Sunni Islamist parties. But Shias objected to the compulsory collection of zakat on the grounds that it was not in accordance with their religious law. Khaled Ahmed, in his book *Sectarian War*, argues that Zia and his fundamentalist advisers—particularly the chairman of the Council for Islamic Ideology, Justice Tanzilur Rehman—knew that the Shia would not pay the poor tax to the state, but they attempted to impose it across the board anyway. They either did not anticipate a Shia backlash or calculated that such a backlash would help consolidate Sunni opinion in favor of the regime.

Instead of zakat, the Shia paid *khums*—twice the amount the Sunnis paid. According to Ahmed, "It was traditionally aid to the Shia clergy, clearly a throwback to the history of Shias living as a suppressed majority or a minority in Sunni states." After the enforcement of the zakat ordinance, Pakistan's Shia staged a massive protest led by Mufti Jafar Hussain (1916–1983), an erudite Shia scholar considered the head of the Shia community in the country. The Mufti had served as a member of the Council of Islamic Ideology numerous times under Ayub and Bhutto and again under Zia. But he resigned his seat on the council in 1979 to protest "the inclusion of majority Deobandi and Ahle Hadith members who nursed a particular animus against his community."[25]

Led by Mufti Jafar Hussain, on July 5, 1980, tens of thousands of Shias marched in Rawalpindi, near the capital, shutting down Islamabad. Violence ensued: one protestor was killed while fourteen were wounded. Zia amended the zakat decree to allow anyone who considered compulsory deduction of zakat as being against his faith to seek exemption from the tax.[26]

Although the Shia had won the argument over zakat, Zia and his fellow generals were angered by the Shia's ability to defy martial law. Moreover, they were fearful that Pakistani Shias would now rely on the new Islamic revolutionary regime in Iran for support. Zia's regime responded by cultivating Sunni extremist groups that called for declaring Shias non-Muslim with proscriptions similar to those that had earlier been issued against Ahmadis. Syed Vali Nasr cites reports that "the martial law administrator of Punjab, General Ghulam Gilani, deliberately turned a blind eye to growing Sunni militancy and the rise of armed bands centered in *madrasas* after 1980, to address the problem of Shia resurgence."[27]

Notwithstanding Zia's harsh treatment of critics, the process of Islamization did not move forward without some resistance from secular Pakistanis along with widespread international criticism. Advocates of Islamization described it "as essential therapy to resolve a longstanding national crisis of identity." Reporting from Islamabad, the *New York Times* reporter Michael Kaufman quoted

> a liberal and worldly Pakistani official, who like many intellectuals here worries about parts of the Islamization campaign but sympathizes with its overall aims as posing the question "If we are not Moslems, what are we, second-rate Indians?" But critics, including former Chief Justice Mohammed Munir, insisted that the forms of Islam advocated by Zia were not only "inimical to progress and scientific inquiry but also corruptions of true Islamic ideals."

Munir, who had confronted obscurantists as a judge while heading the inquiry into the 1953 anti-Ahmadi riots, asserted that the greatest growth and spread of Islam came when it was an adaptive movement encouraging free inquiry. "The Koran constantly urges Moslems to study nature, to investigate things to find out for themselves the order with which God has created the universe, but knowledge has no limits," the jurist wrote. "Now if you subordinate the acquisition of knowledge to any ideology, political, economic or religious, you reduce the field of knowledge to what the ideology teaches you because the ideology has to run through a groove or a defined channel and does not let you get out of it," Munir pointed out.

Kaufman also cited "private expressions of dissatisfaction with specific parts of the Islamization package," such as a banker who pointed out that Pakistan was closed on Friday while foreign banks and stock markets and exchanges closed Saturday and Sunday, leaving Pakistanis only four days to do business involving international transactions. An economist argued against calls for interest-free banking, which "does not mesh with a world system." But the US reporter suggested that "Zia had through the affirmation of Islam rallied the nation and brought a measure of unity."[28] Zia's status as a frontline ally against Soviet communism convinced western observers to avert their gaze from the human rights violations that were being perpetrated in the name of Islamization.

Rumors that Zia planned to repeal the Family Laws Ordinance of 1961—legislation that was seen by many feminists as the first step toward a bill of rights for Pakistani women—provoked a backlash from women's rights groups. The Islamic Ideology Council, created to recommend Islamization of laws, endorsed the repeal, albeit with the dissenting vote of its lone woman member. From the women activists' point of view, the status of women in Pakistan was already deplorable and the removal of protections offered by the 1961 law would only worsen matters.

The Family Laws Ordinance had raised the minimum marriageable age for women from fourteen to sixteen. Before the 1961 decree, a man could divorce his wife simply by pronouncing the word for divorce three times, without legal recourse. The Family Laws Ordinance provided for a three-month effort at reconciliation with the help of an arbitration council designated by civil authorities. The 1961 law also tightened the regulations governing polygamy. These reforms were opposed by conservative clerics from the day they were introduced. Zia's calls for Islamization emboldened the clerics in seeking repeal of the relatively progressive family laws.

For his part, Zia remained shrewdly ambiguous while talking about the role of women in a Muslim society. He spoke of the need for women to "participate fully" in the affairs of the nation and promised the creation of a high-level government commission regarding the status of women. But he also called for separation of the sexes at social events and endorsed conservatives' demands for new universities exclusively for women.[29]

In an orchestrated campaign that relied as much on appealing to conservative religious sentiments and promoting allied Islamist factions as it did to his being the head of the country's military, Zia had ruthlessly suppressed all significant opposition by 1980. After former prime minister Zulfikar Ali Bhutto was executed, his daughter Benazir Bhutto was imprisoned in order to deny leadership to the military regime's opponents. In the view of the world's liberals, Zia was "an isolated dictator lacking even a semblance of popular legitimacy." The Pakistani-American academic Eqbal Ahmed pointed out that "Zia-ul-Haq is specially burdened by a record of disloyalty, broken oaths, betrayed promises, illegal acts and extreme violations of human rights." Zia's Islam, Ahmed wrote, was "shorn of the spiritual, moral and civic virtues that had assured Islamic civilization its richness and humanity. It revives a medieval penal code and outdated social practices."

Ahmed cited the fusing of Pakistan's civic and political culture with institutionalized brutality as "the most reprehensible aspect of the Zia Government." He noted, "For the first time in living memory, highly publicized public executions have been carried out, and people have been flogged publicly and in prisons." He continued:

> Arbitrary arrests and imprisonments without trial have become the norm. During the six weeks that I have been here, at least two men— Nazir Abbasi, who was suspected of distributing opposition literature, and Inayat Masih, a Christian trade unionist who demanded better safety measures after two mask-less sanitation workers had died of asphyxiation while cleaning a sewer—have died under torture.[30]

For most western governments, however, the massive violations of human rights by the Zia dictatorship were less important than Zia's willingness to sponsor jihad against the Soviet Union in Afghanistan. Millions of Afghans were taking refuge in Pakistan and with covert US funding, Zia's intelligence service was arming and training a massive guerrilla army, the Mujahedeen, to transform Afghanistan into the Soviet Union's Vietnam. Zia's strategic cooperation with the United States and its Central Intelligence Agency (CIA) was crucial in persuading the United States to turn a blind eye to the impact of his Islamization policies on Pakistan's women and religious minorities. The 1980 "State Department Country Report on Human Rights for

Pakistan" was rather tepid in describing the deteriorating situation of minority rights.

"Minority religious groups and their adherents are denied certain rights enjoyed by the majority Muslims, but were allowed to participate in the 1979 local elections, in which certain seats were reserved for them," said the State Department report. It added that

> Christians, Parsis, Hindus and others including followers of the Ahmadiyya sect, are considered to be minorities whose members cannot be elected as president or prime minister. (Although the Ahmadiyyas consider themselves Muslims, the government does not, because they are unable to certify they believe Mohammed was the last prophet.)[31]

In the 1981 report, the State Department added another paragraph to its understatement. It said,

> Upon leaving office in September, the president's adviser on minority affairs regretted that during his tenure he was unable to do much for the sweepers and scavengers, most of whom are Christians. He said they constituted "the largest segment of our society" which has suffered continued deprivation of rights and privileges.[32]

But the 1980 and 1981 human rights assessments of the US State Department failed to describe the isolation, marginalization, and threats of violence against religious minorities that were being encouraged by Zia's policies.

General Zia-ul-Haq's western allies also did not notice the momentous changes he introduced in school and college curricula that fostered Islamist prejudices in young Pakistani minds. This was Zia's quest to indoctrinate the country's youth in Islamist ideology; it would have far-reaching adverse consequences for Pakistan's religious minorities. And it would thwart the efforts of those who would cultivate a tolerant, more liberal ethos within the country. Zia's quest began with a 1981 University Grants Commission (UGC) directive to prospective textbook authors. The directive told textbook authors to demonstrate through their writings "that the basis of Pakistan is not to be founded in racial, linguistic, or geographical factors but rather in the shared experience of a common religion."[33]

The stated purpose of the curricula changes was "to get students to know and appreciate the Ideology of Pakistan, and to popularize it with slogans." The new textbooks were meant "to guide students towards the ultimate goal of Pakistan—the creation of a completely Islamicized state."[34] But their real impact was to falsify history, glorify jihad and warfare, denigrate religious minorities, and instill religious prejudice into children's minds in a systematic manner. Years later, experts find Pakistani textbooks educating children "into ways of thinking that makes them susceptible to a violent and exclusionary worldview open to sectarianism and religious intolerance."[35]

A study on Pakistan's textbooks found that "the curricula and textbooks are insensitive to the religious diversity of Pakistani society." In addition to making the learning of Islamiat (Islamic studies) compulsory for Muslim students, the curricula changes resulted in the use of Islamic religious material to teach Urdu as a language and formed a quarter of the Urdu-language texts. Even textbooks for the English language were laced with religious content. Islamiat was also taught in social studies classes, making the syllabus heavily religious. This reflected the "very narrow view held by a minority among Muslims that all the education should be essentially that of Islamiat."[36] Pakistani nationalism was defined in a manner that excluded non-Muslim Pakistanis from either being deemed Pakistani nationals or "from even being good human beings."[37]

Under the new educational policy, the subject of Islamiat was made compulsory for all levels from primary school to college. Teaching of Arabic, a language hardly spoken in Pakistan, was made compulsory in all schools to students belonging to all religions on the grounds that it would help in understanding the Quran. Schools now emphasized the ideology of Pakistan, and teachers and professors deemed opposed to the ideology were weeded out. The Zia regime also encouraged *madrasa* education, declaring *madrasa* certificates equivalent to normal university degrees. This endorsement ignored that the pedagogy in these traditional religious schools was seriously flawed by contemporary standards, on account of its emphasis on learning by rote.

According to the physicist A. H. Nayyar, the redesigned curricula created a monolithic image of Pakistan as an Islamic state and taught students to view only Muslims as Pakistani citizens. Muslim majoritarianism in Pakistan, in Nayyar's view, amounted to creating an environment for non-Muslims in which they became second-class citizens with lesser rights and privileges; their loyalty to the state became suspect, and their contribution to the society was ignored. "The result is that they can easily cease to have any stake in the society," he concluded.

New textbooks in social studies, English, Urdu, and civics from Class I to Class XII were introduced over the several years that followed to shape "children's identities and value systems."[38] A subsequent study on Pakistani textbooks found that they contained substantial distortions of history, insensitivity to the existing religious diversity of the nation, and incitement to religious militancy and violence. Moreover, the textbooks encouraged jihad and martyrdom and advocated perspectives inciting prejudice, bigotry, and discrimination toward fellow citizens, especially women and religious minorities, and often toward nations.[39]

Besides making the learning of Islamiat compulsory for Muslim students, Zia's regime ensured that religious material was interpolated in books used for teaching the Urdu and English languages. Islamic concepts were also included in textbooks for social studies, reflecting the view of orthodox Sunni *ulema* that all education should essentially be about Islam. Pakistani nationalism was repeatedly presented in school books in a manner that excluded non-Muslim Pakistanis from being considered virtuous or patriotic citizens.[40] Children were introduced to the idea of an Islamic global community, the *ummah*, confronting a modern world dominated by Jews and Christians. A distorted narrative of Pakistan's history was taught in schools that blamed western and Hindu conspiracies for events like the 1971 separation of Bangladesh. Bigotry was being methodically inculcated in young minds through textbooks.

Nayyar cited curriculum documents beginning with Zia, but continuing well after his decade in power, to show that the government had now set "specific learning objectives" to promote religious prejudice. Textbook writers were told to write books that would enable children to "understand the Hindu and Muslim differences and the resultant need for Pakistan" as well as to learn about "India's evil designs against Pakistan." The textbooks taught ideas like "Hindu has always been an enemy of Islam" and "the religion of the Hindus did not teach them good things."[41]

One junior school textbook said, "Hindus worship in temples which are very narrow and dark places, where they worship idols. Only one person can enter the temple at a time. In our mosques, on the other hand, all Muslims can say their prayers together." Young students were told, "Hindus thought that there was no country other than India, nor any people other than the Indians, nor did anyone else possess any knowledge." A story in an Urdu-language textbook, titled "The Enemy Pilot," told of a captured Indian pilot of Hindu faith who had "only been taught never to have pity on Muslims, to always bother the neighboring Muslims, to weaken them to the extent that they forget about freedom, and that it is better to finish off the enemy."[42]

The same story spoke of Hindus pleasing their goddess Devi Kali by slaughtering innocent people of other faiths at her feet and said that Hindus regarded those who followed other religions as untouchables. Social studies texts narrated the history of British rule in India with words like "The Hindus, who have always been opportunists, cooperated with the English." The horrors of Partition were also used to fuel hatred. "While the Muslims provided all type of help to those wishing to leave Pakistan, the people of India committed cruelties against the Muslims (refugees). They would attack the buses, trucks, and trains carrying the Muslim refugees and they were murdered and looted," claimed one textbook.[43]

The rewritten curricula created a monolithic image in the minds of young students of Pakistan as an Islamic state with exclusively Muslim citizens. Doubtlessly, as a result, a whole generation of Pakistan's non-Muslim children had to contend with a sense of isolation and alienation from their motherland. And although Pakistan had always had a sense of Muslim majoritarianism, greater hostility toward non-Muslims was now being generated through propaganda in the schools' textbooks. Further, non-Muslim teachers—especially Christians, who had been prominent in the educational sector during Pakistan's early decades—were gradually weeded out of schools and colleges.

The prevailing belief that Pakistan's non-Muslim citizens were of a lower status than their Muslim compatriots—and were not to be trusted in civil or military office—was congruent with the opinions proffered by extreme Islamists in the early years of the nation. Islamists had argued before the Munir commission in 1953 that non-Muslims could live in an Islamic state only as *dhimmis*, liable to pay *jizya*, a tax that ensured their protection and exemption from military duty. According to this view, non-Muslims could only have limited rights and equal national identity could be denied to religious minorities in an Islamic Pakistan. The educational process introduced by General Zia-ul-Haq in the form of curricula and textbooks reinforced this denial. It also encouraged extremists who sought to take the law into their own hands to enforce their vision of a purer Islamic state and society.

One of the many unfortunate consequences of Islamization of the educational system was the attacks by Islamists on free-thinking scientists and academics on campuses. When Pakistan's only Nobel laureate, the physicist Dr. Abdus Salam—an Ahmadi—visited the country, his lecture at the Quaid-i-Azam University in Islamabad was picketed by Islamic fundamentalists. As the *New York Times* reported, the protestors' objections were "not directed at Dr Salam's research but at the religious beliefs of the small community into which he was born."[44] In other cases, fundamentalist students attacked professors teaching evolution or social science theories considered blasphemous by Islamist clerics.

Some professors, such as Sultan Bashiruddin Mahmood, tried to teach what they called "Islamic science," a concept openly embraced by Zia. Mahmood was a nuclear engineer who proposed nurturing the power of *jinn* (genies) mentioned in the Quran to solve the world's energy shortage. "Mahmood was fascinated by the links between science and the Koran," reported the *New York Times*. "He wrote a peculiar treatise arguing that when morals degrade, disaster cannot be far behind" and was fascinated by "the role sunspots played in triggering the French and Russian Revolutions, World War II and assorted anticolonial uprisings."[45] Thus, while students were being indoctrinated with the Islamist ideology of Pakistan, the country's scientific community was also being undermined by pseudo-science. The stage had been set for conflict between Pakistanis' aspiration for modernity and the idea of a puritanical Islamic state advocated by the clerics and their supporters.

This conflict may be largely ascribed to the perennial dissatisfaction of the Islamist extremists, whose worldview was, in many ways, anchored in the seventh century. No amount of reverting to medieval practices or promoting their cause, though, seemed to sate their religious fervor. Neither were they assuaged by the dwindling of the religious minorities in the country. By the time of the 1981 Census, Pakistan's population was 96.67 percent Muslim. Christians constituted 1.56 percent of the population; Hindus amounted to 1.51 percent, and Ahmadis numbered only 104,245—or a mere 0.12 percent of the population.[46] But the Islamists—and Zia himself—were not satisfied with the level of purification they had been able to accomplish within Pakistani society.

While the country's Islamists could not be placated by his campaign of Islamization, Zia was unable to forever curb the dissatisfaction of a broad sector of Pakistani society that wished for a return of democracy. Zia had managed to govern with an iron fist for six years, committing innumerable human rights abuses under the guise of Islamization when, in 1983, he faced the first significant challenge to his rule. The political opposition—a coalition of parties forming the Movement for the Restoration of Democracy—was able to mobilize with strikes, boycotts, and mass demonstrations in a demand for elections. The dictator responded by brutally suppressing the movement and, additionally, by calling for greater Islamization.

Pakistan under Zia was compared by western reporters at the time with seventeenth-century England. "Charles I was beheaded as a result of [Puritan leader Oliver] Cromwell's rise to power; former Prime Minister Zulfikar Ali Bhutto was the principal victim of the advent of General Mohammad Zia-ul-Haq to power here," one report read. "Cromwell and General Zia shared the same overriding objective: To set society 'straight on the path of righteousness,' as General Zia put it recently. What Cromwell thought he was doing for Christianity, General Zia is doing for Islam."[47] But Pakistan was being administered "a bigger dose of government-enforced Islam than England had of Puritanism." In 1983, General Zia's unelected autocracy had already lasted a year longer than Cromwell's.[48] Its impact also lasted much longer. The religious and sectarian minefields laid by Zia are even now debilitating the country—and innocent Pakistanis are being killed on account of their faiths—well into the second decade of the twenty-first century.

Whether the general was aware that decades of internecine strife would result from his policies is open to conjecture. There is no doubt, however, that he intended permanent, state-sponsored Islamization for Pakistan; in his zeal, Zia appeared indifferent to the harm suffered by religious minorities as a consequence. While he—like most extreme Islamists in the country—conflated "Pakistan" with "Islam," the version of Islam that he propounded was narrower, sterner, more obscurantist, and bigoted than that favored by the country's earlier military dictators, and it left no space for religious minorities. Moreover, his determination to impose his extreme brand of Sunni Deobandi Islam was matched by an indissoluble will to remain in power. Zia-ul-Haq would not meekly step down from office and retire from public life as had Ayub Khan and Yahya Khan had before him.

General Zia told his handpicked "Parliament"—the Majlis-i-Shura—that he would stay in power indefinitely to complete his program of Islamization. "If God grants me life you and I both will be here and together we will serve this country in a manner behooving a Pakistani and a Muslim. God willing, we will certainly succeed," he said.[49] Indeed, like Cromwell, only Zia's untimely death would remove him from office.

Zia believed his attaining and consolidating virtual absolute power was legitimated by his ongoing Islamization in the country. The military dictator insisted that his martial law regime was constitutional and Islamic, and he justified his rule—perhaps unsurprisingly—by resorting to Islamic scripture. According to the Canadian scholar Khalid bin Sayeed, Zia argued "that it was the duty of Pakistanis as Muslims to obey his government because it was pursuing Islamic principles. He cited the Quran and a Hadith in support of the idea that as long as the head of State followed the injunctions of Allah and his Prophet obedience became mandatory for his subjects." Zia claimed to derive his authority from the Quran and asserted that "those who opposed or demonstrated against his government could be accused of waging war against an Islamic government and therefore indulging in anti-Islamic activities."[50]

By the time that Zia faced the Movement for the Restoration of Democracy campaign against his dictatorship in 1983, he had implemented most of the legal and administrative changes that could be imposed as Islamic law. But there was still room for manipulating sectarian divisions among Muslims. In this year, Pakistan witnessed the beginning of an intensification of violence against Shia Muslims as well as new laws against Ahmadis. Sunni hard-liners clamored publicly to declare Shias *Kaffirs* as had been done by the constitutional amendment proscribing Ahmadis in 1974. Attacks and riots against Shia Muslims began in a manner similar to those against the Ahmadis in 1953, albeit with the difference that neither the civil administration nor the judiciary were willing to stand up to protect the Shias.

On August 12, 1983, in a move intended to head off the push for civil elections launched by the Movement for the Restoration of Democracy, Zia announced what he described as the blueprint for an Islamic political order. His plan comprised substantial changes in the basic structure of the 1973 constitution, which would be significantly amended before being restored. The power of the president was enhanced, including giving him the authority to nominate the prime minister and to dissolve the lower house of Parliament when he thought the government was performing inadequately.

General Zia claimed that his August 12 plan was for "promotion of Islam, elimination of the evil of interest, maintenance of peace and order, promotion of *chadar* [head-covering for women—a metaphor for female chastity] and *chardiwari* [four walls of the house], and provision of cheap and easy justice for masses." He said he could not leave the country to disorder and was determined to transform it into an Islamic welfare state. Zia also asserted that future candidates for elective office "must possess some fundamental qualities, education, age, knowledge of basic principles of Islam and [a] clean past record."[51]

As Zia opened the door for electoral politics, he made every effort to ensure that his ideological legacy would prevail through the new political system. Many scions of conservative business and landowning families were encouraged to seek election in nonparty general elections held in 1985. Zia ensured the influence of Islamists in political debate by funding new magazines and newspapers, notable among them being the fundamentalist weekly *Takbeer*, in addition to giving prominence to hard-line clerics on state-owned television. Among the new actors on the national scene were sectarian extremists, who baited Shias and Ahmadis as a means of securing and consolidating support.

According to Vali Nasr, who has studied the Shia revival in several Muslim-majority countries, the anti-Shia campaign in Pakistan was backed by Saudi Arabia, which was concerned about the regional influence of Iran's Shia clerical regime. "With Saudi encouragement, self-styled Islamist thinkers and the Ahl-e-Hadith mounted a strong anti-Shia campaign through publication of books, pamphlets and magazines such as *Takbeer*," Nasr noted. Israr Ahmed, popularized by his frequent television appearances, gave Friday sermons in Bagh-i-Jinnah Park in Lahore, criticizing Shias. He and Allama Ihsan Ilahi Zahir, the chief of Jamiat-e-Ulema-e-Ahl-e-Hadith, "formulated the first anti-Khomeini critiques from within Islamist/Islamic circles but more important, began to produce a new style of language in critiquing Shiaism, one that depicted that branch of Islam as outside the pale of the religion." This campaign transformed doctrinal and theological disputes into communal ones. Thus, "The line of attack became increasingly focused on Shias as a people and not Shiaism as an interpretation of Islam."[52]

An anti-Shia strain had existed among Sunni clerics long before Pakistan's creation. Some Sunni Islamists had opposed the demand for Pakistan and cited the prominence of Shias, including Jinnah, among the leaders of the Muslim League as one of their reasons for doing so. Immediately after the anti-Ahmadi riots of 1953, some of the witnesses had told the Munir commission of their belief about Shias being outside the fold of Islam. At the time, prominent Shia clergymen were part of the anti-Ahmadi coalition, which made it difficult for their extremist Sunni detractors to focus their sights on Shias immediately. But books and pamphlets against Shias continued to circulate, though before the 1980s such hate literature was often proscribed by the state to prevent sectarian conflict.

After the Iranian revolution of 1979, the Zia regime gave a freer hand to Saudi-funded Sunni clerics. Although the government pursued a tougher censorship policy in relation to political material, its approach to religious literature changed significantly. Anything about Islam that did not meet with the Sunni *ulema*'s approval was readily banned, but hate literature against religious minorities as well as sects such as the Ahmadis and Shias was not. Zahir's Urdu-language book *Shias and Shiaism*, published in Lahore in 1980, sold widely. The book made the argument that an Islamic state could not accept Shias as Muslims because their reverence for Prophet Muhammad's family amounted to polytheism. It was translated into Arabic and English, and its international distribution was facilitated by Saudi Arabia. Zahir also wrote a book against Barelvi (Sufi) Muslims, making similar arguments. There was much material in this literature for those wanting the state to define who is or is not a pure Muslim. It was a recipe for unending sectarian conflict.

Soon other titles against Shias hit religious bookshops and began to be aggressively distributed or sold outside mosques. Among them were *Shia Hazraat ki Quran se Baghavat* (The Shia rebellion against the Quran) by Azhar Nadim (Lahore: Tehrik Nifaz Fiqh Hanafiya, 1983) and *Deen Main Ghulluw* (Deviant exaggeration in the True Faith) by Maulana Abdul Ghaffar Hasan (Karachi: Ribatul Ulum ul Islamiyah, 1983).[53] After laying out their argument, the anti-Shia agitators also supported the formation in 1983 of a militant group, Sipah-e-Sahaba Pakistan (Army of the Prophet's Companions), which soon became widely known by its initials SSP.

The name of the organization alluded to the view that Shias were non-Muslims, partly because of their refusal to accept the legitimacy of the first three Sunni caliphs, who were all companions of the Prophet Muhammad. The SSP also insisted on describing Yazid, the second ruler of the seventh-century Umayyad dynasty, as an Islamic hero—though Shias (and most Sunnis) blame Yazid for the brutal killing in AD 680 at Karbala (Iraq) of the Prophet Muhammad's grandson, Husain. The Shias commemorate Husain's martyrdom in the Muslim month of Muharram, and the SSP's pointed reverence for Yazid was contrived to create a flashpoint for Sunni-Shia discord during the annual Muharram observances.

The SSP found a strong base in the central Punjab district on Jhang, on the east bank of the river Chenab. The politics of the district had been dominated for years by Shia landed families, whose members managed to claim Sunni votes in Pakistan's sporadic elections, primarily due to the landowners' tradition of patrimonialism. Sunni traders in the area supported SSP as a means "of loosening the hold of the Shia landed elite over Sunni peasants,"[54] enabling the anti-Shia extremist group to organize for a nationwide battle against Shias.

Jhang was already the center of anti-Ahmadi activity—Rabwah, the community's headquarters, fell in the Jhang district—but local Deobandi clerics had started attacking Shias there as far back as the early 1950s. By the time the SSP was founded three decades later, several local clerics in the Jhang area were ready to make their careers through sectarian agitation. The most prominent among them was Haq Nawaz Jhangvi (1952–1990), who aligned himself with Zia's intelligence agencies as part of a plan "to teach the Shias of Jhang a lesson" for having opposed Zia's zakat laws. The SSP also "served as the mother of all the Deobandi militias" fighting the war in Afghanistan and later in Kashmir.[55] The SSP's task was also made easier by apostatizing fatwas by Indian as well as Pakistani scholars, ostensibly funded by Saudi Arabia, saying that the Shia were not Muslims.[56]

Anti-Shia militancy was strengthened by Pakistan's official policy of recruiting and training Afghan as well as Pakistani students from Deobandi madrasas to fight the Soviets in Afghanistan throughout the 1980s. Volunteering for jihad in Afghanistan enabled Sunni extremist groups to get training in guerrilla warfare and terrorism that they could later utilize to advance their goal of ridding Pakistan of Shias and Ahmadis. In some cases, officers of Pakistan's Inter-Services Intelligence (ISI) actively supported the Sunni extremists against Shia Muslims, whom they found unwilling to participate in the jihad against the Soviets in Afghanistan. The Shias' opposition to fighting in Afghanistan stemmed from the Sunni jihadis' commitment both to fighting the Soviets there and to eliminating the Shias in Pakistan. But Zia and his intelligence service had little sympathy for the perspectives of the embattled Shia minority.

The sectarian tensions between Sunnis and Shias—which had been stoked for some time by Zia's Sunni Islamist supporters—flared in Karachi, the country's cosmopolitan financial capital, and the Kurram tribal region along the border with Afghanistan, where the Shia Turi tribe had a strong presence. Parachinar, the headquarters of the Kurram tribal agency, was an important launching pad for Mujahedeen attacks into Afghanistan. The Turi tribe were not only unwilling to cooperate with the Mujahedeen, but they had also become prominent in

Pakistan's national Shia organizations. The Shia organization Tehrik-e-Nifaz-e-Fiqh-e-Jafaria, founded by Mufti Jafar Hussain (the leader of protests against the Zia regime over the forcible deduction of zakat) was now led by a Turi Shia, Allama Ariful Hussaini.

"In the spring of 1983, violent clashes occurred between Muslims of the majority Sunni and minority Shia sects in Karachi" reported the State Department human rights report for that year. The issue that sparked the disturbances was reported to be "the unauthorized construction by Shias of a mosque on land belonging to the city." The Shias accused extremist Sunnis backed by authorities of attacking them. The army was called in to intervene, and it imposed press censorship and a curfew. The violence caused hundreds of injuries, extensive damage to property, and more than twenty deaths.[57] Sunni-Shia violence in the Kurram tribal agency left at least forty persons dead.[58]

In 1986, Zia allowed the Sunni Afghan Mujahedeen to attack Parachinar amid reports that the Shia were leaving for Iran "by the truckload" for military training. Besides harboring a deep-seated prejudice against Shias, which may only go some way to explaining his actions, Zia feared that Iran-trained Shia militants could weaken the flow of Mujahedeen through Kurram into Afghanistan. Strategic considerations took priority over the lives and human rights of Kurram's Shia residents. The result was a "massacre of the Shias" in Kurram in September 1986 that left two hundred people dead.[59] In May 1988, a similar slaughter of Shias occurred in Gilgit in the northern areas of Pakistan abutting the Kashmir region. Pakistan had declared jihad here against India, much as it had done against the Soviets in Afghanistan.

The mass killings in Kurram and Gilgit were intended to cow the Shias into submission: Zia wanted them to be kept from interfering with his strategic plans. Nevertheless, the Shias responded by creating their own groups of militants to fight back and counter the SSP. The Shia leader Allama Hussaini was murdered in 1988, less than a fortnight before Zia's own death in a mysterious air crash on August 17. Zia's governor in the northwest province, General Fazle Haq, whom the Turis (a subtribe of the Khogyani Pashtun tribe, inhabiting primarily the Kurram Valley, with a smaller number across the Afghanistan-Pakistan border in the Paktia Province of Afghanistan) blamed for complicity in the murder of Allama Hussaini, was ambushed and killed a few years later in 1991.[60] Jhangvi and other prominent SSP leaders also died violent deaths, apparently at the hands of Shia militants, but that did not stop the anti-Shia terrorism. If anything, the Sunni extremists could now cite the killing of their leaders as justification for killing more Shias in what would become a perpetual cycle of revenge.

Khaled Ahmed explained the Shia-Sunni violence in Pakistan. "It is often said that the people of Pakistan are not sectarian," he wrote, adding that this was meant to point to the lack of a general anti-Shia animus at the popular level. But he points out that Pakistan has seen a lot of sectarian violence in recent years. "The truth of the above statement," Ahmed adds,

> is substantiated by the pattern of killings: the Sunnis kill Shia at large, targeting congregations, and the Shias target-kill—with some exceptions—the self-proclaimed anti-Shia clerics. This pattern tells us that the Shias are aware that the Sunni majority does not hate them. It rather proves that Shia-baiting is a specialized function carried out in the tradition of certain schools of thought among the Sunni-Hanafi confession.[61]

While General Zia unleashed deadly violence against Shias during his rule, he introduced further legal restrictions on Ahmadis, issuing decrees that made it difficult for them to publicly profess their faith. The hard-line clerics who were calling for Shias to be declared non-Muslims were also not satisfied with the 1974 constitutional amendment that had declared Ahmadis non-Muslims for legal purposes. They wanted criminal penalties for Ahmadis who practiced their religion as if they were Muslims. Thus, it was clear that if the Shias were to be declared beyond the pale of Islam, as demanded by Sunni extremists, it was only a matter of time before additional measures against them would also be made. Pakistan's Islamists had been working toward gradually marginalizing all religions and sects other than orthodox Sunni Islam. The campaign against Shias and new laws against Ahmadis composed the latest stage of their plans.

Using his sweeping powers under martial law, Zia issued a presidential ordinance in 1984 that barred Ahmadis from performing *azan* (the call to prayer) and from describing their places of worship as a mosque or masjid. Zia's ordinance went further than the 1974 constitutional amendment in defining the terms "Muslim" and "non-Muslim." The new definition described a "Muslim" as someone who believed "in the unity and oneness of Almighty Allah, in the absolute and unqualified finality of the Prophethood of Mohammad (PBUH: peace be upon him), and who does not believe in or recognize as, a prophet or religious reformer to be a prophet, in any sense of the word or of any description whatsoever, after Mohammad (PBUH)."[62]

"Non-Muslim" was now defined by law to mean "a person who is not a Muslim and includes a person belonging to the Christian, Hindu, Sikh, Buddhist or Parsi community, a person of the *Qadiani* group or the Lahori group (who call themselves 'Ahmadiyas' or by other name), or a *Bahai*, and a person belonging to any of the scheduled castes [of Hinduism]." A second decree, the Prohibition and Punishment Ordinance of April 26, 1984, inserted two new sections (298-B and 298-C) in the Pakistan Penal Code. The new section 298-B prescribed punishments for "misuse of epithets, descriptions and titles, etc., reserved for certain holy personages or places."

According to the new law,

Any person of the *Qadiani* group, or the *Lahori* group (who call themselves "Ahmadiyas" or by any name), who by words, either spoken or written, or by visible representation: (a) Refers to, or addresses, any person, other than a Caliph or Companion of the Holy Prophet Mohammad (PBUH), "Ameer-ul-Momineen," "Khalifa-tul-Muslimeen," "Sahaabi" or "Razi Allah Anho"; (b) Refers to, or addresses, any person other than a wife of the Holy Prophet Mohammad as "Ummul Momineen"; (c) Refers to, or addresses, any person, other than a member of the family (Ahle Bait) of the Holy Prophet Mohammad as "Ahle-Bait," or (d) Refers to, or names or calls, his place of worship as "masjid," shall be punished with imprisonment of either description for a term which may extend to three years, and shall also be liable to fine.[63]

The ordinance also stated that

any person of the *Qadiani* group or the *Lahori* group (who call themselves Ahmadiyas or any other name), who by words, either spoken or written, or by visible representation refers to the mode or form of call to prayers followed by his faith as "Azan" or recites Azan as used by the Muslims shall be punished with imprisonment of either description for a term which may extend to three years—and shall also be liable to fine.

The new 298-C was even more sweeping. Under this provision,

Any person of the Qadiani or the Lahori group, who directly or indirectly, poses himself as a "Muslim" or calls, or refers to, his faith as Islam, or preaches or propagates his faith, or invites others to accept his faith, by words, either spoken or written, or by visible representation, or in any manner whatsoever outrages the religious feelings of Muslims, shall be punished with imprisonment of either description for a term which may extend to three years, and shall also be liable to fine.

The provisions of Ordinance XX made it virtually impossible for Ahmadis to practice their faith publicly in Pakistan. It was a law reminiscent of the Middle Ages, when public profession of faith by a sect other than that of the ruler elicited state retribution. Moreover, the ordinance allowed an Ahmadi to be subjected to criminal proceedings based on little more than the whim of a member of the religious majority. An orthodox Muslim could go to the police and simply complain that an Ahmadi had outraged his religious feelings, and the Ahmadi in question could be arrested. It should be remembered here that several sects around the world use religious terminology for their leaders that is similar to the words used to describe holy figures of other religions.

The Church of Jesus Christ of Latter-Day Saints (Mormons), for example, call the head of their church a "Prophet" and his closest advisers are "Apostles." Yet the State of Israel does not forbid them to do so for fear of offending Jewish orthodoxy, nor do any of the world's Christian majority states have laws that provide imprisonment and fines for the use of such terminology.

Zia's new laws were received stoically by the Ahmadi community in Pakistan. Its head, Mirza Tahir Ahmad, instructed members of his community to stop performing azan from the minarets of what they considered to be mosques, which were renamed "places of worship." The community also sought judicial review of the laws by challenging their validity in court. Their expectation of fairness from the judiciary, however, was soon proved naïvely optimistic. The government asked that the case be heard, not by the regular High Court, but by its sharia bench. This precluded Ahmadi lawyers, as "non-Muslims," from being able to represent their community because only Muslim lawyers were allowed right of appearance before sharia courts.

A leading Ahmadi civil rights lawyer, Mujibur Rahman, became the plaintiff so that he could argue the Ahmadi case in person. The High Court Sharia Bench found Ordinance XX in conformity with Islamic canon law and the decision was upheld by the sharia bench of the Supreme Court. The judiciary's conclusions in the case of *Mujibur Rahman v. Federal Government of Pakistan* (1986 F.S.C. 1051) exhibited the depth of officially sanctioned prejudice over religious matters. The federal shariat court was asked to judge the validity of the anti-Ahmadi laws under Islamic law. The court recognized that there "was no bar Constitutional, legal or [in sharia] against the right of a non-Muslim to declare the unity of Allah, to acknowledge the Holy Prophet (P.B.H.) as truthful in his claim, to acknowledge the Quran as furnishing a good way of life and to act upon its Injunctions." But it ruled that the prohibition against Ahmadis calling themselves Muslims or posing as such does not amount to turning them out of their religion, namely Islam, since the ordinance merely "restrains them from calling themselves what they are not."[64]

Even though there was no precedent for such legislation in Islamic juridical history, the court justified the ordinance in its entirety on grounds that Ahmadis needed to be prohibited from "posing as Muslims" because they had not accepted the obligation to call themselves non-Muslims, which had been created by the amendment to Article 260 of the constitution in 1974. The judges of the federal court, later supported by the Supreme Court, reasoned that a threat to law and order had been created by the hostility of Muslims to Ahmadis. In the view of the court, the Ahmadis should after the amendment to Article 260 "have refrained from directly or indirectly posing as Muslims but they obstinately persevered in trying the patience of the Muslim Ummah by acting contrarily" and because of this persistence it became necessary to prevent Muslims from being deceived into thinking Ahmadis were Muslims.

In the court's view, Zia's laws that penalized Ahmadis for practicing their religion publicly were justified as part of implementing the 1974 amendment to the constitution. It was also justified because Ahmadis

> by posing themselves as Muslims try to propagate their religion to every Muslim they come across. They outrage his feelings by calling Mirza Sahib [Mirza Ghulam Ahmad] a Prophet because every Muslim believes in the finality of Prophethood of Muhammad (P.B.H.). This creates a feeling of resentment and hostility among the Muslims which gives rise to law and order problems. His claim of being a promised Messiah and Mehdi was also resented.[65]

The assertion that Ahmadis offend the religious sentiments of other Muslims by the mere fact that Ahmadis consider themselves Muslims was deemed a major deviation from internationally accepted norms of human rights in the area of religious freedoms. Karen Parker of Human Rights Advocates visited Pakistan in 1987 and comprehensively documented the violations of the fundamental rights of Ahmadis. "By providing for arrests and imprisonment of persons for the exercise of protected rights," she wrote of the anti-Ahmadi law, "the Ordinance also violates the right to liberty and the right to freedom from arbitrary arrest and detention." Parker explained that for purposes of human rights law, arrest or detention was arbitrary if incompatible with the right to liberty and the free exercise of other human rights. "The fact that the arrest or detention is under provision of national 'law' is irrelevant for purposes of international law," she pointed out, adding that Ordinance XX also violated international human rights law because it barred any judicial remedy.[66]

The International Commission of Jurists (ICJ) pointed out that the prohibitions created by the ordinance "clearly strike at the heart of the practice of the Ahmadiyya faith" and weighed the arguments used by the federal shariat court to justify them. The government and the

Pakistani courts had said the prohibitions were necessary "because the Ahmadis would not deny that in which they believe, namely, that their faith is part of the broad spectrum of Islam." According to the ICJ,

> The other justification for taking these particular measures against one of an estimated 150 sects in Islam was a concern to maintain law and order. This is undoubtedly a factor to be balanced against the exercise of freedom of religion as Article 20 of the [Pakistan] Constitution itself provides. However, the Court's explanation as to why there is any threat is solely in terms of the outrage, resentment and hostility which non-Ahmadi Muslims are said to feel towards Ahmadis practicing their faith; there was certainly no suggestion by the Court that the Ahmadis were themselves seeking to instigate disorder. It is not clear, therefore, why the State should be justified in backing the refusal of some Muslims to tolerate the religious practices of others any more than it would be in supporting an assailant against his victim.[67]

The ICJ also disputed the public order considerations said to be behind the restrictions imposed on Ahmadis by pointing to "the way in which the government itself appears to encourage the resentment felt by some Muslims towards Ahmadis." According to the ICJ, all official references to Ahmadis employed the pejorative term "Qadiani" and an application form for a passport required all Muslims to declare that they believe in the finality of the Prophethood of Muhammad, that they do not recognize any person who claims to be a prophet after Muhammad as a Muslim, and that they "consider Mirza Ghulam Ahmad Qadiani to be an imposter nabi and also consider his followers . . . to be non-Muslim."

A similar declaration, the ICJ observed, was required when applying for government employment. Furthermore, many members of the government were reported as having made statements in speeches that were extremely hostile toward Ahmadis. For example, Zia, in a message to the International Khatm-e-Nabuwwat conference in London (August 1985), referred to the measures taken against Ahmadis and said, "We will, Insha'Allah, persevere in our effort to ensure that the cancer of Qadianism is exterminated." Ghulam Dastgir, the federal minister for labor, was reported in the *Daily Wifaq* (May 20, 1984) as saying

"Qadianis should recognize their minority status and end their conspiracies against Islam." And Malik Khuda Buksh Tiwana, the provincial minister for *auqaf*, was reported in *Mashriq* (February 28, 1986) as saying that life for Qadianis in Pakistan would be made impossible and the *ulema* were urged "to guide the Government for the eradication of this issue."[68] If the Ahmadi religion posed a threat to law and order, it was primarily because of the instigation of intolerance toward Ahmadis by anti-Ahmadi agitators and the government, argued the ICJ.

The anti-Ahmadi laws also received criticism from the United Nations Commission on Human Rights Sub-Commission on Prevention of Discrimination and Protection of Minorities. In its resolution 1895/21 (Annex 5), the commission observed that Ordinance XX constituted a prima facie violation of the "rights to liberty and security of the person, the right to freedom from arbitrary arrest or detention, the right to freedom of thought, expression, conscience and religion, the right of religious minorities to profess and practice their own religion, and the right to an effective legal remedy." Ordinance XX was also condemned at the UN Commission on Human Rights and in the US Congress.[69] But international condemnation had no effect on the implementation of the law in Pakistan, which was often accompanied by vigilante "justice"—unchecked violence perpetrated against Ahmadis.

By 1987, at least twelve Ahmadis were reported murdered. In most instances, the victims were professionals or community leaders. Qamrul Haq and Khalis Suleman were knifed and axed to death in broad daylight in Sukkur on May 11, 1986. Chaudry Abdul Hamid, the president of the Ahmadi community in Mehrabpur, was killed in April 1984; no one was arrested for the murder. Likewise, no one was arrested for the killing of Abdul Rehman, the president of the Ahmadi community in Sukkur, who was stabbed to death. Other Ahmadi murder victims included Najm-ul-Haq, an attorney shot to death on January 28, 1985, in Sukkur; Rehman Anwar, murdered on March 15, 1985, in Sukkur; Abdul Razzaq, the president of the Ahmadi community in Nawabshah, murdered on April 7, 1985; Dr. Aqil-bin-Abdul Qadir, murdered on June 9, 1985, in Hyderabad; Sheikh Nasir Ahmed murdered on September 18, 1985 in Okara (Punjab); Dr. Abdul Qadir stabbed to death on June 16, 1984, in Hyderabad; Rana Sultan Mahmood, murdered in Jhelum on November 28, 1984;

Chaudhry Munawar Ahmad, the president of the Ahmadi community in Khairpur, stabbed to death on April 24, 1985; and Anwar Ahmad, shot on February 28, 1985, in Sukkur.[70]

In some instances, attacks on Ahmadis resulted in Ahmadis being arrested for disturbing the peace or even being implicated in murder. In the city of Sahiwal, a group of between thirty and forty "orthodox" Muslims went to an Ahmadi mosque at 4:45 AM one morning in 1985 to verify that the Ahmadis were violating Ordinance XX by giving the call to prayer and by inscribing the Muslim profession of faith—the *kalima*—on the building. The group brought along a bucket of blue paint and brushes, which they used to paint over the kalima on the outer gate of the mosque. The group then entered the Ahmadi building's compound and began painting over other Islamic inscriptions. The caretaker of the compound, Naeem-ud-Din, urged them to leave, finally firing a warning shot from his gun. The mob turned on him, resulting in the firing of more shots and the death of two of the attackers, Qari Bashir Ahmed and Azhar Rafiq. While no one was charged in relation to any of the numerous murders of prominent Ahmadis, the caretaker was charged with murder. Moreover, several other Ahmadis faced trumped-up charges in the wake of the incident.

Karen Parker, a human rights advocate, listed the case as an instance of persecution of Ahmadis. According to her inquiries, the prosecution admitted that the group of attackers came from the madrasa Jamia Rashidia, which was located seven kilometers from the Ahmadi building, and that the attackers considered Ahmadis "infidels who should be beheaded." Eleven Ahmadis were arrested and charged with murder and unlawful assembly (the unlawful assembly charge being necessary to make each accused liable for the acts of others). Evidence revealed that several of the Ahmadi accused were not even present at the compound at the time of the attack, while others were present but not present at the scene of the violence. Charges against several defendants were dropped after the Sahiwal Bar Association passed a protest resolution. But a special military court, headed by a lieutenant colonel as judge, convicted six Ahmadis and sentenced them to death.

In another case, in the southern city of Sukkur in Sindh Province, multiple murders and arrests of several Ahmadis for wearing Muslim insignia followed the bombing of a mosque on May 23, 1985. Twenty-seven

Ahmadis from Sukkur and the surrounding areas were arrested for alleged involvement in the bombing. All were released by the first week of June, except for seven who were tried by a special military court. Two of the accused were sentenced to death while the other five were acquitted. Legal experts felt that the conviction was "impossible by law." Apparently, the two men sentenced to death "could only be convicted under vicarious liability, but there could be no vicarious liability if the other defendants were acquitted." But General Zia-ul-Haq upheld the Ahmadis' death sentences even though the international community expressed grave concern.[71]

According to Parker, the head of the Ahmadi community in Sukkur and another Ahmadi had been murdered in the year prior to the bombing. Five other Ahmadis were murdered in surrounding areas of Sindh Province during the same period. A number of Ahmadi "places of worship"/mosques had been defaced and many Ahmadis were arrested for wearing Muslim insignia. The authorities, however, paid no attention to the attacks on the Ahmadis while singling them out for legal harassment. Here, Ordinance XX provided a pretext for blatant prejudice and the officially sanctioned maltreatment of the Ahmadis. The cases in Sahiwal and Sukkur were the more egregious of their kind, but they were not the only instances of gross miscarriage of justice against followers of the Ahmadi religion.

In Kunri, a subdivision of Tharparkar district in Sindh, 101 Ahmadis were arrested between April and May 1985 for displaying the kalima and otherwise professing their belief in Islam. "The complaining parties were generally part of a religious faction that was able to persuade the police to make the arrests," Parker noted in her report. Also, between April 26 and May 1, 1985, thirteen Ahmadi leaders in Tharparkar were arrested under the West Pakistan Maintenance of Public Order Ordinance of 1960 and ordered to be detained for thirty days. The orders and memoranda of grounds, issued by District Magistrate Rasool Bakhsh Baloch, charged that the Ahmadis courted arrest by wearing the kalima, "which [was] hurting the feelings of Muslims."[72]

In many instances, a considerable number of Ahmadis were charged. An Ahmadi leader was arrested for injuring the feelings of Muslims in Karachi, arising from the display of Islamic insignia at an Ahmadi mosque. This was followed by the arrest of another forty-one Ahmadis from the mosque, on the grounds that they were "likely to commit a breach of peace." A further five members of that faith in Karachi were charged with preparing a Friday congregation. Similarly, between March 8–11 and March 16–26, 1986, twenty-six Ahmadis were arrested in Sargodha (Punjab) for wearing the kalima.

Many of the "offenses" for which the Ahmadis faced criminal sanction were remarkable for their triviality. A non-Ahmadi schoolteacher was arrested for failing to stop Ahmadi students from wearing the kalima. A number of Ahmadis were even arrested throughout the country for using the Muslim greeting "Assalam Alaikum," used by Pakistanis—non-Muslim and Muslim—as an equivalent for "hello." One such arrest occurred in Mansehra on June 5, 1984, when a shop-keeper gave the greeting to passersby. This person was convicted and handed a six-month prison sentence.

Furthermore, harshly disproportionate sentencing and even blatant overstepping of judicial provisions at the expense of the Ahmadis were a hallmark of many official proceedings conducted under Ordinance XX. The *Daily Jang* (September 19, 1986) reported that Shah Husain Afridi, the assistant commissioner of Mardan in the Northwest Frontier Province, had sentenced two Ahmadis to five years' rigorous imprisonment and had imposed a 50,000-rupee fine under offenses relating to Ordinance XX, even though the ordinance laid down a maximum sentence of three years. In Toba Tek Singh (Punjab), nine Ahmadis were reportedly in district jail in August 1986 for displaying the kalima. In Sargodha, three Ahmadis were sentenced to two years' rigorous imprisonment for wearing the kalima. In Peshawar, an Ahmadi tailor was accused of displaying the kalima in his tailoring shop. He was sentenced to ten years' rigorous imprisonment with a 10,000-rupee fine. The magistrate indicated that posing as a Muslim was a cognizable offense under Ordinance XX but gave no explanation why his sentence exceeded the three-year prison term provided for in Ordinance XX.[73]

"Since the promulgation of Ordinance XX, Ahmadis in all areas have been subject to government persecution in the form of arrest and detention for acts such as wearing religious insignia (*kalima*), and including a prayer on a wedding invitation in violation of the terms of the anti-Ahmadi Ordinance," Parker wrote in her report. According to her research, the government also arrested many people under other laws, such as the West Pakistan Maintenance of Public Order Ordinance (1960). "These arrests clearly illustrate the government's position that the mere presence of Ahmadis 'acting like Muslims' would cause 'real' Muslims to be 'legitimately' offended," she observed. More ominously, it gave Muslims "legitimate" grounds for violent retaliation.

Ironically, the government of Pakistan responded to criticism by the United Nations and international human rights organizations over its treatment of Ahmadis by insisting that "Ahmadis enjoy all rights, including those of worship, assembly and expression." The restrictions on "certain Ahmadi practices" were justified on the grounds that the Ahmadis "offend[ed] orthodox Muslims." Pakistani officials also continued to persist in public incitement of anti-Ahmadi sentiment at home. In a public speech on December 7, 1984, Zia proudly expressed his intolerance toward Ahmadis and stated that "there is no place for infidels in Pakistan. . . . If a man's honor is attacked he does not even hesitate from committing murder. . . . If someone is put against him [the Prophet Muhammad], what should be the reaction of the people?"[74]

During the proceedings of the case involving the Ahmadi challenge to Ordinance XX before the federal shariat court, the deputy attorney general brought virulent anti-Ahmadi rhetoric into the courtroom. "Death is the penalty for those who do not believe in the finality of Prophethood and in Islamic countries it is a heinous crime," he declared. "It is not necessary that the government should take action, but on the contrary any Muslim can take the law in his own hands." This was a bold incitement—which was astounding given his high post in the government judiciary—for Muslims to kill Ahmadis. Official sanction for what may only be described as murder emboldened anti-Ahmadi agitators. In a broadcast on state television in January 1986, Allama Tahir-ul-Qadri, a pro-Zia Sunni religious scholar, urged that those disrespectful of the Prophet Muhammad should be killed instantly.

In another ugly incident, an attorney, Muhammad Ismail Qureshi, attempted to disrupt the annual Pakistan Bar Association meeting by demanding that a banner provided by an Ahmadi businessman be removed from the hall and that Ahmadi lawyers be disbarred. The Bar Association voted down the proposal with only two dissenting votes. This was a clear illustration that, much as targeting Shias did not enjoy much popular support beyond the Islamist hard-liners, many citizens were quite unwilling to engage in the gratuitous persecution of minorities such as the Ahmadis.

Nonetheless, the Pakistani government was accused internationally of abetting religious intolerance through legal formalities and requirements that encouraged private citizens to engage in intolerant or discriminatory acts in order to receive a government benefit. One example was the government requirement that Muslims sign an oath denouncing Ahmadis in order to get a passport or obtain government employment. The standard passport form issued by the government both in Pakistan and in other countries contains a paragraph declaring that the signatory deems the founder of the Ahmadi sect to be an imposter.[75] Although the denunciation paragraph, which remains in force, is described as a declaration that sets Muslims apart from Ahmadis, it amounts to making it obligatory for other Muslims to denounce Ahmadis if they are to obtain a passport.

The international human rights community's response to the anti-Ahmadi laws also drew attention to the discrimination against other religious minorities. In its 1985 report on human rights in Pakistan, the State Department changed its tone somewhat from its earlier findings by acknowledging "reports of discrimination against minority groups." According to the report, "Although conversions are permitted, the government prohibits proselytizing among Muslims and has refused to renew the residence permits of some foreign missionaries who have ignored this ban." The State Department also brought on record "sporadic clashes between the Ahmadis and anti-Ahmadi groups" and the murder of prominent Ahmadis in Sindh Province. "In what appeared to be deliberate efforts to court arrest," the State Department reported, "a number of Ahmadis were detained at various locations throughout the country for wearing badges bearing the Islamic profession of faith. Most were quickly released, but some complained of brutal treatment by the authorities."[76]

In 1986, General Zia-ul-Haq lifted martial law and restored the constitution, albeit with several amendments that maintained his power. An elected Parliament and civilian government headed by a prime minister were also allowed. But elected officials were warned by Zia not to overturn or weaken his policies of Islamization. An ICJ mission to Pakistan in 1987 heard about

> a number of attacks on Hindu temples and a Christian church that had occurred during and since the lifting of martial law. These attacks, which were said to have been perpetrated by Muslims and which resulted in the destruction of these places of worship, took place in Jacobabad, Rahimyar Khan and Sukkur in the provinces of Punjab and Sind.

According to the ICJ, "On every occasion the authorities had failed to take any action to force the attackers to desist" and "the local police had appeared to turn a blind eye to what was happening."[77]

The State Department also mentioned the continuation of attacks on non-Muslims after the end of martial law in its annual report for Congress. "Following reports of anti-Muslim violence in India, there were scattered acts of violence against Hindus and Christians, but these were immediately condemned by the responsible provincial government," the report said. The US government was exercising cautious diplomacy here in maintaining the US alliance with the Zia regime, rather than bluntly pointing out the regime's shortcomings in protecting religious minorities, as it otherwise might have done. The report also said, "Conservative government estimates list more than 130 killed in sectarian clashes in July between Sunnis and Shias in the Kurram Tribal Agency." American diplomats also noted that "in 1986 Parliament passed legislation, apparently aimed at Ahmadis, making blaspheming the Prophet Muhammad a capital offense. Thus far, no Ahmadis have been brought to trial under this provision."[78]

Although a new political order was taking shape in Islamabad, with greater political freedoms than before, its benefits would not be extended to non-Muslims and minority Muslim sects. In 1987, the US embassy reported mob attacks on the Ahmadi mosque in Khushab and raids on Ahmadi shops in Rabwah and Bahawalnagar. In Peshawar, the police intervened to prevent mob action against an Ahmadi place of worship. The Ahmadis were prohibited from holding their annual meeting in December 1986 in Rabwah, and according to the State Department's annual report on human rights, "there [were] credible reports of discrimination against Ahmadis in the military and civil service."[79]

In the eleven years that Zia held power, his regime was the recipient of massive international military and economic assistance, around four and a half billion US dollars that came primarily from America. US support for his dictatorship weakened somewhat, however, once the Soviet Union announced its intention to withdraw its forces from Afghanistan as a result of the Geneva Accords of May 1988. Like all Pakistani rulers and leaders, Zia never admitted that his policies amounted to discrimination against religious minorities. In fact, he argued strongly to the contrary. In a speech on August 12, 1983, he declared, "In Islam minorities are not regarded as suppressed classes, rather they are the most privileged ones. In fact in a Muslim society their rights are more than Muslim populations. In Islamic system of government their rights will be fully protected."[80]

But Zia's assurances bear a particularly hollow ring in view of the bigotry inculcated in Pakistan's children as part of his educational reforms, the Ordinances against Ahmadis and the Blasphemy Ordinance. Further, as the scholar Ian Talbott pointed out, the impact of the law of evidence and the introduction of separate electorates for the minorities in themselves amounted to severe discrimination against the minorities. The minorities were marginalized from the political mainstream under Zia. In all, only 10 out of 237 seats in the lower house of Parliament were reserved for them. This led "some minority leaders to fear that their position would be reduced from that of citizens with full rights to the protected *dhimmi* status and repudiate Jinnah's famous foundational statement in the Constituent Assembly."[81] Under Zia's rule, Pakistan's legal system was methodically stacked against religious minorities, and legislation was passed that gravely impinged upon their right to maintain or openly profess their beliefs.

Furthermore, the Pakistan Penal Code (PPC) and the Criminal Procedure Code were amended under Zia's rule, through ordinances in 1980, 1982, and 1986. These criminalized any act that could cause dishonor to the Holy Prophet (SAW), *Ahle Bait* (the family of the Prophet [SAW]), *Sahaba* (companions of the Prophet [SAW]) and *Sha'ar-i-Islam* (Islamic symbols). A simple complaint to the police about any action that may constitute a crime under the dubiously wide-ranging provisions of these ordinances could result in an arrest and trial leading to punishments of imprisonment or a fine—or both.

It would perhaps be an understatement to describe these amendments and other related legislation as draconian. Article 295A of PPC states that a deliberate and malicious act to outrage the religious feelings of any class by insulting its religion or religious beliefs will be punishable by up to ten years' imprisonment or a fine or with both; 295B makes the defiling of the Holy Quran punishable by imprisonment for life; 295C mandates that the use of derogatory remarks in respect of the Holy Prophet be punished by death and a fine; 298A makes the use of insulting remarks in respect of holy personages punishable by three years' imprisonment or a fine or with both; 298B prescribes punishment of three years' imprisonment and a fine for the misuse of epithets, description, and titles reserved for certain holy personages or places of Islam by Ahmadis; and 298C makes an Ahmadi calling himself Muslim or preaching or propagating his faith or outraging the religious feeling of Muslims or posing himself as a Muslim a punishable crime attracting three years' imprisonment and a fine.[82]

These legal changes enabled bigoted Muslims to persecute, settle scores, or otherwise seek advantage against non-Muslims and Ahmadis by bringing false cases under the vaguely worded blasphemy law. In addition to false cases of blasphemy or of posing as Muslims, the Zia era also saw a plethora of cases concerning the abduction and forcible conversion of Hindu women from the Sukkur, Larkana, and Mirpurkhas districts of Sindh. The law was manipulated by powerful men who would kidnap a non-Muslim woman, then—with the connivance of false witnesses—claim that she had converted to Islam. They would then threaten the woman with the dire consequences of apostasy if she denied her conversion to Islam.

As an ally and benefactor, Washington turned a blind eye to Zia's domestic politics and his pursuit of nuclear weapons for Pakistan. Pakistan's religious minorities suffered without much protest in the world's capitals, where Zia was feted as a frontline ally against Soviet expansion. But it is unclear how much influence international protest might have had in diminishing the effects of Zia's bigotry in any event. Given his stranglehold on power in Pakistan and the geopolitical climate of the era, international pressure against Zia's treatment of the country's minorities would have been confined to moral appeals and petitions for human rights. And these would have fallen on deaf ears, for Zia's prejudices were deeply ingrained. Upon being told that his ordinances against Ahmadis had violated global human rights norms, Zia expressed his views toward such matters in a characteristically tren-chant manner: "Ahmadis offend me because they consider themselves Muslim. . . . Ordinance XX may violate human rights but I don't care."[83]

General Zia-ul-Haq died in a mysterious plane crash on August 17, 1988. His death opened the way for general elections and civilian rule. But the constitutional amendments put in place by Zia created a hybrid system of governance, with considerable powers in the hands of the president, including the authority to dismiss an elected government. Zia also left behind a powerful religious establishment and conservative politicians who remained committed to his Islamist vision.

Over the next eleven years, power alternated between Zia's protégé, Nawaz Sharif, and Benazir Bhutto, the daughter of Zulfikar Ali Bhutto, the man whom Zia hanged. The Pakistani military played a critical role during the period following Zia. Pakistan deployed Islamist militants for influence in a post-Soviet Afghanistan and in continuing attempts to seize control of the Indian-administered parts of the disputed terri-tory of Jammu and Kashmir. Religious minorities suffered now under the discriminatory legal order left behind by Zia and at the hands of jihadist groups, which were nurtured and encouraged by the Pakistan military.

6

Global Jihad and Pakistan's Minorities, 1988–1999

ON FEBRUARY 12, 1989, thousands of protestors attacked the American Cultural Center in Islamabad to denounce Salman Rushdie's novel *The Satanic Verses*. Five people were killed and more than one hundred wounded in the attack.[1] The book was not available for sale in Pakistan and none of the protestors had actually read it. They had only been told by clerics and opposition politicians that the book was blasphemous and belittled Islam's Prophet and his companions.

The international media noted that the protests were meant to "undercut" the newly elected prime minister, Benazir Bhutto, who had come to office after the elections in November 1988 that followed General Zia-ul-Haq's death. It was the first of many incidents over the next decade that reflected the resilience of the alliance Zia had forged between Pakistan's establishment and Islamists. Powerful forces were now at work to maintain the Islamist order that Zia had introduced, and life would not be easier for the country's religious minorities after the dictator's demise.

Benazir Bhutto had campaigned strenuously against Zia's Islamization before and after Zia's death. Bhutto particularly objected to what she perceived as the antifemale bias in the Islamization program, and this theme became a major issue of the Pakistan Peoples Party (PPP) campaign in 1988. She declared in a speech in 1987 that she represented a progressive vision for Pakistan. "I like to think I am carrying on my father's dream of a federal democratic Pakistan," she said, adding that her father had "set the way for a society in which there should be no discrimination on the basis of sex, race or religion, and I too am fighting for this."[2]

Those who voted for Bhutto's PPP in the 1988 election did so with the expectation of turning away from Zia's Islamization. "Indeed the issue of Islamic reform and particularly the issue of the status of women in Islam became one of the most visible issues of the 1988 National Assembly campaign," wrote Professor Charles Kennedy at the time. Benazir Bhutto's "successful management of the issue can be partly credited with providing her with the margin of victory in the election," he added.[3]

But the legacy of Zia was carried forward by an alliance of religious and pro-establishment political parties, assembled hastily by the Inter-Services Intelligence (ISI), called the Islami Jamhoori Ittehad (IJI Islamic Democratic Alliance). The Pakistani military and its intelligence arm wanted to continue the jihad in Afghanistan started by Zia and hoped to start one against India in Jammu and Kashmir. They were also wary about the prospect of a pro-western Bhutto government accepting American terms concerning Pakistan's nuclear program. Although not all Pakistani generals were committed Islamists, their strategic policies necessitated encouraging the country's Islamic militants.

Moreover, although Bhutto had formed the federal government, her PPP did not have a clear majority in Parliament. Separate electorates created by Zia deprived the party of its non-Muslim vote bank and limited the number of non-Muslims in the lower house of Parliament, the National Assembly, to 10 out of 237. Nawaz Sharif, who led the Muslim League, the largest component of the IJI, had retained his position as the chief minister of Punjab, the country's largest province. Like many Muslim League leaders before him, Sharif was not an Islamist like members of the Jamaat-e-Islami or the Jamiat Ulema Islam; he was more interested in protecting the interests of the Punjabi business elite nurtured by Zia. But under his control, Punjab became a bastion of Zia's Islamist legacy, and the repression and exclusion of religious minorities were thus perpetuated in Pakistan's most influential province.

The clerics within the IJI began their attack on Bhutto with fatwas, backed by ulema from Saudi Arabia, against a woman leading an Islamic country. Demonstrations against a "woman's rule," on the purported basis that a woman leading the country contravened sharia, started as soon as Bhutto took her oath of office as prime minister. Then, a series of religious issues were raised and the violence over the Rushdie book was its culmination. Bhutto described the agitation as "a protest by those who lost the election or those who were patronized by martial law to try and destabilize the process of democracy." She said, "The dying order always likes to give a few kicks before it goes to rest."[4]

But subsequent events proved that the order created by Zia did not die, and secular political forces were eventually forced into pragmatic compromises over Islamization. Beginning with the anti-Rushdie protests, Pakistan witnessed "a rising tide of religious fervor" that weakened the newly elected government's ability to change any of the laws imposed as part of Zia's Islamization. "Perhaps more difficult for Ms. Bhutto to deal with over the coming days, however, is the accusation that she is out of touch with Pakistani religiosity," observed a reporter for the *New York Times*. It was pointed out that the Bhutto cabinet lacked "a strong religious thinker with ties to the Muslim establishment."[5]

After putting Bhutto on the defensive from the very start of her tenure, the Islamist clerics went about their usual business of trying to cleanse Pakistan of its non-Muslims. At the same time, the ISI organized training for militant jihadis with the aim of securing control of Afghanistan following the Soviet withdrawal, as well as for attacks inside the disputed Kashmir region controlled by India. Many of these jihadis, who were trained for attacks across the border, doubled as sectarian terrorists in targeting minority communities at home. In short, the well-entrenched Islamist power base established by General Zia remained, and the Islamists' ability to influence events in the nation was largely undiminished by his death. This meant that for the most part, Bhutto's ostensibly secular government was cast as a helpless observer while the Islamists thwarted its leader's vision of a society that did not discriminate on the basis of religion.

Incidents of persecution of religious minorities thus continued in a pattern that had become familiar under Zia's rule. In addition to targeted attacks on Shias, the Ahmadis continued to be persecuted under the draconian Ordinance XX. There were several new cases of sect members being imprisoned for using Islamic symbols. Local officials in several jurisdictions paid little attention to the prime minister's calls for greater religious tolerance. For example, the District Magistrate in Abbottabad charged fifty-five Ahmadis on January 12, 1990, for holding "a prayer meeting in a private household." The charges were brought upon the complaint of a local Islamic group, the Khatm-e-Nabuwwat Youth Force, which objected to the Ahmadis "offering prayers and citing from the Holy Quran."[6]

The actions of the Abbottabad authorities in their pursuit of the matter betrayed at least as much prejudice against the Ahmadis as the complaint itself. Not to be outdone by the complainant's prejudice, the authorities piled on charges against the Ahmadis of disturbing law and order in purported violation of Section 16 of the Maintenance of Public Order Ordinance and Section 107 of the Criminal Procedure Code. This was despite the apparently peaceful nature of the prayer meeting that was, in any event, held in a private home. Five of the accused Ahmadis were arrested and were only released on bail three and a half months after their arrest.

Such incidents increased religious polarization and by August 1990, the *New York Times* noted that Bhutto was having to confront her foes over the volatile issue of religion. The paper's reporter, Barbara Crossette, observed that the opposition IJI had managed to pass a bill in the Senate that would "impose the sharia, a conservative code of Islamic law and practice, on a nation still struggling against all odds to become a democracy." Members of the Senate had taken their seats under Zia and the purpose of the "Sharia Bill" was to dare Bhutto's PPP to vote against it in the lower house, the National Assembly. "Bhutto cannot afford to appear anti-Islamic," Crossette wrote, adding that the prime minister had proposed introducing her government's own version of a sharia bill.[7]

The debate over sharia created several difficulties for Bhutto. The conservatives could use religious courts to challenge her right to govern under sharia as a woman, an issue they had continually raised since the 1988 election. Moreover, Bhutto held only a very narrow majority in the National Assembly, and opinion polls published in the Pakistani press showed overwhelming support for the introduction of Islamic law. Bhutto had "already stirred up religious protest by remarking . . . that it was inhuman for a modern country to cut off the limbs of criminals as the sharia demands. Several religious leaders immediately declared her an infidel."[8]

Before she could resolve the dilemma posed by the opposition's sharia bill, Bhutto was removed from the prime minister's office on August 6, 1990, by presidential decree, under provisions inserted into the constitution by Zia. Fresh elections were ordered for Parliament, but their result was a foregone conclusion. Years later, Pakistan's Supreme Court determined that the Pakistani military and ISI had raised money from businessmen for a slush fund to help the IJI win. The ISI had also operated behind the scenes to manipulate the poll results and had waged a campaign of dirty tricks against Bhutto's PPP.

The disputed 1990 elections resulted in Nawaz Sharif, now head of the Muslim League, becoming prime minister. The ISI had backed Sharif for the greater freedom that a Sharif-led government would afford it in encouraging jihad in Afghanistan and Kashmir. For his part, Sharif, a Punjabi businessman, was interested primarily in opening up the economy and advancing free enterprise. But both the ISI and Sharif depended heavily on Islamist factions for support in the streets, which ensured the preeminence of the Islamist agenda. Soon after Sharif's election, it became apparent that the ISI would get its jihad and Sharif would be able to advance his economic agenda only if they conceded greater space to the Islamists. Further, they would have to allow the Islamists to continue their systematic marginalization of religious minorities.

Even during the 1990 election campaign, the minorities had expressed dismay at being left out of the national mainstream.[9] Under the system of separate electorates, Hindus, Sikhs, Christians, Parsis, and other minority groups were denied the right to vote for Muslim candidates. The IJI thus had to win only a majority of Muslim votes on the overwhelming number of seats allocated for Muslims in the National Assembly. The non-Muslims could vote only for people of their own faiths. The religious minorities shared ten seats in the lower house of Parliament from which the prime minister is drawn, while 217 seats in that house were filled by parliamentarians voted for by Muslims. Four of the ten seats were reserved for Hindus, four for Christians, one for Ahmadis, and one was shared by Parsis, Sikhs, and Hindu untouchables (described as "scheduled castes"). The Ahmadis refused to participate in elections as non-Muslims, insisting that they should be treated as one of Islam's many sects, which was what their religion proclaims.

The separation of franchise that was foisted on religious minorities was unsatisfactory for both the candidates who stood for office and their communities. R. M. Lawrence, a retired army officer who was competing with several dozen others for one of the four Christian seats, described the regime of separate electorates as "a very unfair system." He explained that because Christians are denied constituencies and must campaign nationwide, they can never serve their electorates effectively. Further, they are always cast as competitors with each other. The campaigning itself takes its toll. Another Christian candidate, Shamshad Sanaullah, the principal of a private school, told The *New York Times* that he collapsed physically because he could not keep up with reaching out to Christians scattered all over Pakistan, sometimes two or three families to a village.

Sanaullah also voiced the concern of Pakistani Christians about the cost of their effective exclusion from politics. "For some reason, electricity stops before it gets to them," he said. "The same for roads. Somehow development stops where Christian communities start." This could be changed, he said, only by giving Christians more political power by allowing them to vote for Muslim candidates. Christian candidates also complained about unreliable census figures about their numbers in Pakistan. According to Sanaullah, the government's figure of 1.2 million Christians was ludicrously low and was intended to keep the Christians' political representation at a minimum.[10] But no one was paying attention to the minorities' complaints. With the election of Nawaz Sharif, Pakistan saw a revival of momentum in Zia's Islamization.

Soon after coming to office in November 1990, Nawaz Sharif faced the difficulties of restarting the economy while also advancing the goals of his political allies: the military and the religious parties. When Saudi Arabia and the United States assembled a coalition to confront Iraq in the aftermath of Saddam Hussein's occupation of Kuwait, Sharif supported the Saudi view. To him it made economic sense, as all of Pakistan's major aid donors were allied with the United States and Saudi Arabia. But General Aslam Beg, who had succeeded Zia as Army Chief of Staff, made a speech in which he said that the Gulf War was part of a "Zionist" strategy that also guided Washington. Reflecting the view that any Muslim leader was preferable to an assortment of infidels and heretics, he argued that "the United Nations had allowed the allied forces to liberate Kuwait and not to destroy Iraq economically and politically."

Beg's statement encouraged Islamists to take to the streets in support of Saddam Hussein, and Pakistan was soon "awash in anti-Western polemics." Christian churches were stoned because "Washington is in charge of the war" and a daily diet of visceral anti-Americanism and crude anti-Semitism was served in the press, both English and Urdu. "Imagine, $13.5 billion for losing half a dozen lives and some houses," a columnist in the *Muslim* newspaper wrote today of the Israeli aid request because of its role in the conflict. "Trust a Jew to make big money out of a minor mishap."[11] The Gulf War helped consolidate Pakistani anti-Americanism, which previously was mostly about foreign policy, as an anti-Jewish and anti-Christian ideology championed mainly by the country's Islamist parties.

Once the Gulf War was over, Sharif's IJI government focused on catering to its religious constituency. It took credit for passing the sharia bill in May 1991 and the twelfth amendment to the constitution in July. The sharia bill declared the Quran and Sunnah as the law of the land, not just the guideline for legislation as had been the case since the Objectives Resolution of 1949. The language of the bill was such that it could render legislatures superfluous, notwithstanding that they remained both at the federal and provincial levels as the only lawmaking bodies in the country. The sharia bill opened the way for courts to base their judgments on Islamic law, citing sayings attributed to the Prophet or to medieval Islamic jurists, instead of adjudicating cases on grounds of Pakistan's laws. Opponents of the bill, including minority and women's groups, saw it as a further step toward making Pakistan a theocracy.[12]

Critics saw Sharif as following in Zia's footsteps in playing the Islamic card. Addressing a gathering of religious leaders at Islamabad, Sharif announced his resolve to amend the constitution to ensure the supremacy of the shariat as the law of the land, even though the National Assembly had already enacted the sharia bill. "The prime minister's policy seemed to be 'hunting with the hounds and running with the hare,'" commented Rais Khan, an academic. "On Independence Day, he declared himself to be the standard bearer of Jinnah's principles and on Zia's anniversary three days later he pronounced himself the guardian of Zia's legacy," Khan said, adding, "It did not bother him that Jinnah, the father of Pakistan, was a democrat and a secularist and Zia was a ruthless military dictator and religious bigot."[13]

One of the legacies of Zia-ul-Haq that found special resonance under the IJI government related to blasphemy laws. In October 1990, the federal shariat court had determined that "the penalty for contempt of the Holy Prophet . . . is death and nothing else." The court directed the government of Pakistan to change the law to reflect its determination and added, "in case this is not done by 30 April 1991 the words 'or punishment for life' in section 295-C, PPC, shall cease to have effect on that date." Decisions by the federal shariat court are binding on the government under Article 203-D (3) of the constitution. The government could have appealed the decision to the shariat appellate bench of the Supreme Court but chose not to do so. In July 1991, it announced that it had decided to amend section 295-C as directed.[14]

Once it became known that the death penalty was the only punishment in cases involving blasphemy or insult to Islam's Prophet, the floodgates opened for the abuse of the relevant provisions. And rampant abuse of these laws was by no means restricted to the authorities, though the police as well as political and sectarian organizations were most often involved. In Pakistan, bail is restricted in cases involving the death penalty; a person accused under section 295-C would therefore face immediate imprisonment before the case was heard in court. The blasphemy statute thus became a convenient tool for retribution or to gain an advantage against anyone with whom one might have a dispute—regardless of the nature of the dispute. Soon, there were instances of blasphemy complaints being lodged to force the hand of business rivals or even to exact revenge against someone who had spurned an unwanted sexual advance.

The legal amendment that was to follow the sharia court's judgment was never enacted. A bill was placed before Parliament in 1992 to make death the only punishment for blasphemy or insult to the Prophet. While the Senate unanimously adopted the bill in July 1992, it was discussed at length but rejected in the National Assembly and eventually taken off the parliamentary agenda. The opposition parties considered it "too vague and liable to abuse." In February 1994, the Law Commission of Pakistan, presided over by the Chief Justice of Pakistan and the Minister for Law, Justice and Parliamentary Affairs, decided to send the draft of the blasphemy law amendment bill to the Council for Islamic Ideology for further scrutiny.

According to Amnesty International, "The legal situation in respect of the blasphemy law is confusing and this confusion has frequently been used by the Government of Pakistan to confound human rights activists and critics." Following the directive of the federal shariat court of 1990, the alternative punishment of imprisonment for life contained in section 295-C became void. The death penalty is the mandatory punishment for blasphemy. But as Parliament has not passed the legislation required of it by the federal shariat court, the clause "or imprisonment for life" is still part of section 295-C, though without force.[15] But this legal confusion offered no relief for those charged with blasphemy, who now, amid the legal uncertainty, faced even greater hostility from a society ever more preoccupied with enforcing religious homogeneity.

Not to be outdone by the federal shariat court in pronouncing legal sanctions against heterodoxy, the government introduced Ordinance XXI of 1991 on July 7, 1991, to increase the maximum punishment for outraging the religious feelings of any group from two years to ten years. As was the case with Zia's Ordinance XX, this new law was primarily directed against the Ahmadis. Amnesty International noted that

> the amendments of the Pakistan Penal Code introduced in 1991 are applicable to anyone defiling the name of the Prophet Mohammad or outraging the religious feelings of certain groups. They are of significance particularly in the context of the Pakistan Government's policy towards the Ahmadiyya community, as its members are frequently charged under these two sections of the PPC.[16]

Amnesty International documented that 3,113 Ahmadis had been charged under Ordinance XX up to September 1988. The enhanced punishment was likely to affect the cases of hundreds or possibly thousands more who were likely to be charged, tried, and convicted to prison terms solely for their religious beliefs, which were legally considered offensive to Muslims since Zia's days. Human rights activists feared that Ordinance XXI and prescribing the death penalty as the mandatory punishment for defiling the name of the Prophet Muhammad would virtually criminalize the Ahmadi faith. "The Ahmadis' reference to the Prophet Mohammad is by orthodox Muslims considered to be defiling his name," Amnesty International pointed out. It added that

> legislation which provides for imprisonment and even the death penalty on grounds of religious conscience violates the right to freedom of religion contained in Article 18 of the Universal Declaration of Human Rights. It is contrary to the 1981 United Nations Declaration on the Elimination of All Forms of Intolerance and of Discrimination Based on Religion and Belief.[17]

By the time of Sharif's second year in power, attacks on religious minorities had become frequent and widespread. International human rights organizations listed several such attacks on Christians. Niamat Ahmer, a teacher, poet, and writer, was murdered by extremists in 1992. Bantu Masih, aged eighty, was stabbed and killed in the presence of the police in 1992. Apart from Ahmadis and Christians being victimized by blasphemy laws, violence against Shias also worsened. The army was called out in Gilgit and Quetta after attacks on Shias. But instead of clamping down on militant Islamists, the government announced an allocation from zakat of 250 million rupees ($10 million) for Sunni madrasas, which were incubating the anti-Shia hatred. *Dawn*, Pakistan's newspaper of record, editorially described these sectarian schools as "theological time capsules buried somewhere in the fifteenth century, out of which step young fanatics programmed to spread sectarian hatred."[18]

Also in 1992, for the first time in Pakistan's history, candidates fielded by an openly militant sectarian group, Sipah-e-Sahaba Pakistan (Army of the Prophet's Companions) (SSP), won by-elections in Jhang and won representation in both the National Assembly and the Punjab Assembly. "How much the government and the country are held hostage by religious obscurantists," said Rais Khan, "can be judged from the fact women's events from the Barcelona Olympics could not be telecast and women cannot appear on television without their heads covered."[19]

The renewed emphasis on Islamization affected all religious minorities. It exacerbated the prosecution and persecution of Ahmadis and Christians over alleged blasphemy and gave way to a rise in militant attacks on Shias by a politically legitimated SSP. Pakistan's Hindus became the focus of Islamist violence again when India's Hindu fanatics destroyed the historic Babri Masjid in Ayodhya in December 1992. Pakistani Islamists portrayed the Hindu attack on the mosque as symbolic of the contest between Muslim Pakistan and Hindu India. Retaliatory assaults were immediately organized on Hindu temples and other property in Pakistan and in addition to the severe outbreak of communal strife throughout much of the subcontinent, there were bombings in both India and Pakistan.[20] The destruction of temples extended to ancient Jain temples, including one in Rawalpindi, even though Jains had nothing to do with the Babri Masjid incident.

Any hope that Pakistan's state institutions would offer protection to religious minorities against Islamist legislative adventurism was dashed by the attitude of the country's judiciary, which ruled in favor of the Islamists most of the time. The Supreme Court dismissed the constitutional challenge to laws directed at Ahmadis on grounds that the Pakistani state was entitled to "protect" Islamic terms from use by non-Muslims. The court ruled that laws limiting Ahmadi religious practices were necessary for law and order given that "Ahmadi religious practice, however peaceful, angered and offended the Sunni majority in Pakistan." This opened the door for district magistrates and lower courts to forbid public observance of other religious communities on grounds of protecting the majority from being offended.

The situation did not change when Bhutto returned to power as prime minister in October 1993 after the dismissal of the Sharif government a few months earlier. Once again, an election was won by a liberal political party, but Pakistan's political environment favored the Islamist viewpoint even without the Islamists winning a significant number of votes. Pakistan was deeply involved in the civil war in Afghanistan, in which various Mujahedeen groups were pitted against each other following the collapse of the Soviet-installed regime in Kabul. Militancy in Indian-controlled parts of Jammu and Kashmir, which began in 1989, was also at its height. Both of these external operations involved

Islamist jihadis, many of whom maintained close ties with sectarian militants attacking religious minorities within Pakistan.

Although the government and the ISI both voiced disapproval of domestic sectarian violence, their covert operations across the border were inexorably strengthening religious militancy at home. Moreover, in addition to its usual targeted attacks on Shia professionals in major cities, the SSP was becoming much more engaged in harassing non-Muslim minorities. One such instance began when Maulvi Fazl-e-Haq, an SSP leader in Gujranwala (central Punjab), accused three Christians in his town of blasphemy. Manzoor Masih, Rehmat Masih, and Salamat Masih were arrested in May 1993. Maulvi Fazl-e-Haq had accused Salamat Masih, who was only thirteen, of writing blasphemous slogans on the wall of the local mosque.

But testimony emerged that Salamat Masih could not read or write. Still, he and his two older companions were charged under section 295-C of the Pakistan Penal Code, which provided a mandatory death penalty for anyone defiling the name of the Prophet Muhammad. Human rights campaigners took up the case and protested against the three Christians' imprisonment. It was pointed out that they could not be fairly tried in Gujranwala where the safety of the prisoners could not be guaranteed. SSP held frequent demonstrations in and outside the courtroom, demanding the execution of the three Christians accused.

The case of the three Christian prisoners was transferred to Lahore and the child Salamat Masih was released on bail in November 1993. Manzoor and Rehmat Masih got bail in January 1994, although the charges remained against them. On April 5, 1994, in Lahore, Manzoor Masih was shot dead and his co-accused, Rehmat Masih and Salamat Masih, were seriously injured. Their assailants were three gunmen identified by eyewitnesses as SSP members. The attack took place near the Lahore High Court—and about two hundred meters away from a police station—just after the Christians had left a court hearing.[21] From around this time, attacks against Pakistan's religious minorities would no longer be solely characterized by the mob violence of the variety witnessed throughout Pakistan's history. It would be now backed by well-trained militias and terrorist groups that could carry out massacres with modern weaponry and sophisticated explosives.

Religion-motivated mob violence would continue, however. Just a few days after the shooting of the Christians in Lahore, on April 21, 1994, a Muslim practitioner of indigenous medicine was stoned to death by a mob in Gujranwala, which believed him to have burned some pages of the Quran. They tried to set his body on fire while he was probably still alive and dragged his dead body through the streets. According to Amnesty International, the government of Pakistan did not publicly condemn such acts and failed to take all possible measures to ensure the safety of members of religious minorities. "None of the major political parties have publicly condemned the incidents," it noted.

The extremists did not stop at killing Manzoor Masih. One of the judges in the trial of Manzoor Masih and his family members, Arif Iqbal Bhatti, was later murdered in his chambers by an extremist assassin simply because he acquitted the accused Christians on the basis of weak evidence.[22] The murder of a judge who dared to rule in support of members of a minority community—and thus against the militants' diktat—served as a warning to officials that they should not sympathize with non-Muslims, even within the confines of laws that were already stacked against minority communities. Once militants had accused someone of blasphemy, trial before judges would now be a mere formality; a guilty verdict was a foregone conclusion. The accusation itself was tantamount to a death sentence, with the militants, instead of the state, acting as the executioner.

During a debate in the National Assembly following the murder of Manzoor Masih, retired Supreme Court Judge Dorab Patel, chairman of the nongovernmental Human Rights Commission of Pakistan, called for amendments to the blasphemy law as it contributed to religious fanaticism. He was interrupted by a Sipah-e-Sahaba member of Parliament, Azam Tariq, who shouted that "anyone who commits blasphemy will meet the fate of Manzoor Masih."

The exchange between Tariq and Patel, a Parsi (Zoroastrian), was cited in a July 1994 report titled "Pakistan: Use and Abuse of the Blasphemy Laws," by Amnesty International, which also compared the Bhutto and Sharif governments and their attitudes toward minorities and blasphemy. According to the report, "During the first period of government of Benazir Bhutto (1988 to 1990) no further steps towards Islamization were undertaken." But the IJI government of Prime Minister Nawaz Sharif (1990–1993) used its clear majority in Parliament to pass the Enforcement of Sharia Act in 1991. It declared that "the Injunctions of Islam . . . shall be the supreme law of Pakistan" and provided for the Islamization of education and the economy while ensuring that none of the provisions of the act would "affect the personal laws, religious freedoms, traditions, customs and way of life of non-Muslims."[23]

Amnesty International pointed out that "in elections in October 1993 the Islamic parties obtained considerably fewer seats in the National Assembly than in the two previous elections while the secular Pakistan People's Party obtained a clear majority and formed the government under Benazir Bhutto." The new government announced that steps would be taken to amend the penal code and the code of criminal procedure to curb the abuse of the blasphemy laws. But the situation on ground deteriorated before concrete legislative measures could be initiated.

According to Amnesty, religiously motivated attacks on members of minority groups began to increase soon after the election. At least thirteen attacks were recorded against members of the Ahmadiyya community in late 1993 and in the early months of 1994. "It is not known to Amnesty International at present if these and other reported instances of religiously motivated attacks are spontaneous outbreaks of violence or if any militant groups plan, support, condone or coordinate them," said the report.

The report also stated that

> several dozen people have been charged with blasphemy in Pakistan over the last few years; in all the cases known to Amnesty International the charges of blasphemy appear to have been arbitrary, founded solely on the individuals' minority religious beliefs or un-founded and malicious accusations brought by individuals against others in the majority Muslim community. The available evidence in all of these cases suggests that charges were brought as a measure to intimidate and punish members of minority religious communities, or as a consequence of accusations brought by individuals motivated by personal enmity or a desire to gain political advantage.[24]

As a consequence, Amnesty International concluded that "most of the individuals now facing charges of blasphemy, or convicted on such charges, are or could become prisoners of conscience, detained for their real or imputed religious beliefs in violation of their right to freedom of thought, conscience and religion." The global human rights organization pointed out a common feature of accusations of blasphemy in Pakistan as "the manner in which they are uncritically accepted by prosecuting authorities, who themselves may face intimidation, threats and accusations should they fail to accept them." Amnesty International voiced concern that trial procedures in cases involving charges of blasphemy, including pretrial procedures, did not meet international standards of fairness.

When the Bhutto government announced its intention to make changes to the blasphemy law, a one-day strike was organized in May 1994 by both Sunni and Shia fundamentalist groups, and the prime minister and her law minister were threatened with death. One proposed amendment to the law would have mandated a ten-year prison sentence for falsely accusing anyone of committing blasphemy. Given that the blasphemy law carried an automatic death penalty, this was perhaps a reasonable measure to curb its abuse. But the Islamists' ability to mobilize street power against the contemplated changes forced the government to offer negotiations with the ulema before introducing the new legislation. But before these discussions could advance, a major development in Afghanistan provided impetus to Islamist militancy in Pakistan.

The stalemated civil war in Afghanistan came close to a conclusion with the rise of the Taliban in late 1994. Journalist Ahmed Rashid described the Taliban phenomenon as "a Messianic movement made up of *taliban* (lit., students) from Islamic *madrasas* (seminaries) who were living as refugees in Pakistan." The Taliban "vowed to bring peace to Afghanistan, establish law and order, disarm the population, and impose sharia (Islamic law)" and were welcomed by the war-weary Pashtun population in the south and east of Afghanistan, along the border with Pakistan.[25]

The Taliban were backed by Pakistan and Saudi Arabia with the objective of ending strife in Afghanistan. They were also supported by the Saudi-born Islamist radical Osama bin Laden and other Arab extremists who had fought alongside the Afghan Mujahedeen during the war against the Soviets. In areas they controlled, the Taliban imposed their own interpretation of Islam, which had "emerged from an extreme and perverse interpretation of Deobandism, preached by Pakistani mullahs (clerics) in Afghan refugee camps."[26] Since Independence, the Deoband branch of Sunni Islam had been behind the efforts to purify Pakistan's society on the basis of religion. They have expressed harsh views of non-Muslims and Shias and deemed Ahmadis as apostates deserving of death. Now, with control over territory in Afghanistan, they could forcibly impose their version of sharia rule, while arming and training militants to do the same in Pakistan.

The rise to power of the Taliban across the border instigated a religious revolt in the Malakand Division of Pakistan's northwest Pashtun region. On November 2, 1994, the Tehrik-i-Nifaz-i-Shariat-i-Muhammadi (TNSM), a movement to enforce sharia, blocked roads and took over official buildings. The rebels took civil court judges and government officials hostage and murdered a PPP National Assembly member. The Saidu Sharif airport in Swat Valley was captured by TNSM activists, and roads linking the area to the rest of the country were blocked. The government agreed to the creation of sharia courts locally, and the combination of concessions and threats of force to the militants brought back a semblance of normalcy to the affected territory. But Islamists now knew that they could force the government's hand by using tactics that had brought their ideological kin to power in Afghanistan.[27]

According to one authoritative account, members of the TNSM were referred to as "Black Turbans" because of their distinctive headgear. They composed a force of approximately forty thousand men, armed and equipped with Russian-manufactured wireless equipment that dated to the Soviet occupation of Afghanistan. "The Black Turbans also had some outside support—Arab and Afghan mercenaries left over from the Afghan civil war," noted Robert La Porte Jr., in an academic journal soon after the events in Malakand.[28]

The war against the Soviets had already resulted in the proliferation of hundreds of madrasas in Pakistan's Pashtun belt to provide Afghan refugees and young Pakistanis free education, food, shelter, and military training. Most of these madrasas were run by barely literate mullahs who had an overly simplistic understanding of Islam and its tradition.

Saudi funding during and after the anti-Soviet war brought them closer to ultraconservative Wahhabism, which emphasized religious purity. After the 1993 elections, the relatively small Deobandi party, the Jamiat Ulema Islam (JUI), joined Bhutto's ruling coalition, giving its leaders access to the corridors of power. Just as the Jamaat-e-Islami had done during the Zia era, the JUI established close links with the army, the ISI, and the Interior Ministry. The party became a key interlocutor between Pakistan's establishment and the Afghan Taliban, most of whom had studied at madrasas under the party's leaders.

Around the same time that the Taliban were expanding their control of Afghanistan, the United States was pressing Pakistan to shut down training camps for militants fighting in Indian-administered parts of Jammu and Kashmir. Taliban-controlled Afghanistan was a convenient place to relocate these camps. Because of the JUI's links with the Taliban as well as Bhutto's civilian government, its militant factions (including extreme sectarian groups such as the SSP) ended up controlling the jihadi training camps in Afghanistan. The JUI and many Deobandi factions such as Harkat-ul-Ansar, Harkat-ul-Jihad-al-Islami, Harkat-ul-Mujahideen, and Sipah-e-Sahaba became the main recruiters of Pakistani and foreign (mainly Arab) madrasa students to fight for the Taliban.

According to Ahmed Rashid, between 1994 and 1999, an estimated eighty thousand to one hundred thousand Pakistanis trained and fought in Afghanistan.[29] Many of these battle-hardened militants also fought in Kashmir and were inclined to attack religious minorities and impose their brand of sharia within Pakistan.

The role of madrasas in nurturing militancy and inspiring extreme Islamization in the country could barely be overlooked. In the decades following Independence, there had been phenomenal growth in madrasas all across Pakistan, swelling the ranks of young men who had no vocational skills and little academic capability beyond the rote learning of the Quran and medieval religious texts. In 1947, Pakistan had only 137 seminaries, whereas by the year 2000 the number of madrasas had reached close to 29,000. Several of these madrasas received financial support from outside the country,[30] mainly from orthodox individuals and charities in Saudi Arabia and other Gulf Arab countries.

The rationale behind the bankrolling of the madrasas was quite transparent: it was a clear and unabashed attempt—and a successful one at that—to propagate a preferred religious ideology. "There is little doubt that most Deobandi madrasas were funded by Saudi Arabia because of the affiliation of Arab scholars with that school of thought," the author and newspaper editor Khaled Ahmed pointed out. He cited an article in the monthly Wahhabi religious publication *Nida al-jihad*, which explained that Saudi donors took philosophy and reason out of the madrasa syllabus and emphasized Hadith—sayings attributed to the Prophet Muhammad, not all of which are deemed accurate.[31] This lessened the educational and accentuated the indoctrinational aspects of the madrasas, transforming them from outposts of religious conservatism to bastions of religious militancy.

Benazir Bhutto's own account of the events during this period shows that she and her civilian government felt embattled, as the Kashmiri insurgency continued and the Taliban consolidated their grip on Afghanistan—with the help of Pakistan's military and ISI. "The extremists had not given up," she wrote in the revised edition of her autobiography, *Daughter of the East*. According to her, they attempted to burn down Pakistan's National Assembly building, kidnapped a bus full of schoolchildren in 1994, and bombed the Egyptian embassy.

Bhutto also spoke of discovering "a massive underground culture of so-called madrasas that were churning out hate-filled and paramilitary-trained young terrorists" after the arrest of Ramzi Youssef, a nephew of Al-Qaida's operational commander, Khalid Shaikh Mohammed, who had bombed New York's World Trade Center in 1993. Youssef had detonated a truck loaded with explosives in the building's basement before leaving New York for Pakistan. He managed to hide for several months before being tracked down by the CIA and was arrested and deported with the help of Pakistani law enforcement officials. The fact that an Al-Qaida operative could hide among fellow believers in Pakistan after setting off a bomb in New York pointed to a jihadi network, which was exposed further in the aftermath of the September 11, 2001, World Trade Center attacks, culminating in the discovery of Al-Qaida leader Osama bin Laden in a Pakistani garrison town in May 2011.

Bhutto asserted that she tried to put radical madrasas "under governmental scrutiny, control and regulations and required them to teach math, science and literature." According to her, the government asked the madrasas "to stop brainwashing young students to 'kill the Hindus, Christians, Jews and Shias and anyone else that deviated' from their interpretation of religion." Mullahs resisted the demand for government regulation of religious schools at first but accepted the requirement for registering madrasas with local authorities after Bhutto shut down the Islamic university in Peshawar for refusing to do so. Bhutto said she sought to make a distinction between "traditional madrasas which taught students how to read the Holy Quran and also taught mathematics, philosophy, law and astronomy" and "the new, hardline madrasas created by the extremists of the Mujahideen and ISI" that sought to take on the west and also oppressed other Muslims.[32]

But the efforts Bhutto describes obviously did little to curb Islamist extremism, which continued to rise with the backing of elements within the government and state institutions. In January 1994, SSP extremists killed six and injured twenty-one Shias in an attack on a Shia mosque in Multan. Over the next couple of months, there were five retributive assassinations of Shia and Sunni leaders in Punjab.[33] On February 25, 1995, gunmen opened fire on worshippers in two Shia mosques in Karachi, killing eighteen men and wounding many more. These massacres were part of a wave of attacks by trained terrorists, in which innocent Shias were killed during prayers—a reprehensible tactic that became more frequent in subsequent years. It is ironic that worshippers at prayer in a mosque were no longer safe in a country that was created to provide security to South Asia's Muslims.

The two attacks were choreographed for maximum effect. In the first attack, six men were killed and several injured when four gunmen began shooting with automatic weapons in the Abu al-Abbas Mosque in Karachi East. The attackers struck at 6.00 A.M., targeting worshippers gathered for morning prayers. Half an hour later, twelve more people were killed and six injured when gunmen fired on worshippers who had been herded into a room in the Mehfil Murtaza Mosque two miles away. Officials believed that both shootings were carried out by the same gunmen, but there was no explanation for how they moved between their target locations without being detected by law enforcement personnel.[34]

On March 10, 1995, ten Shias were killed and twenty-two wounded in a brutal sectarian attack on another Shia mosque in Karachi. A bomb was exploded outside the mosque after Friday prayers, and masked gunmen stormed into the smoke-filled courtyard, letting loose "volleys of automatic rifle fire at the panicked survivors." The attack came just one day after extremist gunmen ambushed a United States consulate van in downtown Karachi, killing two American diplomats and injuring a third.

Both attacks appeared to be carefully planned and coordinated, and there was speculation of a connection between them. The armed men who had attacked the Shia mosque may, at least, have received similar training to that of the Americans' assailants. And while the local media downplayed the killings of the Americans, the outpouring of emotion following the mass killing at the mosque was immense. "Twelve people were killed, including eight children, and 28 others wounded when a powerful bomb exploded outside a Shia mosque in Malir just after the Friday congregation," reported *Dawn*. The victims were "children and teenagers, aged between two and 15 years." According to the report, "the explosion triggered sectarian tension with reports of scattered shooting in parts of the city. Roads wore a deserted look while in Malir masked armed men forced shopkeepers to pull down shutters and set ablaze a bus. The Tehrik-i-Jaffaria Pakistan held the provincial government responsible for the attack, described it as incompetent, callous and helpless."[35]

A month later, on April 9, 1995, a violent mob attacked two members of the Ahmadiyya community in the town of Shab Qadar in the Khyber-Pakhtunkhwa Province (then known as the Northwest Frontier Province). Dr. Rashid Ahmad and his son-in law, Riaz Khan, were about to attend a court hearing when the frenzied mob set upon them after being egged on by extremist Sunni clerics. Riaz Khan was stoned to death and his dead body stripped and dragged through the town on a rope. Rashid Ahmad was taken to a hospital in Peshawar with serious injuries. A third Ahmadi, advocate Bashir Ahmad, escaped unhurt.

The three men had come to the small town from Peshawar, the provincial capital, to help another Ahmadi, Daulat Khan, who had been suffering harassment at the hands of local extremists following his conversion to the sect several months earlier. Police had detained Daulat

Khan ostensibly "for his own safety," before charging him with disturbing public tranquility by joining an unlawful assembly. In addition to the brutal attack in Shab Qadar, at least seven Ahmadis were attacked and killed with impunity by religious extremists in other parts of Pakistan. Though most of these killings took place in broad daylight and before many eyewitnesses, in none of the cases were those responsible for the killings arrested and charged.[36]

Emboldened by their "success" in attacking hapless religious minorities, some Islamists plotted in the same year to overthrow the Pakistani government. The conspiracy involved at least thirty-six army officers, including a major-general and several brigadiers. Their plan was to kill the prime minister and senior generals and then install an Islamic government modeled on the early Islamic caliphates. The planned coup was foiled by military intelligence, which was alarmed at attempts by Islamists to subvert the armed forces chain of command and aghast that they would even consider killing top generals. The military was not averse to using Islamist sentiment for strategic objectives, but the generals had no intention of relinquishing authority to clerics and military officers tied too closely to religious factions. At any rate, the episode highlighted the weakness of civilian power. Reporting on the Islamist plot, the *Economist* stated that "widespread corruption, a sputtering economy and a state of near anarchy in Karachi, the main commercial city do not help [Benazir Bhutto] in trying to promote Pakistan abroad as a moderate Islamic country, opposed to fundamentalism."[37]

By the autumn of 1996, Bhutto's second term had lasted longer than her first term or Nawaz Sharif's first stint as prime minister. But she spent most of her tenure negotiating crises such as the TNSM revolt, the rise of the Taliban in Afghanistan, a faltering economy—and the sporadic violence that flared in various parts of the country but especially blighted Pakistan's commercial capital, Karachi. In September 1996, two hundred Shias were killed in Parachinar, while the next month saw the lives of forty-eight Sunnis extinguished in two separate retaliatory mosque attacks in Multan.[38] In such an environment, there was little room for policy and legislative changes that were needed to end the widespread abuse and harassment of the various religious minorities.

Bhutto's government was dismissed—again by presidential fiat—in November 1996, and new elections in February 1997 brought Nawaz

Sharif back to power with an overwhelming majority of seats in Parliament. On the eve of the 1997 elections, a bomb killed nineteen Sunni militant leaders in a courthouse in Lahore.[39] Any hope that a new government would rid the country of religious or sectarian terrorism was dashed by the prospect of further retaliatory violence between the SSP and its Shia nemesis, the Sipah-e-Muhammad. While the latter's fortunes declined simply because it did not have the establishment support system that the SSP enjoyed, the sectarian killing persisted. The Islamists continued their targeted violence against minority-Muslim sects as well as against non-Muslims.

The blasphemy laws also continued to wreak havoc in the lives of ordinary people, especially those from the lower strata of society. In a reprise of a familiar pattern of cases involving Christians, Ayub Masih was accused on October 14, 1996, of praising Christianity and speaking favorably of Salman Rushdie's controversial novel *The Satanic Verses*. He was thus charged with blasphemy. "Masih" (a reference to Jesus) is the surname adopted by members of lower Hindu castes after their conversion to Christianity. Apparently, the accusations against Ayub Masih were the culmination of a disagreement with a Muslim neighbor.

On November 6, 1997, Ayub was shot and wounded outside the court by one of his accusers, Mohammad Akram. Notwithstanding eyewitness accounts of the crime, the police refused to investigate or charge Akram, indicating the authorities' unwillingness to prosecute vigilante violence against those accused of blasphemy. Many of the lawyers and judges in the case also received death threats. On April 27, 1998, a court in the Punjab town of Sahiwal sentenced Ayub to death for alleged blasphemy, relying solely on the complainants' uncorroborated statement. A lower appeals court upheld the sentence, as did the High Court. During his six years in prison, there were at least two attempts on his life. Several years later, on August 16, 2002, Ayub Masih was acquitted by the Supreme Court after his lawyer was able to prove that Akram had used the conviction to acquire Ayub's land after the entire Christian population of his village—including Ayub's family—was forced to evacuate the village in the wake of the charges against Ayub.[40]

Although Nawaz Sharif's Pakistan Muslim League did not need the parliamentary support of Islamist groups, his government continued to appease them. Sharif himself seemed eager to burnish his credentials as a champion of Islam during his second term. The Taliban had by now taken control of most of Afghanistan, including the capital city, Kabul. Sharif's government formally recognized the Taliban regime, and Pakistan became the only country where that regime was allowed to establish an embassy. The nexus between the Taliban and ISI deepened once Pakistan recognized the Taliban as the de jure rulers of Afghanistan. In addition to jihadi terrorists who traveled freely to receive training across the border, Pakistan's hard-line Sunni clerics and ISI officials regularly traveled between the countries. The Pakistani media was awash with stories that quite incredibly presented the Taliban's brutal regime as the reincarnation of the decidedly more pious caliphate of Islam's earliest days.

In May 1998, Pakistan conducted nuclear tests within a week of similar tests by India. Sharif took credit for leading Pakistan into the "nuclear club," and the government encouraged hyper-nationalist sentiment over Pakistan's emergence as the world's only Islamic nuclear power. International sanctions following the nuclear tests created serious economic challenges. But the government decided to distract the public with doses of propaganda about economic hardship being a small price to pay for the glory of Islam and Pakistan. By August, Sharif was ready to amend Pakistan's constitution "to create an Islamic order in Pakistan and establish a legal system based on the Quran."

The country's opposition, led by Benazir Bhutto, pointed out that further Islamization "would deepen strife in a country where religiously motivated violence has killed hundreds of people." But Sharif insisted that his proposed new order would create a "true Islamic welfare state." He said all laws would be based exclusively on the Quran and Sunnah. "Simple changes in laws are not enough," he said in a televised address to the nation. "I want to implement complete Islamic laws where the Quran and Sunnah are supreme." Under the amendment, the federal government would be "obliged" to enforce prayers five times a day and collect annual tithes as zakat.[41]

This attempt at sweeping Islamization was similar to that undertaken by General Zia-ul-Haq, with one crucial difference. While Zia was a military dictator who lacked legitimacy, Sharif was an elected leader who was trying to move Pakistan further along the path toward theocracy through an act of Parliament. Like Zia, Sharif sought to assure minorities and women that the new Islamic laws would not violate their rights. But human rights advocates accused Sharif of using Islam to buttress his power at a time when he seemed globally isolated and embattled at home. "In the name of Islam, Nawaz Sharif is trying to perpetuate a fascist rule," warned Asma Jahangir, a prominent human rights activist and lawyer. She also warned that militant Muslims will use the new law to impose their brand of Islam on the populace.[42]

Sharif, however, was unmoved by the criticism. He declared at one point that he admired the Taliban and wanted the introduction of swift Islamic justice in Pakistan, including the hanging of rapists within twenty-four hours of being arrested. He said his "goal was a system of justice like that followed by the Taliban movement in Afghanistan," which would "rid the country of crime and corruption."[43] Sharif told a public meeting that "in Afghanistan, crimes have virtually come to naught. I have heard that one can safely drive a vehicle full of gold at midnight without fear." He added that he wanted the same kind of system in Pakistan where "justice will end oppression and bring prosperity."[44]

Sharif's comparison between his vision of sharia law and that of the Taliban created an uproar. The Taliban's use of executions, amputations, and floggings handed down by Islamic "courts" had outraged western governments as well as forward-thinking Pakistanis. "That will doubtless bring peace, the peace of the graveyard," the Human Rights Commission of Pakistan said in a statement. "I think he is treading a very dangerous path that could decimate the country," a spokesman for the PPP told Reuters. The *New York Times* reported the feeling in the country that Sharif had "just tried to eliminate democracy from the Constitution." The newspaper's reporter, Barry Bearak, reported from Pakistan that Sharif had sought legislation that "gave the prime minister more power, all in the name of Allah," which represented "a tactical mix of politics and religion with a long history here."

" 'We must go down on our knees and bow before Allah,' " Bearak quoted Sharif, "a millionaire industrialist" as saying. "By his reckoning, holy practices were the only way to end the nation's many years of 'corruption, gratification and maladministration.' What he meant by full Islamic law was left vague, although he did promise to protect individual and minority rights," the reporter continued. According to Bearak, "Even a number of the devout questioned the need for the proposal. The Constitution already proclaims Pakistan an Islamic state, subject to the religion's fundamental principles. For many, the true motive for Mr. Sharif's bill rested less in piety than in politics."

Changes to the constitution proposed by Sharif would have changed some essential numbers: in matters of Islam, a simple majority in both houses of Parliament—rather than the current two-thirds—would suffice to amend the constitution. Also, Bearak noted, "The prime minister would be empowered to issue decrees that further entrenched Islamic practices. What would then stop him, critics asked, from pushing bills through the legislature in the name of Allah? Could he dissolve Parliament if he considered its actions un-Islamic?"[45] Interestingly, some of the country's established Islamist parties did not support the move. "He is exploiting the Quran to serve his own interests," a spokesman of the Jamaat-e-Islami was quoted as saying. "If the government really wants to enforce Islamic law, the laws are now sufficient. The problem is in the practice not in the laws." Eventually, Sharif's proposed legislation was watered down amid the opposition clamor.

Sharif insisted he was motivated by his own strong beliefs. But some scholars, such as Lawrence Ziring, see Sharif's moves for further Islamization as simply part of an effort to amass more power. Soon after his election for a second time, Sharif had thwarted efforts by Supreme Court Chief Justice Sajjad Ali Shah to hold him accountable by installing a new chief justice. Later he secured the resignation of the army chief general Jehangir Karamat and appointed a handpicked successor, General Pervez Musharraf, as commander. According to Ziring, this made Nawaz Sharif more powerful than any of his predecessors and gave full rein to Pakistan's more extremist Islamist organizations. Sharif named his own election commissioner and strengthened his legitimacy by "surrounding himself with ultra-orthodox Islamic clerics."

Through the Fifteenth Amendment to the constitution, Ziring wrote, Sharif "aimed to bypass the parliament, the judiciary, and the provincial governments by emphasizing the elevation of sharia above secular law." He wanted to be unrestrained by the common law and "anticipated achieving maximum power as the leader of a Muslim people who were wholly subject to Islamic jurisprudence." Ziring argues that Sharif "had his sights on transforming Pakistan into an Islamic state only slightly different from Afghanistan under the Taliban."[46]

Others, such as Hasan-Askari Rizvi, see Sharif's turn to Islam in light of the "dangerous polarization" between the federal government, dominated by Sharif's home province Punjab and by Pakistan's other provinces. According to Rizvi, "The polarization sharpened when the Sharif government unveiled its plan to introduce a constitutional amendment (15th) to amass more powers at the expense of the Parliament, the judiciary, and the provinces under the pretext of introducing sharia." In his view, Sharif had mobilized orthodox Islamic groups to counterbalance his political adversaries.[47]

Whether out of conviction or expediency, the prime minister's embrace of orthodox clerics and the Afghan Taliban emboldened Pakistan's jihadi groups. They began collecting funds in mosques and bazaars and openly published the list of foreign and Pakistani martyrs killed in action in Afghanistan and Kashmir, even though Pakistan officially denied the presence of jihadi groups on its soil. That jihad was now officially sanctioned was affirmed by a visit in April 1998 by the governor of Punjab to the headquarters of the Lashkar-e-Taiba, a Wahhabi militant group. The official media described the jihadis fighting in Kashmir as "freedom fighters." The Pakistani information minister was quoted as saying that "the government had strengthened the national defence by launching [the nuclear capable] Ghauri missile. . . . Now [the] country's fate was not decided by the superpowers."[48]

The inevitable consequences of the government nurturing the jihadi groups were unabated religious militancy and sectarian terrorism across the country. The academic Anwar Syed gave a crisp summation of the pattern of violence: "Militant groups belonging to the Sunni and Shia sects within Islam, bombed each other's mosques and assassinated each other's religious and professional leaders and other notables. Police officers and high ranking civil servants were among those killed, and the police became reluctant to investigate because of fear of reprisals." According to Syed, "Many observers saw the Sunni-Shia conflict as a 'proxy war' between Saudi Arabia and Iran on the soil of Pakistan."[49]

The vast majority of the casualties in this war were Pakistani civilians. In the first seven months of 1997, one hundred people were killed in attacks on Shias and retaliatory attacks on Sunnis. In the first ten days of August 1997, seventy people were killed. According to Vali Nasr, 862 incidents of anti-Shia violence between 1989 and 1994 had already claimed 208 lives and injured another 1,629. Now there was armed communal conflict such as a five-day "war" in Parachinar in northwest Pakistan, in which the combatants' use of mortars, rocket launchers, and anti-aircraft missiles claimed the lives of some two hundred people. Nasr documented the assassination of seventy-five Shia municipal leaders and prominent community figures in rural Punjab between January and May 1997 and the killing of seventy people amid sectarian violence in and around Lahore between August 1 and 10, 1997. In January 1998, twenty-two Shias were killed and fifty injured in an attack on a Shia religious ceremony in Punjab. In March 1998, fifteen people were killed in two days of sectarian violence in Hangu in the Northwest region.[50]

Unable to stop the bloodletting, primarily of Shias, the Sharif government at least voiced its concern about it. No such condemnation was made in relation to the persecution of Ahmadis. Amnesty International reported that Ahmadis charged with religious offenses found it difficult to obtain bail. It cited the example of Riaz Ahmed (a village headman), his son, and two nephews from Piplan village, Mianwali district, who had remained in detention since their arrest in November 1993. "Their bail application was turned down by the Sessions court, then the Lahore High Court, and has been pending without being heard in the Supreme Court since 1994," the human rights organization observed. It pointed out that as of the summer of 1997, "Their trial [had] not yet begun. They [had] been charged with blasphemy, for allegedly claiming that the founder of their faith was a prophet and had worked miracles."

According to Amnesty, more than two thousand Ahmadis faced various criminal charges relating to their religious activities, though most had eventually made bail. Although no Ahmadi was executed for blasphemy, many spent long years in prison or in pretrial detention. "Even when bail is granted, Ahmadi prisoners are sometimes not released," Amnesty reported. In one case, two goldsmiths from Pattoki, Punjab Province, Bashir-ul-Haq and his nephew, Mubashir Javed, were arrested for "having displayed in their shop—and thereby supposedly defiled—the words 'There is no God except Allah and Mohammad is his prophet' and to have preached their faith." When a magistrate in

Pattoki granted them bail, local Islamists protested against the Ahmadis' release and their bail was canceled.[51]

Islamists, backed by militants trained in Afghanistan, increasingly took the law into their own hands. Amnesty reported that thirty-four Ahmadis had been killed between 1984 and 1996 in Pakistan, "sometimes in the presence of police who have stood by passively without making any attempt to protect the victims." In June 1997 another targeted killing of an Ahmadi took place when Ateeq Ahmad Bajwah—an Ahmadi lawyer and local leader of the Ahmadiyya community in the town of Vihari in Punjab—and his driver were shot dead in broad daylight. "It is imperative that the Government of Pakistan ensures that citizens at risk are adequately protected and that inquiries into attacks and killings of members of minority religious groups are investigated with a view to bringing perpetrators of abuses to justice," Amnesty International said.[52]

Pakistan, however, was by now indifferent to international expressions of concern about its treatment of its religious minorities. Some leaders of minority communities felt they had to take drastic steps to force Pakistan's rulers to notice their community's plight, and not all of these involved revenge assassinations. The most noteworthy incident in this respect during Nawaz Sharif's second stint in power involved a Christian clergyman in Punjab.

Ten days after Ayub Masih was sentenced to death for alleged blasphemy in the Punjab town of Sahiwal, the Bishop of Faisalabad, Dr. John Joseph, shot himself with a pistol in front of the local court building. Bishop Joseph committed suicide in a dramatic protest against the patent injustice of the charges and proceedings against Ayub. He had long campaigned against Pakistan's blasphemy laws and had sent a letter to the newspaper *Dawn* shortly before his death, calling on Christians and Muslims to act together in bringing about the lifting of Ayub Masih's death sentence and the repeal of the laws.[53] Unfortunately the bishop's sacrifice, which was alluded to in his letter to *Dawn*, made no impact on the country's entrenched attitudes.

Ziring narrated the incident with powerful commentary. "The veneer of sophistication and civility that projected a global personality for the modern Pakistan," he wrote, had rubbed thin with the sustained emphasis on Islamization. Forces never judged mainstream had become a mighty river and in the circumstances associated with national catharsis a different standard had been established for the measurement of Pakistani behavior. Religious minorities were at particular risk in the new circumstances. Long the targets of majority community abuse, Ahmadiya and Christians were prominent victims of the self-appointed purifiers of Islamic spirituality.[54]

According to Professor Ziring,

Punjabi villages, where minority groups had lived side by side with orthodox Muslims for generations were almost overnight transformed into hamlets of communal bloodletting. Subject to vilification, beatings and death, minorities looked to the government for assistance but the latter failed time and again in its mission to defend the persecuted. Not only were Christians assaulted as never before, but sectarian contests between Shiites and Sunnis attained new levels of violence. Again officials were slow to react to maintain law and order, let alone to mete out justice. The breakdown of civil society was also seen in the rising levels of criminal behavior. No one could claim security on the nation's highways or in their homes as gangs of thieves and cut-throats operated at will and without fear of retribution.[55]

In October 1999, Nawaz Sharif was overthrown in a coup d'état that brought the army back into power. The constitution was once again sidelined and the Army Chief of Staff ruled by decree. General Pervez Musharraf took over first as "chief executive" of the country and later declared himself president. Although he organized legislative elections in 2002 and appointed a prime minister, Musharraf ruled as Pakistan's dictator until September 2008. He styled himself as a reformer and promised to push back religious extremism.

Musharraf described his policies as "enlightened moderation" and often announced reforms that were diluted after initial publicity. For example, he announced his intention to change the procedure for initiating criminal proceedings under blasphemy laws, making it difficult to file false charges. The announcement fell far short of ending blasphemy laws but was nonetheless welcomed by minorities as an improvement. Eventually, however, Musharraf failed to introduce the promised changes after protests from Islamist groups.

Similarly, he ended the separate electorates, allowing non-Muslims to vote and run for office alongside Muslims in general elections. Some seats in Parliament and provincial legislatures were still reserved for non-Muslims and for that purpose a non-Muslim voter register was created. Ahmadis still could not vote because they refused to put their names in the non-Muslim register of voters, insisting that they were Muslims notwithstanding what Pakistan's law declared them to be. Musharraf initially also expressed sympathy for Christians and Hindus and promised the end of religious militancy. But overall the situation did not improve for Pakistan's minorities during his decade in power.

Musharraf's regime was wedded to national security strategies that involved support for the Afghan Taliban as well as jihadi groups targeting India. These groups recruited and trained hardened militants who were not content with attacking American troops in Afghanistan or Indian soldiers in the disputed Kashmir region. Their jihad for a purer Islamic state also prompted many of them to terrorize Pakistan's non-Muslims and to attack Muslims they considered hypocrites or insufficiently committed to Islam. Officially backed Islamist militant groups splintered to spawn deadly offshoots that refused to be controlled by Musharraf's military or intelligence service.

After 9/11, some Islamists even targeted military and intelligence officers who had trained them, accusing them of acting as America's agents at Musharraf's behest. Musharraf himself was targeted twice for assassination but still did not change the policy of supporting some while opposing other jihadi militant groups. Instead of making Pakistan less extreme in religious terms, Musharraf—a personally secular, westernized general—ended up presiding over a Pakistan where armed militants and suicide bombers became the face of Islamist fanaticism.

7

Militancy, Terrorism, and Sectarianism, 1999 and Onward

PAKISTAN HAD BEEN ISLAMIZING gradually for decades by the time General Pervez Musharraf took over as Pakistan's fourth military dictator in October 1999. And with the rise of militancy, religious minorities had borne the brunt of the Islamists' ferocity during the 1990s, suffering greater persecution then than in any earlier decade. Musharraf promised to reverse the policies of the past, which he said had "rocked the very foundation of the Federation of Pakistan."[1]

When Musharraf relinquished power in 2008 after almost a decade at the helm, the religious extremist militants were more entrenched than ever. Conditions for non-Muslims and minority-Muslim sects have continued to deteriorate under civilian rule in subsequent years. The reason why Musharraf's promise of reining in religious extremism went unfulfilled lies in his support for jihad as an instrument of Pakistan's foreign policy. The pursuit of regional influence, especially in countering India's ascendancy, has remained central to Pakistani political strategy under the civilian governments since 2008. Likewise, jihadis have continued to play a significant role in maintaining the country's posture on territorial issues. There has thus been no genuine effort to root out Islamist terrorism.

As a consequence, persecution of Christians and Ahmadis under blasphemy laws and attacks on Sufi Sunnis and Shias—as well as the forcible conversion of Hindus—persist. Pakistanis often debate questions such as how to return Pakistan to Jinnah's ideals or whether the large-scale elimination of Shias can be described as genocide. But these arguments change little in the lives of minority community members, who live under the constant threat of Islamist militancy. In recent years, Muslims rising to the defense of the minorities have also been targets of Islamist violence; the militants have thus ruthlessly forestalled any broad discussion in Pakistani society about legal and policy reform.

Soon after the coup that brought him to power, Musharraf acknowledged religious extremism as a problem that had to be dealt with by the government and the military. In his first address to the nation as Pakistan's ruler, Musharraf criticized what he described as "exploitation of religion." He said, "Islam teaches tolerance, not hatred, universal brotherhood and not enmity, peace and not violence, progress and not bigotry." Urging the ulema "to come forth and present Islam in its true light," Musharraf asked for their help in curbing "elements which are exploiting religion for vested interests and bringing [a] bad name to our faith." He also reassured "our minorities that they enjoy full rights and protection as equal citizens in the letter and spirit of true Islam."[2]

Musharraf also invited leaders of minority religions for a meeting during which he personally held out a pledge to uphold the rights of non-Muslims in the country. He spoke of giving "equal opportunities in nation building to religious minorities," and he appointed Derrick Cyprian, a Catholic, as federal minister for sports, culture, and minorities' affairs. According to the meeting's participants, Musharraf promised that he would abolish the separate electorate system in favor of a joint electorate, to "bring minorities into the national political mainstream." He also made a commitment to return Christian schools and colleges that had been nationalized several years earlier to their respective communities' ownership and management. Interestingly, the official press release issued by Musharraf's office made no mention of these two critical promises.[3] Bold statements about limiting the role of religion in Pakistan led to speculation that Musharraf's role model was Kemal Ataturk, the founder of the secular Turkish Republic.

But while Musharraf fulfilled his promises of ending separate electorates and returning Christian educational institutions to Christian control, his legacy would not reflect a championing of minorities' rights in a more secular Pakistan. With the passage of his dictatorship, Musharraf reverted to defining the role of Islam in Pakistan's life in ways similar to those adopted by earlier leaders after Jinnah. Upon being asked what role Islam should have in Pakistan, he replied,

> This is an Islamic republic and that has to be clear. My view is of a tolerant Islam, Islam in the true sense, and not an Islam which is manipulated for political gains. Islam is a *deen*, a way of life. I am a believer in taking Islam in its real, progressive form—a much broader, futuristic view rather than a dogmatic and retrogressive one.[4]

The new dictator was using language similar to that of earlier rulers. He did not wear Islam on his sleeve, like Zia-ul-Haq, but he also was not willing to embrace Jinnah's vision of religion having nothing to do with the business of state. Some of his rhetoric resembled that of Ayub Khan, Pakistan's first military dictator, who was not an Islamist but inadvertently strengthened the Islamist cause while pursuing his external and domestic policies.

Within a few months of Musharraf's assumption of power, hopes of significant change in Pakistan's treatment of minorities began to fade. As the scholar Iftikhar Malik pointed out, "Pakistan's own unresolved ideological dilemmas fed into the country's social discords" as "religio-political forces with their own agendas of majoritarian/minoritarian rule and pursuing jihad in Afghanistan and Kashmir kept up the pressure."[5] Amnesty International recorded "a wide range of abuses" against Christians and Ahmadis and noted that the blasphemy laws were being used under the new government "to arbitrarily detain members of the minorities" as they had done since the 1980s.

Charges against Ahmadis under laws specifically directed at them (Ordinances XX and XXI) increased during the first twenty months of Musharraf's military regime. These charges now entailed trial by special antiterrorism courts, which did not provide a fair trial in accordance with international standards. Amnesty protested that charges against Ahmadis and Christians appeared to have been brought solely on the basis of membership within these minority groups.

"Latent or overt hostility against religious minorities is often exacerbated by professional rivalry or quest for economic gain, particularly over land issues," an Amnesty report observed. It complained about the manner in which blasphemy accusations were uncritically accepted by "members of the criminal justice system who themselves sometimes face threats and abuse if they do not accept them." The Amnesty report also pointed out that

> threats and use of violence against members of the minority communities by private persons or members of non-governmental groups are widely condoned by the State, and have led to a climate of fear for the minorities while perpetrators feel encouraged by the impunity with which they can abuse minority members.[6]

Although the country was ostensibly being run by a military strongman, the government seemed helpless against religiously motivated terrorists. A year into Musharraf's regime, gunmen shot dead five members of the Ahmadiyya community on October 30, 2000, as they left their mosque after early morning prayers in Ghatialian village, near Sialkot in Punjab's northeast. Among the dead was a sixteen-year-old boy. Ten others were injured. No one was arrested for involvement in the attack.

Another five Ahmadis, including two children, were murdered in their mosque by a mob in Sargodha on November 10. The murders were instigated by the local mullah. The police refused to act on telephone requests to preempt the attack. The mob broke into the mosque and attacked and killed four Ahmadis, mutilated their bodies with axes, then ransacked the building and set it alight. A fourteen-year-old schoolboy injured in the attack later died of his injuries. The police apparently only arrived after the attack was over. Not only did authorities fail to protect the Ahmadis against such attacks, they also prosecuted them for their beliefs. In 2000 in Sialkot district alone, criminal cases based on religion were brought against twenty-three Ahmadis.[7]

In some instances, the accusations of blasphemy took on a bizarre tone, reminiscent perhaps of the witch hunts of early modern Europe and North America. In one incident in Okara—also in Punjab Province, where most blasphemy cases seemed to arise—a Muslim and five Christian boys were arrested on blasphemy charges on July 28, 2001. According to an authoritative account, the boys, ten to fifteen years old, were treating a wounded donkey with liquid medication, which they massaged on its wounds. A group of Islamists declared that the boys had used the medicine to write holy names on the donkey with the intent of insulting Islam. The boys were detained and even the donkey was briefly taken into custody. The children were eventually released after many people submitted affidavits attesting their innocence. But the absurdity of the charge, coupled with the fact that the police felt compelled to act on it, reflected the depth of extremism in Pakistani society as well as the irrational sentiments aroused by the country's blasphemy laws.[8]

Although most blasphemy prosecutions involved Ahmadis or Christians, in July 2001 a Hindu living in the southern Punjab district of Bahawalpur also became ensnared by the blasphemy ordinance's vague provisions and overzealous application. Ram Chand, a manual laborer, was constructing a bathroom floor for Mohammad Safdar at the latter's home in a village. Safdar accused the laborer of defiling the name of the Prophet Muhammad by carving it on a brick, and he took the brick to the village head. Deeply offended by this so-called act of blasphemy, local Muslims attacked homes and other property belonging to Hindus and also beat up Hindu women and children. Chand and his son, Ram Yazman, were arrested and charged with blasphemy. Islamists incited local Muslims to block the roads in the district for hours and demand that all Hindus be expelled from the area.[9]

In August Dr. Younus Sheikh, a Muslim homeopathic doctor and lecturer, was charged with blasphemy for answers he gave to his students about whether the Prophet Muhammad followed Muslim practices before he declared his Prophethood. The charges against him were filed by persons who had not been present in the lecture hall and were known for their sectarian bias. "The blasphemy laws of Pakistan are a handy tool to silence debate and dissent," Amnesty International asserted. Amnesty has repeatedly highlighted the cruel truth of blasphemy accusations; that is, they are often leveled as a brutally effective tactic to gain personal or material advantage. "In the interest of justice, the blasphemy laws should be abolished or as a first step amended to prevent abuse,"[10] Amnesty insisted, echoing the sentiments of Pakistan's own human rights activists.

Musharraf responded to the calls for repeal of blasphemy laws by promising to amend the procedure for their implementation. Instead of allowing the police to take cognizance of blasphemy allegations on its own, the proposed amendments would require the matter be brought before a judge, who would then ascertain whether a person ought to be charged. But this change alone could not ensure justice for those accused of blasphemy. Given the bigotry and hatred that had been fomented against minorities, especially in Punjab, there was no guarantee that judges would not be as biased as the police. In any case, the proposed legal reform did not offer any solution to the mob violence that followed almost every instance of blasphemy accusation.

Nonetheless, just as they had opposed Benazir Bhutto's proposed reforms, the clerics railed against Musharraf for attempting to "weaken" protections against insults to Islam and its Prophet. The government consequently dropped the idea of changing the law, as the Islamists were regarded as its allies—especially in the context of the war in Afghanistan and the ongoing insurgency in Kashmir.

The year 2001 began with an assembly in support of the Taliban and Kashmiri jihadis at Akora Khattak near Peshawar. For the liberal newspaper editor Khaled Ahmed, the assembly represented those who "have for the past eight years tyrannized and murdered tens of thousands of innocent Afghans, destroyed countless hundreds of Afghan villages, burned untold acres of Afghan farmlands and orchards, torched thousands upon thousands of ancient Afghan texts and artifacts, and basically ruined that which had survived the Soviet scourge." The congregation was meant to be a show of "anger" and "defiance" against fresh United Nations sanctions against the Taliban militia. The list of attendees in Akora Khattak's Haqqania seminary included leaders of Pakistan's three major Islamic political parties: Maulana Samiul Haq and Maulana Fazlur Rehman of the two factions of Jamiat Ulema Islam and Qazi Hussein Ahmad of Jamaat-e-Islami. The militant leader Masood Azhar of Jaish-e-Muhammad also spoke at the meeting, as did a former army chief general, Aslam Beg, and the former Inter-Services Intelligence (ISI) head lieutenant General Hamid Gul.[11] The event showcased the enthusiasm for jihad in Pakistan's clerical and military establishment.

Amid such orchestrated shows of public support for jihad, Musharraf enthusiastically defended his support for the Taliban and insisted that the jihadis fighting in Afghanistan and Kashmir were crucial for Pakistan's national interest. The dictator did not seem to recognize that the rise of religious extremism and militancy inside the country was a direct consequence of the government's embrace of Islamist ideologues and jihadists in the region. He had to change tack quickly when, on September 11, 2001, terrorists belonging to Osama bin Laden's Al-Qaida attacked the Pentagon in Washington, DC, and the World Trade Center in New York. Bin Laden and Al-Qaida operated out of Taliban-controlled Afghanistan, and the United States now pressured Pakistan to join the rest of the world in bringing to justice those responsible for the 9/11 attacks.

As the United States planned a military operation against Al-Qaida and the Taliban in Afghanistan, it demanded intelligence cooperation, use of airspace, and logistics support from Pakistan. Musharraf readily acceded to the American demands. But Pakistan's intelligence service assumed that American involvement in Afghanistan would be limited to punitive action against bin Laden and would not result in the overthrow of the Taliban regime. Once the Americans started bombing Afghanistan, Musharraf said that Pakistan had taken the decision "of being part of the world, of the world community and a part of a coalition to fight terrorism." But he still insisted that Pakistan had interacted with the Taliban regime "in [its] best national interest."

According to Musharraf, the "ideal scenario" for Afghanistan was "a short, sharp action, targeted action, followed as fast as possible through a very balanced political dispensation and rehabilitation effort." He later said that "because we were the only country who were interacting with them, we tried to bring moderation to the Taliban Government." Pakistan, he claimed, had made all possible efforts to extradite Osama bin Laden, and it was unfortunate that he was unable to avert war through his diplomatic efforts with the Taliban.[12] But US President George W. Bush decided to pursue a wider "global war on terrorism." This dashed Musharraf's hopes, and the ISI's expectation, of a short American intervention in Afghanistan that might eliminate Al-Qaida but leave Pakistan's jihadi clients intact.

The American-led alliance ousted the Taliban regime, replacing it with an Afghan government backed by the international community. The destruction of their operating bases in Afghanistan led both Afghan and Pakistani militants, as well as jihadis from distant countries, to pour across the border into Pakistan. Many groups raised and trained by the ISI splintered into factions, some of which turned on Musharraf and the Pakistani government, whom they accused of collaborating with the United States against Islam and Muslims.

As the Taliban were being ousted in Afghanistan by US coalition forces—and within weeks of the 9/11 terrorist attacks—the Kashmiri jihadi group Jaish-e-Muhammad carried out a terrorist attack on October 1, 2001, at the state legislature building in Srinagar. Forty-one people, including three militants, were killed in the suicide bombing and subsequent small-arms assault on the legislature complex. The Indian Parliament in New Delhi was likewise attacked less than three months later on December 13, 2001. Fourteen people were killed and twenty-two injured in this strike by five heavily armed terrorists. Another Kashmiri jihadi group, Lashkar-e-Taiba, along with Jaish-e-Muhammad, was accused of involvement in this attack.

Both groups had close ties to the Pakistani intelligence service. India responded by mobilizing troops along its border with Pakistan. The United States, which thought it had won Musharraf over as an ally, stepped in to avoid the escalation of tensions on the subcontinent. President Bush pressured Musharraf to act against Pakistan-based jihadi groups and offered much-needed economic and military assistance as an inducement for doing so. Musharraf subsequently announced that he was banning terrorist groups, including some involved in jihad against India in Jammu and Kashmir; but he downplayed America's hallmark "carrot and stick" diplomacy in influencing his actions.

"We have been taking measures against terrorism from the beginning, not because of any outside pressure," Musharraf said on national television. He reiterated that "Kashmir runs in our blood. No Pakistani can afford to sever links with Kashmir" but also said that "no organizations will be able to carry out terrorism on the pretext of Kashmir."

Musharraf asserted that those "involved with such acts in the future would be dealt with strongly, whether they come from inside or outside the country." His words raised expectations of a crackdown on all religious militant groups. He spoke of ridding the nation "of hatred, of religious intolerance." In a particularly moving sentence he declared, "Violence and terrorism have been going on for years and we are weary and sick of this Kalashnikov culture," he said, adding, "The day of reckoning has come."[13]

The Pakistani government helped the Americans in arresting several leading members of Al-Qaida from towns and cities across the country. Several militant groups and charities associated with them were banned, though many were allowed to reorganize under new names amid assurances by their leaders to restrain their members. The banned groups included Lashkar-e-Jhangvi, a vicious offshoot of the Sunni extremist Sipah-e-Sahaba, and the Shia Sipah-e-Muhammad. The fact that Sipah-e-Sahaba was not immediately banned enabled Sunni militancy to persist even after the Shias had lost their ability to fight fire with fire. Even when a ban on Sipah-e-Sahaba was eventually announced, the group endured under new names: its membership overlapped with legal Deobandi political parties, as well as with jihadi groups that were still being protected, reserved to fight across Pakistan's borders when the need arose.

Musharraf was apparently playing a double game after 9/11, supporting the United States and the Taliban at the same time. Several years later, Musharraf confessed that Pakistani spies in the ISI directorate cultivated the Taliban after 2001 because Afghanistan's post-Taliban government led by Hamid Karzai was dominated by non-Pashtuns, the country's largest ethnic group, and officials who were thought to favor India. "Obviously we were looking for some groups to counter this Indian action against Pakistan," he told the *Guardian* in an interview in February 2015, acknowledging something that was widely known but never admitted by Pakistan's government.[14]

At the time, however, many observers believed that he was serious about shutting down Islamist militancy. "Musharraf has tried to rein in the country's jihadi elements," wrote one scholar, arguing that the intricate networks and linkages of jihadis throughout the establishment, including the military and the ISI agency, did not allow the general to accomplish his objective.[15]

In his autobiography, Musharraf painted himself as a leader committed to ending religious extremism in Pakistan. "Earlier Pakistan governments had been hesitant about taking on the militant religious groups that were spreading extremism and fanaticism in our country," he wrote. According to Musharraf,

General Zia had openly courted them for political support and Nawaz Sharif was in the process of setting himself up as a "commander of the faithful" sort of a national imam. For my part, I have always been a moderate Muslim, never comfortable with the rhetoric or ways of extremists. I moved against them when I banned a number of extremist religious organizations in February 2001 because they were involved in sectarian militancy. But now here [post-9/11] was a chance to confront them more boldly and openly. Second, even though being a frontline state fighting terrorism would deter foreign investment there were certain obvious economic advantages, like loosening the stranglehold of our debt and lifting economic sanctions. Third, after being an outcast nation following our nuclear tests we would come to center stage. What of the domestic reaction? The mullahs would certainly oppose joining the US and would come out into the streets.[16]

The mullahs, though, did not just come out into the streets. The militant groups began planning large-scale terrorist attacks across Pakistan. One of their first targets was the St. Dominic's Roman Catholic Church in Bahawalpur, a southern Punjab town known for ties with the Kashmir jihadi group, Jaish-e-Muhammad. The group's founder, Masood Azhar, had been released from an Indian prison in December 1999 as part of a deal to free hostages from an Indian Airlines jet hijacked to Taliban-controlled Kandahar. He had returned to Pakistan to organize jihad with support from the ISI.

Such jihadis had long shown their penchant for killing innocents at prayer. In this latest militant assault, eighteen Christian worshippers at St. Dominic's, their minister, and a Muslim policeman were killed during a Sunday service on October 28, 2001, by six masked gunmen. The victims—a number of whom were young children—were from a Protestant congregation that lacked its own building and had long used St. Dominic's by arrangement with the Catholic community. The attack was assumed to be "a protest against United States airstrikes over Afghanistan," though poor Pakistani Christians in a Punjab town clearly had nothing to do with US policy. Survivors said worshippers had tried to hide under pews or flee from the gunmen, who sprayed the interior of the church with rounds from automatic weapons. Musharraf said in a statement that "the method used and the inhuman tactics employed clearly indicate involvement of trained terrorists of organizations bent on creating discord and disharmony in Pakistan."[17]

That, however, did not prevent further terrorist attacks on the Christian community. On August 5 and 9, 2002, successive attacks were carried out by Islamist terrorists on a Christian missionary school at Murree and the chapel of a Christian hospital in Taxila, which left ten people dead. Another attack on September 25 on the Karachi offices of the Christian welfare organization Peace and Justice claimed seven lives.[18]

Although Pakistan under Musharraf was once again an ally of the United States in the war against terrorism, its policies in relation to Islamists changed little. Extremist madrasas continued to proliferate in an alarming manner even after the ouster of the Taliban from Afghanistan in 2001. The number of madrasas—ideological hothouses that almost invariably took a harsh view of unbelievers and apostates—had risen from 6,761 in 2000 to 11,221 in 2005. Thus, in the five years that also saw the terrorist attack of 9/11, the number of apostatizing seminaries had almost doubled in Pakistan. There were now 448 madrasas for women too. The greatest number of madrasas were now in the city of Bahawalpur (where the October 2001 church attack on Christians had been perpetrated), followed by Lahore, Bahawalnagar, and Faisalabad.[19]

As the madrasas minted more and more extremist mullahs, religious vigilantism intensified. In one of many such incidents, a mentally ill man was stoned to death in a village near Chak Jhumra in 2002 at the urging of the local Imam. The victim of the stoning had been charged under blasphemy laws "for desecrating the Holy Quran and using objectionable words against the holy Prophet." He had been arrested and subsequently released on bail after three years in prison.[20] A mob of around four hundred people killed a man accused of blasphemy in Nowshera district two years later.[21]

In 2006, a prisoner charged with blasphemy was stabbed to death while in police custody at the District and Sessions Court of Muzaffargarh. Five attackers continued to stab the prisoner until they were certain of his death. Two policemen who tried to overpower the attackers were injured while other policemen nearby did not even bother to intervene. A sixty-year-old retired schoolteacher, Mohammad Sadiq, was also killed by a mob for alleged blasphemy the same year.[22] Numerous such cases were reported year after year, but no clear strategy was proffered by the government to deal with religiously motivated mob lynchings.

The US State Department reported in 2002 that since Musharraf's coup in 1999, 316 purported religiously motivated criminal cases, including charges of blasphemy, had been brought against Ahmadis. Some of these cases were based on decidedly trivial allegations, such as wearing an Islamic slogan on a shirt. In July 2002, Zulfikar Goraya was arrested and charged for "posing as a Muslim" based on greeting cards he had sent out that included a verse from the Quran and the Islamic salutation, Assalam Alaikum. In October 2006, police charged Mohammad Tariq with blasphemy because he had allegedly removed anti-Ahmadi stickers placed inside a bus.[23]

According to an Ahmadi-related website, between April 1984 and December 2008, hundreds of Ahmadis faced prosecution. There were 756 Ahmadis charged with illegally displaying the *kalima*, the Islamic testament of faith; 37 with offering a call to prayer, 44 with posing as Muslims, 161 with using Islamic words and epithets, and 679 for preaching. The same estimate reported over nine hundred other charges of violating sections 298-B and 298-C and 258 cases under 295-C and more than twenty-four for distributing pamphlets criticizing the laws against them.

Among the most absurd cases brought against Ahmadis involved allegations of building a minaret and a niche in a mosque that had existed for decades. The judge concluded that a Quran had been found in the mosque, as had Ahmadi literature, and that was sufficient reason to punish Attaullah Warraich, the Ahmadi whose house was adjacent to the mosque. The judge then inexplicably added that the mosque may have been built before the passing of section 298-C made it a criminal offense but added, quite preposterously, that Warraich "should have changed the shape of the mosque after the said amendment." Since he was a first-time offender and an illiterate farmer, the judge claimed to be exercising leniency in sentencing Warraich to rigorous imprisonment for two years with a fine of two thousand rupees. In another case, Ahmadis were charged over watching an Ahmadiyya television program in a private garage that had its door open because of the mid-summer heat.[24]

Although Musharraf declared "enlightened moderation" to be his vision for Pakistan, his government did little to end the widespread prejudice in society against religious minorities. One of Musharraf's much touted accomplishments was the opening up of the media. After ending the state monopoly of radio and television, private channels were allowed, a move that could theoretically allow the airing of plural-ist ideas in Pakistani society. But even this liberalization of the airwaves could be deleterious to minority communities. Most channels broad-cast religious shows that espoused extremist Islamist views. News was also often presented to reflect the Islamo-nationalist belief that non-Muslims, and some Muslim sects, were instruments of influence of major world powers and that Islam and Muslims were under constant threat. This motif, recurrent throughout Pakistan's history, was now aired by dozens of entertainment and news channels on television.

The threat posed to minorities by extremists inciting hatred and vio-lence on mainstream media was very real indeed. This was exemplified by the case of a religious show anchor on the popular Geo TV outlet. On September 7, 2008, Dr. Amir Liaquat Hussain, a self-proclaimed religious scholar, urged Muslims not to be afraid to kill Ahmadis. Two other ulema on the program supported him. Inspired by the televi-sion program, within twenty-four hours a gang of six Islamist vigilantes found their way into the Fazle Umer clinic in Mirpur Khas and killed forty-five-year-old Dr. Abdul Manan Siddiqui. The vigilantes shot Siddiqui eleven times. He was the district president of the Ahmadiyya Muslim Community in Mirpur Khas.[25] Not only did the government fail to act against Hussain for instigating the murder, but it also made no effort to take his show off the air.

The Shias fared even worse under Musharraf than they had under earlier regimes. The newly invigorated jihadis often found it easier to recruit after arousing extremist sectarian sentiment. They took advan-tage of the government's policy of picking and choosing among jihadi groups, with members of banned groups easily finding protection in alternative groups that were still allowed to operate. Just as attacks on Christians multiplied soon after 9/11, so too did terrorist incidents targeting Shias.

Moreover, the viciousness and mindless cruelty of the acts of terror against Pakistan's largest religious group after the majority Sunnis became even more pronounced. On April 26, 2002, twelve women and children were killed and dozens of others injured when an explosion tore through a Shia mosque in the western town of Bhakkar in Punjab Province. A timed explosive device had been planted in the women's enclosure of the mosque before a mass gathering for an annual religious ceremony. This was perhaps the first attack where women and children had been specifically targeted, and it would by no means be the last. Sunni Islamist militants also adopted a brutal strategy of killing Shia professionals, particularly doctors, around the time of the Bhakkar attack. The statistics of the terrorist campaign against the Shias under Musharraf's military dictatorship are staggering. Between 2001 and Musharraf's resignation in 2008, at least 713 Shias were killed and 1,343 wounded in 86 incidents of terrorism against the community.[26]

Pakistan's political environment changed after lawyers and citizens started to protest in the streets against Musharraf's sacking of the country's chief justice in 2007. The protests provided an opportunity for Benazir Bhutto to end her exile and return to Pakistan. Soon Nawaz Sharif too was able to end his exile, which further weakened Musharraf's control over Pakistan's political scene. Before her return to the country, Bhutto had started drawing attention to "the need for building a moderate Muslim democracy in Pakistan that cares for its people and allows them to elect its leaders." According to her, the war against terrorism could not be won "without mobilizing the people of Pakistan against Islamist extremists, and bringing Pakistan's security services under civilian control."[27]

Bhutto received an exuberant welcome on her arrival in Karachi on October 18, 2007. But her sharp antijihadi message was clearly unacceptable to both the jihadis and Pakistan's establishment. Her welcome rally, attended by at least a million people, was marred by a suicide bombing that killed 160 people. Musharraf's government refused to accept Bhutto's requests for an investigation assisted by the FBI or Scotland Yard, "both of which [had] greater competence in analyzing forensic evidence than Pakistan's notoriously corrupt and incompetent law enforcement."[28] Even after what was clearly an attempt on Bhutto's life, she was not provided enhanced security. On December 27, 2007, Bhutto was killed in a suicide attack following a rally in the garrison city of Rawalpindi, near Islamabad.

When Pakistan went to the polls in February 2008, Bhutto's Pakistan Peoples Party (PPP) emerged as the winner, followed by Sharif's Pakistan Muslim League (Nawaz Group) (PML-N). The two parties collaborated to force Musharraf's resignation. Pakistan was once again under civilian rule with Bhutto's widower, Asif Zardari, as the president and the PPP leader Yusuf Raza Gilani as prime minister. Sharif's party retained control of the provincial government in Punjab with his brother, Shehbaz Sharif, as chief minister. Although the civilians declared the elimination of terrorism as their aim, there was little progress over the following several years either in offering greater protection to religious minorities or in controlling the jihadi groups. The army and the ISI still had virtual control over foreign policy. With Pakistan persisting in its preoccupation with gaining advantage in Afghanistan and Kashmir, and jihadi militancy its means of leverage, there was little room for reining in Islamist militants.

Soon after Zardari's election as president, a massive terrorist attack on Islamabad's Marriott Hotel, not far from the president's official residence, demonstrated the capability of jihadis to strike at will in Pakistan's ostensibly well-guarded capital. A few weeks later, Zardari's initiative for normal ties with India was undermined by coordinated terrorist attacks in Mumbai. Although the government arrested the operational mastermind of the Mumbai attacks, it still could not act against the group that perpetrated the attack—Lashkar-e-Taiba. Besieged by a hostile judiciary and media—fending off charges of incompetence, corruption, and even treason—the civilian government was unable to significantly change the country's direction. The shelving of its reformist agenda was reminiscent of Bhutto's embattled PPP-led governments of the 1990s, which had wished to implement at least some secular reforms but were unable to contain extreme Islamist influence in order to effect change.

Zardari was able to complete his five-year term as president, serving from 2008 to 2013. Gilani, the prime minister, was removed from office by the Supreme Court in 2012 to be succeeded by another PPP leader, Raja Pervez Ashraf. In a development that was seen as positive for the

evolution of democracy in Pakistan, there was no premature dissolu-
tion of parliament; an occurrence that was de rigueur of the country's
political process in the 1990s. The 2013 election was won by PML-N,
resulting in Nawaz Sharif becoming prime minister for the third time.
This consolidation of democracy did not, however, improve things for
the religious minorities. For them, the ever-present threats of violence,
prosecution for blasphemy, and persecution under discriminatory laws
remained, just as they had, in varying degrees of consequence, since
Independence.

Soon after the return of civilian rule in 2008, terrorist attacks on
Shia Muslims resumed with greater ferocity. A car bomb killed twenty-
nine people and wounded scores near a Shia mosque in Peshawar in
December that year. On February 5, 2009, a suicide bomber killed
twenty-four worshippers at a Shia mosque in Multan. Then on February
20, a suicide attack killed twenty-eight people and wounded more than
sixty others, leaving shoes and torn clothing littering a bloodstained
street in the northwest region of the country. Some of the dead and
injured were taken to the hospital in wooden handcarts. Gunfire broke
out afterward, and police said angry Shias fired on policemen rushing
to the scene. Two Sunni Muslims were shot dead in subsequent rioting.[29] In December, a suicide bomber struck a procession marking a
Shia Muslim holy day in Karachi, killing thirty people. Two earlier attacks in the city had wounded forty-nine Shias.[30]

The extremists expanded their targets in 2010, including Sufi shrines
revered by "soft" Sunnis who often share religious observances with
Shias and do not consider them apostates or heretics. On July 1, 2010,
in Lahore two suicide bombers killed forty-two people at the Data
Darbar, a nine-hundred-year-old shrine to Data Gunj Bakhsh Ali
Hajveri. "Thousands of people had gathered late Thursday at the green-
domed Data Darbar shrine in Lahore when bombs went off minutes
apart," said a news report describing the incident, adding, "The blasts
ripped concrete from the walls and left the white marble floor awash
with blood."[31] Astonishingly, given the intense and well-known hostility of jihadi extremists to Sufis and Shias, Pakistan's media tried to de-
flect blame away from the jihadis: the media ludicrously cited Pakistan's
alliance with the United States as a probable cause and even went so far
as to accuse the Ahmadis of the attack.

At any rate, the sectarian killings continued. During the month of Ramadan in 2010, a suicide attack on a Shia procession in Quetta killed fifty-five people and injured over one hundred others.[32] This marked the beginning of a sustained campaign against Shias in Quetta, the capital of Balochistan Province bordering Afghanistan and Iran. Meanwhile, a Sipah-e-Sahaba offshoot, Lashkar-e-Jhangvi al-Aalami, claimed responsibility for a string of blasts that decimated a Shia religious procession in Lahore on September 1, 2010, killing at least twenty-eight people and injuring more than 150.[33] By 2011, the attacks on Shias had become even more brutal. On September 20 in that year, twenty-six Shia pilgrims on their way to Iran were lined up in front of their bus and shot dead in Mastung, Balochistan. Another three people were killed as they tried to bring victims of the attack to a hospital in Quetta, the provincial capital.[34] In the following year, a similar attack took place on a Shia pilgrim bus in the same location, begging an explanation for why better security measures had not been put in place.

Between 2009 and 2015, 1,659 Shias were killed and 2,950 wounded in 320 incidents, a greater toll than that under the preceding military regime.[35] Shias in Quetta, many of whom belong to the Hazara ethnic group, saw the campaign against them as a planned genocide. While human rights experts quibbled over whether the numbers of dead merited the use of the term "genocide," others convincingly argued that the purpose of the anti-Shia attacks in Balochistan was, in fact, similar to that of genocide—to eliminate an entire people.

Hazara Shias joined the ranks of other Pakistani minorities applying for asylum in western countries to escape persecution at home. Several were rescued from boats off the coast of Australia, where they were hoping to find sanctuary after persecution in the land where their people had lived for centuries. "Iran-bound pilgrims," the Human Rights Commission of Pakistan (HRCP) said of the Hazara Shias,

> feel like sitting ducks. Little wonder then that many young people from the community are prepared to take their chances to flee the country in search of safety, often risking travel in rickety boats in shark-infested waters to do so. At least seventy young men from the community had drowned in one such attempt in Indonesian waters in 2011.[36]

The heightening of attacks on Shias in Balochistan after 2008 may also be attributed to Pakistan's national security policies. The Sunni extremists involved in the attacks were seen as the Pakistani military's allies in its campaign against Baloch nationalist and separatist insurgents as well as in its curbing the growing influence of Iran in Pakistani Balochistan. Instead of protecting Shias from the extremists, individuals in the security services chose to let extremist militants have their way against the Shias in return for intelligence on Baloch separatists.

In addition to the Shias, attacks on Christians and Ahmadis have only increased in recent years. There have also been reports of Hindu citizens' migration to India from Sindh and Balochistan. "Some spokespersons of minorities have argued that vested interests are threatening and frightening the non-Muslim citizens with a view to forcing them to migrate," noted the HRCP. It added, "Some of these elements are said to be religious extremists while others have plans to grab the minorities' property. In any case there is little doubt that the minorities have been driven to despair."[37]

The Ahmadis have fared no better than other minorities under the civilian government in recent years. A horrific attack on Ahmadis involved gunmen attacking two Ahmadi mosques or worship centers during Friday prayers in Lahore on May 28, 2010. They fired shots and set off grenades, killing ninety-eight people and wounding 110 worshippers. The attacks took place within minutes of each other at locations several miles apart. The police took several hours to regain control and when they entered the mosque several of the attackers blew themselves up with suicide vests packed with explosives.[38]

"Live broadcasts of the attacks in Lahore were notable on Friday for failing to refer to the Ahmadis as Muslims," noted the *New York Times*. "Reporters and commentators rarely referred to the Ahmadis by name, preferring the phrase 'minority community,'" it said.[39] Such was the prejudice against the Ahmadis that even amid tragedy, the media chose to not refer to them by the name they had given their own sect.

One of the most brutal attacks against Pakistani Christians in many years began on July 30, 2009, in the Punjab village of Korian, home to around one hundred Christian families. A Christian family was accused of throwing torn pieces of a Quran in the air at a wedding ceremony where guests threw money in the air according to custom. Mullahs began calling for attacks against Christians from mosque loudspeakers. An angry mob of extremist Muslims, "armed with guns and explosives used trucks to break through walls and gasoline to start fires." Approximately sixty houses were destroyed, two churches were ransacked, and livestock was stolen. Many families were able to escape and hide in the fields, where they watched their homes burn to the ground.[40]

The blasphemy allegations reached the town of Gojra, where on August 1, 2009, Sipah-e-Sahaba assembled a crowd of around one thousand and attacked local Christians. Over forty homes were razed and at least seven Christians were killed, six of whom (including two children) were burned alive. The independent HRCP found, in a report released on August 4, 2009, that the police had been aware of plans for the attack in Gojra but did not act to stop it. According to the HRCP, calls for Muslims to "make mincemeat of Christians" in retaliation for the alleged blasphemy had come from Gojra mosques the previous night.[41]

The Gojra riots divided the federal and Punjab governments, with the former trying to get the latter to act in support of the Christians. The PPP had appointed Shahbaz Bhatti, a Christian community leader, as the minister of minority affairs, and he declared after the riots that the blasphemy law was being used to terrorize minorities in Pakistan. Bhatti was soon joined by liberal leaders of the PPP in calling for reform of the blasphemy laws. By the beginning of 2010, the PPP federal government was able to initiate some debate on the horrors inflicted on religious minorities by the Islamists' concept of blasphemy. But that did not stop prosecutions being brought by the Punjab provincial government under blasphemy laws.

In February, Qamar David received a twenty-five-year prison sentence for allegedly outraging Muslim religious feelings by disseminating blasphemous text messages concerning Prophet Muhammad and the Quran. In early March, a Christian couple was found guilty of desecrating the Quran after allegedly touching it without first washing their hands and for using Islamic texts in black magic rituals. The couple, Munir Masih and Ruqqaya Bibi, was sentenced to twenty-five-year jail terms. On June 19, 2010, Rehmat Masih, believed to be eighty-five years old, was arrested by police and sent to Faisalabad District Jail after being accused of blasphemy by a Muslim neighbor with whom he had a land dispute.[42]

The case that evoked greatest sympathy for changing the blasphemy laws involved Asia Bibi, a mother of five, who was sentenced to death in November 2010 for purported blasphemy in the town of Nankana in Sheikhupura district, near Lahore. Asia was charged over an incident that occurred in June 2009 when she worked as a farm laborer and was asked by the village elder's wife to fetch drinking water. Some other female Muslim farmhands reportedly refused to drink the water, saying it was sacrilegious and "unclean" to accept water from Asia Bibi, as a non-Muslim. Asia Bibi took offense, reportedly saying, "Are we not human?," which led to an argument.

The village women complained about their altercation to Qari Salim, the local cleric, and claimed that Asia Bibi had made derogatory remarks about the Prophet Muhammad. The cleric informed local police who arrested and charged her with insulting the Prophet, even though Asia Bibi denied the allegations and there was no independent corroboration of the events. The trial judge, Naveed Iqbal, "totally ruled out" the possibility of false charges and said that there were "no mitigating circumstances." Asia Bibi filed an appeal against the judgment in the Lahore High Court. She was detained in prison, held in isolation, and was not given access to a lawyer during her detention and the final day of her trial.[43]

Asia Bibi was a poor illiterate woman, who by most accounts committed no crime; she was simply a victim of Pakistan's culture of targeting non-Muslims for alleged blasphemy. PPP leaders, led by the Punjab governor Salman Taseer, called for compassion for Asia Bibi, arguing that the blasphemy laws were skewed against poor and helpless non-Muslims and were being widely abused. Taseer went to prison to console Asia Bibi in a widely publicized move aimed at exposing the injustice of blasphemy laws. He also called on President Zardari to use his constitutional power of pardons to set her free.

Taseer's defiance of the religious establishment resulted in fatwas against him, declaring him an infidel. As the PPP-appointed governor of a province where executive authority was wielded by the PML-N, Taseer's humanitarian campaign soon got embroiled in politics. The PML-N encouraged the Islamists' campaign against him, with some party leaders going to the extreme of saying that his call for changing blasphemy laws itself amounted to blasphemy. After instigation by mullahs and even otherwise modern news anchors on television, one of Taseer's bodyguards killed him in Islamabad on January 4, 2011. Several mullahs even refused to lead his funeral prayers on grounds that his stance against the blasphemy laws had made him an apostate.

The assassination of a powerful personality for daring to suggest changes in laws he deemed to be man-made signaled what might await anyone who questioned Pakistan's laws on blasphemy. Two months after Taseer's murder, the minorities affairs minister, Shahbaz Bhatti, was also killed. Pakistan's religious parties made Taseer's killer, Mumtaz Qadri, into a hero. When he was brought to court for trial, Islamist lawyers rushed to kiss him and threw flower petals on him in a gesture of admiration. When Taseer's killer was convicted, based on his admission of guilt, a former High Court Chief Justice offered to lead his defense to show solidarity with "a lover of the Prophet" who dared to kill "a blasphemer." The judge who convicted Qadri had to escape the country for fear of reprisals. The debate on the fairness or otherwise of the blasphemy laws had been effectively shut down.

Islamists have sought to purify Pakistan—the land of the pure—but in doing so have embraced bigotry and prejudice instead of invoking the nobler examples from Muslim history. They ignore the Quranic verse "There shall be no coercion in matters of faith" (2: 256), the generosity of Prophet Muhammad toward his non-Muslim adversaries after the conquest of Makkah in 629 A.D., and the insistence of Caliph Umar (ruled 634–644) that injustice is the greatest of sins under an Islamic ruler. Successive governments in Pakistan's sixty-seven-year history have appeased Islamists, failing consistently to protect both non-Muslims and minority-Muslim sects.

Pakistan's religious minorities have often been the target of religiously motivated attacks and persecution—these have risen in tandem with religious extremism in the country. Discrimination, harassment, and violence have been directed against all religious minorities, including Ahmadis, Christians, Shia Muslims, Sikhs, Hindus, Parsis, and Jains.

In its 2013 annual report, the United States Commission on International Religious Freedom described Pakistan's failure to protect its minorities as having reached "crisis proportions." According to the report, "The government of Pakistan continues to engage in and tolerate systematic, ongoing, and egregious violations of freedom of religion or belief." Violations reached unprecedented levels, it said, because of growing incidents of sectarian violence against Shia Muslims. The government also failed to protect Christians, Ahmadis, and Hindus, it said.[44]

In an overall climate of antagonism, Pakistan's blasphemy laws have exacerbated attacks on minorities by fostering religious frenzy, violence, and persecution. Police frequently fail to record and investigate complaints, and justice is impeded by the biased attitude of some judges against religious minorities.[45]

Pakistan's national discourse, aided by its school curriculum, generates religious prejudice against minorities. Although the country's founder, Muhammad Ali Jinnah, envisioned a secular Pakistan, over the years respect for the diversity of beliefs has eroded. Islamist groups have sought to purify Pakistan, which they deem to be the land of the pure. But history shows that these efforts at purification have only made Pakistan vulnerable to conflict, terrorism, and lawlessness.

The pursuit of religious purity is a goal that cannot be attained without widespread violence and chaos. Sectarian and religious wars in medieval Europe led rulers, clergy, and scholars to realize the futility of using force to demand religious conformity. The Muslim world has yet to reach that realization. From North Africa to Pakistan, the greater Middle East is currently embroiled in conflicts fueled by fanaticism. Shias and Sunnis are locked in sectarian wars in Iraq and Syria. Extremist groups such as ISIS in the Levant and Boko Haram in Nigeria are known for their inhumanity toward those who do not share their beliefs.

Enslavement and mass murder of Christians, Yazidis, and Shia Muslims by ISIS; destruction of ancient monuments and manuscripts from Syria to Mali; sectarian brutality in Lebanon and Egypt; and attacks on atheists and Hindus in Bangladesh are all symptoms of the same malaise. It is unlikely that Islamist extremists will ever succeed fully in their efforts for ethnic and cultural cleansing but they will continue to cause considerable suffering and dislocation for large numbers of people.

Just as Pakistan's non-Muslim population declined from 23 percent on the eve of Independence in 1947 to 3 percent today, non-Muslim communities in other Muslim-majority countries have also shrunk. Christians in the Arab Middle East, for example, constituted 20 percent of the population at the beginning of the twentieth century but that figure hovers around 5 percent today. Violence against religious minorities has forced mass migration but has failed to make Muslim societies better or even more pious.

The case of Pakistan demonstrates the failure of religious intolerance as an instrument of state policy. Instead of unifying the nation or making the state more effective, constant attacks on minorities have hindered Pakistan's progress and added to its insecurity. Instead of allowing bigotry to cloak itself in the garb of a state religion, Pakistan would advance better as a nonconfessional state, as imagined by Jinnah, its secular founder. That would require dismantling the constitutional, legal, and institutional mechanisms that have gradually excluded minorities from the mainstream of Pakistani life.

However, Pakistan remains engulfed in religious furies instead of cultivating humanistic passions—a process that shows no sign of abating in the immediate future. When Pakistan started its journey as a nation some seventy years ago, it was alone among majority-Muslim countries in describing itself as an Islamic state. Now, with calls for Islamization having become a regionwide trend, it is difficult to reverse course in the country that was the trendsetter. One ray of hope is the willingness of younger Pakistanis to question official narratives of history and wonder to where their parents' non-Muslim friends and neighbors have disappeared. It will not bring those neighbors back but might enable Pakistan to stop trying to purify itself further.

ACKNOWLEDGMENTS

Loss and the leaving of land are a part of the life of my family: Partition from India, the civil war that created Bangladesh and left Pakistan torn apart, and now the constant departure, death, and life as second-class citizens of the minority Muslim and non-Muslim populations of my country of birth. This book is dedicated to all those who love this land of Pakistan and yet are not seen as of it. The future must belong to all of us—equally. A pluralist Pakistan is the only way forward.

I am very grateful for the example of leadership from my grandfather Mirza Abol Hassan Ispahani and my grandmother Ghamar Azeemi Ispahani. They exemplified what should have been Pakistan's future and what still can be, both in the public, political sphere and in hands-on philanthropy and charitable work.

My maternal aunt Begum Salma Hashim Raza and maternal uncle Syed Hashim Raza were of the Partition generation as well. They brought with them the spirit of community, devoting their lives to the service of their new country and building roots for their future generations.

My elder sister, Dr. Mahnaz Ispahani, encouraged me onward from Wellesley College through the twists and turns of my life and career path. Her love, knowledge, and wisdom have always been with me. My younger sister, Laleh Ispahani, continues the family tradition of contributing to protecting human rights and strengthening democracy. I admire both my sisters greatly.

My brother, Mirza Iraj Ispahani, has seldom lived in proximity but has always been encouraging. My brothers-in-law, Adam Bartos, Hasan Haqqani, Mohsin Haqqani and Tapio Vaskio, have been constant friends.

My nieces, Nur Celeste Bartos, Ameneh Vaskio, Shaha Zehra Haqqani and Sofia Ispahani have given me nothing but love, as has my nephew Adam Ispahani. And for that I am very grateful.

During my journalistic career the late American broadcast journalists David Brinkley and Peter Jennings as well as Ted Koppel and Charlie Gibson showed me that TV news should be informative, insightful, and educational.

My life was transformed by my late leader, Pakistan's first woman prime minister, Benazir Bhutto. As the first woman prime minister in the Muslim world, Ms. Bhutto was a trailblazer and also a great supporter of other women. She asked me to join her team to work for the restoration of democracy in Pakistan during the military dictatorship of General Pervez Musharraf. I packed one suitcase and returned to Pakistan from a life of comfort in the United States.

Her assassination, and the assassinations of the late governor of Punjab Province, Salman Taseer, and my colleague in Parliament and Pakistan's first Christian federal minister, Shahbaz Bhatti, were the inspiration for this book.

My time in the presidency of Pakistan as a media adviser to President Asif Ali Zardari, co-chairman of the Pakistan Peoples Party, gave me firsthand knowledge of tragic attacks on Pakistan's religious minorities, like the Gojra massacre of Christians and the repeated attacks on Balochistan's Hazara Shias. My membership in the Human Rights Committee and Parliamentary Women's Caucus sharpened my worldview and my understanding of the human rights issues facing women and religious minorities in Pakistan.

I would also like to thank Jane Harman, the director, president, and CEO of the Woodrow Wilson International Center for Scholars, for giving me the time and space to write this book. Without the guidance and suggestions of Dr. Robert Hathaway, the former director of the Asia Program, and Dr. Haleh Esfandiari, the former director of the Middle East Program, this book may never have been completed. I would also like to thank Dr. Robert Litwak and Ambassador William Milam.

The many researchers who made this book possible include the librarians at the Woodrow Wilson Center. Led by Janet Spikes, the library team was a dream to work with. Hari Krishna Prasad, Devin Chavira, Leila Gharagozlou, and Amir Hashemian were also of great help. My Pakistan-based research team of Riaz Ali Toori, Ahsan Abbas Shah, and Napoleon Qayyum remained steadfast through good times and bad.

Dr. Aparna Pande and Nina Shea of the Hudson Institute in Washington, DC, were supportive throughout the process.

My most constant companion and guide is my husband, Husain Haqqani. A truer friend and adviser would have been hard to find. Our common purpose to improve the lives and find justice for the two hundred million citizens of Pakistan drives us in everything we do, say, and write.

His children, Huda and Hammad Haqqani, have also been a source of joy at important times in my life.

My editor at Oxford University Press, David McBride, has been encouraging and thoughtful. I could not have chosen or been chosen by a better publishing house for this book.

Thank you all so much.

NOTES

<hr/>

Introduction

1. "Mourning the Unthinkable," *Newsweek* (Pakistan), April 28, 2016.
2. Imran Gabol, "At Least 72 Killed in Suicide Blast as Terror Revisits Lahore," *Dawn*, March 29, 2016.
3. Kenneth Roth, "Twin Threats: How the Politics of Fear and the Crushing of Civil Society Imperil Global Rights," World Report 2016 (New York: Human Rights Watch, 2016), 1.
4. Universal Declaration of Human Rights, December 10, 1948, http://www.un.org/en/universal-declaration-human-rights/.
5. "ISIL May Have Committed Genocide, War Crimes in Iraq, Says UN Human Rights Report," United Nations News Center, March 19, 2015.
6. Aminu Abubaker and Josh Levs, " 'I Will Sell Them,' Boko Haram Leader Says of Kidnapped Nigerian Girls," CNN, May 6, 2014.
7. Jeffrey Goldberg, "Is It Time for Jews to Leave Europe," *Atlantic*, April 2015.
8. M. Zuhdi Jasser and Katrina Lantos Swett, "Russia Should Embrace Its Religious Diversity," *Moscow Times*, July 26, 2015.
9. Sarah Kaplan, "The Serene-looking Buddhist Monk Accused of Inciting Burma's Sectarian Violence," *Washington Post*, May 27, 2015.
10. Eleanor Albert, "Religion in China," Council on Foreign Relations Backgrounder, June 10, 2015.
11. "North Korea," Freedom House Country Report (New York: Freedom House, 2015).

12. "Human Rights Commission of Pakistan, Annual Report 2012" (Human Rights Commission of Pakistan, 2013), 1.

13. I. A. Rehman, "Feathers of a Pariah," *Dawn*, October 24, 2013.

14. M. A. Jinnah's speech, August 11, 1947, in Constituent Assembly of Pakistan Debates, vol. 1. (Karachi: Government Printing Press, 1948).

15. Asma Jahangir, "Pakistan's Tenets of the Faith," *New Statesman*, April 14, 2011.

Chapter 1

1. Note of confidential conversation at Dacca on May 25, 1950, between J. N. Mandal and T. V. Venkatraman, *The Hindu*, Calcutta correspondent, quoted in Durga Das (Ed.), *Sardar Patel's Correspondence, 1945–50*, vol. 10 (Ahmedabad: Navjivan Publishing House, 1972), 136–138.

2. Louis Fischer, *Mahatma Gandhi: His Life and Times* (London: Jonathan Cape, 1951), 130.

3. See P. K. Datta, "Dying Hindus: Production of Hindu Communal Common Sense in Early 20th Century Bengal," *Economic and Political Weekly* (June 19, 1993): 1303.

4. Gene R. Thursby, *Hindu–Muslim Relations in British India: A Study of Controversy, Conflict and Communal Movements in Northern India 1923–1928* (Leiden, Netherlands: Brill, 1975).

5. O. H. K. Spate, "Partition of India and Prospects for Pakistan," *Geographical Review* 38, no. 1 (January 1948): 5–29.

6. Kingsley Davis, "India and Pakistan: Demography of Partition," *Pacific Affairs* 22, no. 3 (September 1949): 254–264.

7. Ibid.

8. Ishtiaq Ahmed, *The Punjab: Bloodied, Partitioned and Cleansed, Unraveling the 1947 Tragedy through Secret British Reports and First Person Accounts* (Karachi: Oxford University Press, 2012), xxxiv–xxxv.

9. Ibid., xxxiv.

10. Ibid., xxxiv–xxxv.

11. Lionel Carter, *Punjab Politics 1 January 1944–3 March 1947: Last Days of the Ministries (Governor's Fortnightly Reports and other Key Documents)* (New Delhi: Manohar, 2006), 151. Cf. Ahmed, *Punjab*, 85.

12. Carter, *Punjab Politics*, 151.

13. Ahmed, *The Punjab*, 88.

14. Ibid., 88–89.

15. Ibid., 98.

16. Ibid., 131.

17. Ibid., 120–121.

18. Ibid., 128.

19. Ibid., 139.

20. Ibid., 156.

21. Ibid., 173.

22. Vazira Fazila-Yacoobali Zamindar, *The Long Partition and the Making of Modern South Asia: Refugees, Boundaries, Histories* (New York: Columbia University Press, 2010), 6.
23. Davis, "India and Pakistan," 254–264.
24. "Full Protection for Minorities in Pakistan," *Dawn*, July 14, 1947.
25. "Competitive Massacre," *Time*, September 8, 1947, 31.
26. Ian Talbott, "A Tale of Two Cities: The Aftermath of Partition for Lahore and Amritsar, 1947–57," *Modern Asian Studies* 41, no. 1 (January 2007): 15.
27. "Competitive Massacre," 31.
28. "Glass Houses in India," *New York Times*, October 22, 1947.
29. "A Second Letter to Mr. Gandhi," *Dawn*, July 20, 1947.
30. Constituent Assembly Debates (Legislature), March 2, 1948, 136.
31. Richard Symonds, "State-Making in Pakistan," *Far Eastern Survey* 19, no. 5 (March 1950): 47.
32. C. H. Phillips and Mary Doreen Wainwright (Eds.), *The Partition of India: Policies and Perspectives 1935–1947* (London: George Allen and Unwin, 1970), 388.
33. Mohammad Munir, *From Jinnah to Zia* (Lahore: Vanguard, 1980), 29.
34. S. M. Burke (Ed.), *Jinnah: Speeches and Statements 1947–48* (Karachi: Oxford University Press, 2000), 14.
35. President's address to Constituent Assembly of Pakistan, August 11, 1947, in G. Allana (Ed.), *Pakistan Movement Historic Documents* (University of Karachi, 1967), 407–411.
36. Ibid.
37. Ibid.
38. A. G. Noorani, "Jinnah's August 11, 1947 Speech," *Criterion Quarterly* 5, no. 2 (June 2012).
39. Note on Field Marshal Viscount Wavell's interview with Jinnah on January 5, 1946, in Nicholas Mansergh (Ed.), *The Transfer of Power 1942–7*, vol. 6 (London: Her Majesty's Stationery Office, 1976), 737.
40. "We Will Make Up for Lost Time," *Dawn*, May 30, 1948.
41. Ibid.
42. "Pakistan Should Be Established on Purely Islamic Concepts Says Ghulam Mohammad," *Dawn*, January 24, 1948.
43. Constituent Assembly Records (Legislature), March 6, 1948, 269.
44. Editorial, "Hindu Capital in Pakistan," *Dawn*, July 10, 1947.
45. Editorial, "Mr. Nehru Again," *Dawn*, June 1, 1949.
46. Constituent Assembly Records (Legislature), March 2, 1948, 136.
47. Ibid., 260.
48. Ibid., 261.
49. Ibid., 262–263.
50. Ibid.
51. Constituent Assembly Records (Legislature), December 16, 1948, 24.
52. Ibid., 222.

53. Constituent Assembly Records (Legislature), February 22, 1948, 114.
54. Ibid., III.
55. "The Objectives Resolution," *Islamic Studies* 48, no. 1 (Spring 2009): 91–119.
56. Constituent Assembly of Pakistan Debates, March 12, 1949, 2–5.
57. See Munir, *From Jinnah to Zia*.
58. Constituent Assembly of Pakistan, Debates, March 7–12, 1949, 7.
59. Maulana Maududi, *Towards Understanding Islam* (Lahore: Islamic Publications, 1960), 131.
60. Constituent Assembly of Pakistan Debates, vol. 5, 1949, p. 45.
61. Khalid bin Sayeed, "Religion and Nation Building in Pakistan," *Middle East Journal* 17, no. 2 (Summer 1963): 283–284.
62. " 'Pakistan Is Secular Democratic State' Ismail Assures Minorities," *Dawn*, January 27, 1949.
63. "Agreement between India and Pakistan on Minorities," *Middle East Journal* 4, no. 3 (July 1950): 344–346.

Chapter 2

1. "Letter from Ahmad Sai'd Nawab of Chatari to Liaquat Ali Khan," October 11, 1947, taken from Durga Das (Ed.), *Sardar Patel's Correspondence, 1945–50*, vol. 10 (Ahmedabad: Navjivan Publishing House, 1972), 56–57.
2. "Pakistan," *Time*, November 8, 1954.
3. Iftikhar Malik, "Relations between the Hindus and Muslims in the Subcontinent of India and Pakistan," *Civilizations* 5, no. 1 (1955): 51.
4. F. M. Innes, "The Political Outlook of Pakistan," *Pacific Affairs* 26, no. 4 (December 1953): 305–306.
5. Ibid.
6. "Membership for Ahmadiyyas," *Dawn*, May 4, 1944.
7. Lawrence Ziring, *Pakistan: At the Crosscurrent of History* (Oxford: Oneworld, 2003), 58–60.
8. Ibid.
9. Khalid bin Sayeed, "Religion and Nation Building in Pakistan," *Middle East Journal* 17, no. 2 (Summer 1963): 283–284.
10. Ibid.
11. Ziring, *Pakistan*, 58–60.
12. Ibid.
13. Herbert Feldman, *Revolution in Pakistan: A Study of the Martial Law Administration* (Karachi: Oxford University Press, 1965), 41–42.
14. Sayeed, "Religion and Nation Building in Pakistan," 283–284.
15. Ibid.
16. S. V. R. Nasr, "The Rise of Sunni Militancy in Pakistan: The Changing Role of Islamism and the Ulema in Society and Politics," *Modern Asian Studies* 34, no. 1 (February 2000): 173–176.

17. *Report of the Court of Inquiry Constituted under Punjab Act II of 1954 to Enquire into the Punjab Disturbances of 1953* (Lahore: Government Printing Press, 1953).

18. Ibid.

19. Feldman, *Revolution in Pakistan*, 41–42.

20. Ibid.

21. Ibid.

22. "Report of the Court of Inquiry constituted under Punjab Act II of 1954 to enquire into the Punjab disturbances of 1953" (Lahore, Government Printing Press Punjab, 1954).

23. Ibid.

24. Ibid.

25. Feldman, *Revolution in Pakistan*, 41–42.

26. G. W. Choudhury, *Documents and Speeches on the Constitution of Pakistan* (Dacca: Green Book House, 1967).

27. Constitution of Pakistan, 1956, Article 198.

28. Huseyn Shaheed Suhrawardy, "Political Stability and Democracy in Pakistan," *Foreign Affairs* (April 1957): 426.

29. Mohammed Ayub Khan, "Pakistan Perspective," *Foreign Affairs* 38, no. 4 (July 1960): 549.

30. Ayub Khan, *Friends Not Masters: A Political Autobiography* (Karachi: Oxford University Press, 1967), 196–197.

31. Khalid bin Sayeed, "Pakistan's Constitutional Autocracy," *Pacific Affairs* 36, no. 4 (Winter 1963–1964).

32. Ibid., 368.

33. Ibid., 369.

34. Javid Iqbal, *The Ideology of Pakistan and Its Implementation*, xi–xii. Cited in S. M. Burke, *Pakistan's Foreign Policy: An Historical Analysis* (Minneapolis: University of Minnesota Press, 1971), 93.

35. Khan, *Friends Not Masters*, 172.

36. Ibid., 187.

37. Herbert Feldman, "The Communal Problem in the Indo-Pakistan Subcontinent: Some Current Implications," *Pacific Affairs* 42, no. 2 (Summer 1969): 157.

38. Feldman, *Revolution in Pakistan*, 213–214.

39. Editorial, *Dawn*, December 20, 1961.

40. Sayeed, "Religion and Nation Building in Pakistan," 287.

Chapter 3

1. Ayub Khan, *Friends Not Masters: A Political Autobiography* (Karachi: Oxford University Press, 1967), 200.

2. P. Sharan, "Islamic State and Pakistan," *Indian Journal of Political Science* 29, no. 2 (April–June 1968): 127–134.

3. Ali Usman Qasmi, "God's Kingdom on Earth? Politics of Islam in Pakistan, 1947–69," *Modern Asian Studies* 44, no. 6 (November 2010): 1228–1229.
4. Sharan, "Islamic State and Pakistan."
5. Qasmi, "God's Kingdom on Earth?," 1236–1237.
6. "Betrayal of Asia," *Dawn*, October 20, 1962.
7. "Nehru Prefers War," *Dawn*, October 27, 1962.
8. "Pakistan and Mr. Nehru's War," *Dawn*, October 31, 1962.
9. "The Peril Is Ours Not India's," *Dawn*, November 8, 1962.
10. Herbert Feldman, "The Communal Problem in the Indo-Pakistan Subcontinent: Some Current Implications," *Pacific Affairs* 42, no. 2 (Summer 1969): 148.
11. Tathagata Roy, *A Suppressed Chapter in History: The Exodus of Hindus from East Pakistan and Bangladesh 1947–2006* (Delhi: Bookwell, 2007), 271–274.
12. Ibid.
13. Lawrence Ziring, *The Ayub Khan Era: Politics in Pakistan, 1958–69* (Syracuse, NY: Syracuse University Press, 1971), 54–55.
14. Husain Haqqani, *Pakistan: Between Mosque and Military* (Washington, DC: Carnegie Endowment for International Peace, 2005), 54.
15. Text of President Ayub Khan's address to the nation, September 6, 1965, in Rais Ahmad Jafri (Ed.), *Ayub—Soldier and Statesman* (Lahore: Mohammad Ali Academy, 1966), 138–139.
16. Haqqani, *Pakistan: Between Mosque and Military*, 55.
17. A. R. Siddiqui, *The Military in Pakistan: Image and Reality* (Lahore: Vanguard, 1996), 107.
18. Khalid bin Sayeed, "1965—An Epoch Making Year in Pakistan—General Elections and War with India," *Asian Survey* 6, no. 2 (February 1966): 83.
19. Ziring, *Ayub Khan Era*, 68–69.
20. Herbert Feldman, *The End and the Beginning: Pakistan, 1969–71* (Karachi: Oxford University Press, 1974), 39–40.
21. Ibid.
22. Ibid.
23. Excerpts from public speech at Mansehra, April 20, 1970, http://www.bhutto.org/1970-1971_speech9.php, accessed September 26, 2015.
24. Haqqani, *Pakistan: Between Mosque and Military*, 58–60.
25. Craig Baxter, "Pakistan Votes—1970," *Asian Survey* 11, no. 3 (March 1971): 216.
26. Altaf Hasan Qureshee, *6 Nukaat ki Sachi Tasveer* (Lahore: Maktaba Urdu Digest, 1969), 101.
27. Ibid.
28. See Major General Farman Ali Khan, *How Pakistan Got Divided* (Lahore: Jang, 1992); Lieutenant General A. A. K. Niazi, *The Betrayal of East Pakistan* (Karachi: Oxford University Press, 1998); and Hassan Zaheer, *The Separation of East Pakistan* (Karachi: Oxford University Press, 1994).

29. Baxter, "Pakistan Votes—1970," 216.
30. Feldman, *End and the Beginning*, 90–91.
31. Ibid.
32. Ibid., 132.
33. Ibid.
34. See, for example, Major General (Retd.) Khadim Hussain Raja, *Stranger in My Own Country: East Pakistan 1969–1971* (Karachi: Oxford University Press, 2012).
35. Lawrence Ziring, *Pakistan: At the Crosscurrent of History* (Oxford: Oneworld, 2003), 120.
36. Ibid., 124.
37. Feldman, *End and the Beginning*, 134.
38. Sydney Schanberg, "Hindus Are Targets of Army Terror in an East Pakistani Town," *New York Times*, June 29, 1971.
39. Robert La Porte Jr, "Pakistan in 1971: The Disintegration of a Nation," *Asian Survey* 12, no. 2 (February 1972): 103.
40. Feldman, *End and the Beginning*, 142.

Chapter 4

1. Malcolm Browne, "Bhutto a Whirlwind on Mission to Restore a Shattered Pakistan," *New York Times*, January 19, 1972.
2. Speech delivered by Zulfikar Ali Bhutto, the foreign minister of Pakistan, to the Pakistan Islamic Council for International Affairs, Karachi, June 13, 1965, http://www.bhutto.org/1957-1965_speech19.php, accessed September 26, 2015.
3. Excerpts from public speech at Mansehra, April 20, 1970, http://www.bhutto.org/1970-1971_speech9.php, accessed September 26, 2015.
4. Herbert Feldman, *The End and the Beginning: Pakistan, 1969–71* (Karachi: Oxford University Press, 1974), 39–40.
5. Akhtar Hasan Khan, Census commissioner, "Population Census of Pakistan 1972: Statistical Report of Pakistan, Population Census Organization, Statistics Division, Government of Pakistan, Islamabad," 1, 20.
6. Malcolm Browne, "The People Went to Mosques to Pray and Weep: India-Pakistan," *New York Times*, December 19, 1971.
7. Lawrence Ziring, *Pakistan: At the Crosscurrent of History* (Oxford: Oneworld, 2003), 131.
8. Feldman, *End and the Beginning*, 39–40.
9. Rafi Raza, *Zulfikar Ali Bhutto and Pakistan, 1967–1977* (Karachi: Oxford University Press, 1997), 182.
10. 1973 Constitution of Pakistan, http://www.pakistani.org/pakistan/constitution/.
11. Raza, *Zulfikar Ali Bhutto and Pakistan*, 216–217.
12. Ibid., 549.

13. Waheed-uz-Zaman's editor's note in "The Quest for Identity" (proceedings of the First Congress on the history and culture of Pakistan held at the University of Islamabad, April 1973), p. iv, cited in William Richter, "The Political Dynamics of Islamic Resurgence in Pakistan," *Asian Survey* 19, no. 6 (June 1979): 551.

14. Interview of Zulfikar Ali Bhutto by Imtiaz Ahmad, managing editor of *Asia Observer*, London, at Larkana, December 24, 1975, http://www.bhutto.org/interview31.php, accessed September 26, 2015.

15. Mubashir Hasan, "The Mirage of Power: An Inquiry into the Bhutto Years 1971-77" (Karachi: Oxford University Press, 2000), 256.

16. "Students Clash at Rabwah Station: 24 Held," *Dawn*, May 20, 1974.

17. Charles H. Kennedy, "Towards the Definition of a Muslim in a Islamic State: The Case of the Ahmadiyya in Pakistan," in Dhirendra Vajpey (Ed.), *Religious and Ethnic Minority Politics in South Asia* (New Delhi: Manohar, 1989), 90.

18. Herbert Feldman, "Pakistan in 1974," *Asian Survey* 15, no. 2 (February 1975): 110.

19. Raza, *Zulfikar Ali Bhutto and Pakistan*, 293–296.

20. "Bhutto Urges Opposition Not to Incite Emotions and Endanger Country," *Dawn*, June 3, 1974.

21. "Declare Qadianis a Minority: NWFP Assembly Resolution," *Dawn*, June 19, 1974.

22. "PM Bhutto Interview," *Dawn*, July 12, 1974.

23. "Qadianis Declared Minority: Preaching against Finality of Prophethood by a Muslim Made Punishable," *Dawn*, September 7, 1974.

24. "Issue Suppressed by Past Regimes Now Solved Well: Maududi," *Dawn*, September 7, 1974.

25. 1973 Constitution of Pakistan, http://www.pakistani.org/pakistan/constitution/.

26. "Decision Reflects Will of Muslims of Pakistan: PM," *Dawn*, September 7, 1974.

27. Ibid.

28. "Issue Suppressed by Past Regimes Now Solved Well."

29. Ibid.

30. Husain Haqqani, *Pakistan: Between Mosque and Military* (Washington, DC: Carnegie Endowment for International Peace, 2005), 107.

31. Raza, *Zulfikar Ali Bhutto and Pakistan*, 293–296.

32. Ibid.

33. Ibid.

34. Lewis Simmons, "Sect Fears for Its Future: Pakistan Rules Ahmadis Are 'Non-Moslems,'" *Washington Post*, September 23, 1974.

35. Raza, *Zulfikar Ali Bhutto and Pakistan*, 293–296.

36. Anwar Syed, "Pakistan in 1976: Business as Usual," *Asian Survey* 17, no. 2 (February 1977): 184.

37. Shahid Javed Burki, *Pakistan under Bhutto* (New York: St. Martin's, 1980), 195.
38. M. G. Weinbaum, "The March 1977 Elections in Pakistan: Where Everyone Lost," *Asian Survey* 17, no. 7 (July 1977): 600.
39. Ibid., 612–614.
40. Ian Talbot, *Pakistan—A Modern History* (New York: St. Martin's, 1998), 241.
41. Ziring, *Pakistan*, 158.
42. Cited in Husain Haqqani, *Pakistan: Between Mosque and Military*, 122.
43. Ibid., 122–127.
44. Gen. Faiz Ali Chishti (Retd.), *Betrayals of Another Kind: Islam, Democracy and the Army in Pakistan* (Cincinnati, OH: Asia Publishing House, 1990), 31.

Chapter 5

1. Text of General Zia-ul-Haq's address to the nation on July 5, 1977, in Hasan Askari Rizvi, *The Military and Politics in Pakistan 1947–86* (Lahore: Progressive, 1986), 289–293.
2. Husain Haqqani, *Pakistan: Between Mosque and Military* (Washington, DC: Carnegie Endowment for International Peace, 2005), 126–128.
3. Text of General Zia-ul-Haq's address to the nation on July 5, 1977, in Rizvi, *Military and Politics in Pakistan*, 289–293.
4. "Text of Gen. Zia's Address to the Nation," *Dawn*, July 28, 1977.
5. "Text of President's Address to the Nation," *Dawn*, August 16, 1977.
6. "General Mohammad Zia-ul-Haq Meets the Press, September 1, 1977, Rawalpindi" (Islamabad: Ministry of Information Directorate of Publications, 1977), 4–5.
7. "Minorities' Rights to Be Protected: Gen Zia's Assurance to Christians," *Dawn*, September 26, 1977.
8. W. Eric Gustafson and William Richter, "Pakistan in 1980: Weathering the Storm," *Asian Survey* 21, no. 2 (February 1981): 166–168.
9. Lawrence Ziring, *Pakistan in the Twentieth Century: A Political History* (Karachi: Oxford University Press, 1999), 449.
10. Ibid.
11. W. Eric Gustafson, "Pakistan 1978: At the Brink Again?" *Asian Survey* 19, no. 2 (February 1979): 159–162.
12. Ibid.
13. Ibid.
14. Ibid.
15. Trevor Fishlock, "Moves to Entrench Islam in Pakistan Face Tough Hurdles," *Times of London*, September 22, 1980.
16. Address by the president of Pakistan, General Mohammad Zia-ul-Haq, to the nation, December 2, 1978, published in *Pakistan Horizon*, 32, nos. 1–2 (First and Second Quarters 1979): 277–280.

17. Address of Zia on the introduction of Nizam-e-Islam in Pakistan, reproduced from *Dawn*, February 12, 1979 (English rendering of speech in Urdu), published in *Pakistan Horizon*, 32, nos. 1–2 (First and Second Quarters 1979): 288–290.

18. Ayesha Jalal, *The Struggle for Pakistan: Muslim Homeland and Global Politics* (Cambridge, MA: Belknap Press, 2014), 222–224.

19. William Richter and W. Eric Gustafson, "Pakistan 1979: Back to Square One," *Asian Survey* 20, no. 2 (February 1980): 191–192.

20. Karen Parker, *Human Rights in Pakistan* (New York: Human Rights Advocate Inc., January 1987), 13–14.

21. Ibid.

22. Ibid.

23. Stuart Auerbach, "Pakistan Moves towards Islamic Authoritarianism," *Washington Post*, October 21, 1979.

24. Ziring, *Pakistan in the Twentieth Century*, 462–470.

25. S. V. R. Nasr, "The Rise of Sunni Militancy in Pakistan: The Changing Role of Islamism and the Ulema in Society and Politics," *Modern Asian Studies* 34, no. 1 (February 2000): 155–157.

26. W. Eric Gustafson and William Richter, "Pakistan in 1980: Weathering the Storm," *Asian Survey* 21, no. 2 (February 1981): 166–168.

27. Nasr, "Rise of Sunni Militancy in Pakistan," 155–157.

28. Michael T. Kaufman, "Pakistan's Islamic Revival Affects All Aspects of Life," *New York Times*, October 13, 1980.

29. Frank J. Prial, "As Pakistan 'Islamizes' Feminists Rise Up in Anger," *New York Times*, November 8, 1980.

30. Eqbal Ahmad, "Zia Is No Spokesman," *New York Times*, October 1, 1980.

31. "Country Reports on Human Rights Practices for 1980: Report Submitted to the Committee on Foreign Relations US Senate and Committee on Foreign Affairs, US House of Representatives by the Department of StateIn Accordance with Sections 116(d) and 502B(b) of the Foreign Assistance Act of 1961, as Amended" (Washington, DC: US Department of State, US Government Printing Office, 1981), 1074.

32. Ibid., 1078.

33. Stephen P. Cohen, *Idea of Pakistan* (Washington, DC: Brookings Press, 2004), 171.

34. Ibid.

35. A. H. Nayyar and Ahmed Salim (Eds.), *The Subtle Subversion: The State of Curricula and Textbooks in Pakistan* (Islamabad: Sustainable Development Policy Institute, 2005), 1.

36. Ibid., vi.

37. Ibid.

38. Ibid., v.

39. Ibid.

40. Ibid., vi.

41. Ibid., 11–12.
42. Ibid., 21.
43. Ibid.
44. Michael T. Kaufman, "Pakistan Has a Conflict between Science and Islam," *New York Times*, February 21, 1982.
45. David E. Sanger, "Obama's Worst Pakistan Nightmare," *New York Times*, January 8, 2009.
46. "Pakistan 1981 Census Report" (Islamabad: Statistics Division Government of Pakistan, 1981).
47. William K. Stevens, "In Pakistan, Islam Leaves Little Room for Freedom," *New York Times*, August 28, 1983.
48. Ibid.
49. Zia's address to the Majlis-i-Shura on August 12, 1983, cited in Khalid bin Sayeed, "Pakistan in 1983: Internal Stresses More Serious Than External Problems," *Asian Survey* 24, no. 2 (February 1984): 219.
50. Sayeed, "Pakistan in 1983," 220.
51. Surendra Nath Kaushik, *Politics of Islamization in Pakistan: A Study of Zia Regime* (New Delhi: South Asian Publishers, 1993), 72–74.
52. Nasr, "Rise of Sunni Militancy in Pakistan," 160–161.
53. Ibid.
54. Ibid., 165–169.
55. Khaled Ahmed, *Sectarian War: Pakistan's Sunni-Shia Violence and Its Links to the Middle East* (Karachi: Oxford University Press, 2012), 32–38.
56. Ibid.
57. "Country Reports on Human Rights Practices for 1983," 1391.
58. Ibid.
59. Eamon Murphy, *The Making of Terrorism in Pakistan: Historical and Social Roots of Extremism* (New York: Routledge, 2012), 133.
60. Ibid.
61. Ahmed, *Sectarian War*, 85.
62. Ordinance XX of April 26, 1984, in Kaushik, *Politics of Islamization in Pakistan*, 135–140.
63. Ibid.
64. "Pakistan: Human Rights after Martial Law, Chapter VIII: Rights of Religious and Other Minorities," International Commission of Jurists' 1987 report, Geneva, 98–105.
65. Ibid.
66. Parker, *Human Rights in Pakistan*, 16–30.
67. "Pakistan: Human Rights after Martial Law," 98–105.
68. Ibid.
69. Ibid.
70. Parker, *Human Rights in Pakistan*, 16–30.
71. Ibid.
72. Ibid.

73. Ibid.
74. General Zia ul Haq public speech, December 7, 1984.
75. Parker, *Human Rights in Pakistan*, 16–30.
76. "Country Reports on Human Rights Practices for 1983," 1357–1358.
77. "Pakistan: Human Rights after Martial Law," 98–105.
78. "Country Reports on Human Rights Practices for 1983," 1275.
79. Ibid.
80. *Al Mushir* 26, no. 1 (1984): 173, cited in Ian Talbott, *Pakistan: A Modern History* (New York: St. Martin's, 1998), 282.
81. Talbott, *Pakistan*, 282–283.
82. Pakistan Penal Code: Act XLV of 1860, as amended from time to time.
83. Parker, *Human Rights in Pakistan*, 16–30.

Chapter 6

1. "Protest against Book: Five Killed in Islamabad Police Firing," *Dawn*, February 12, 1989.
2. *Benazir Bhutto: The Way Out: Interviews, Impressions, Statements and Messages* (Karachi: Mahmood, 1988), 98, cited in Anita Weiss, "Benazir Bhutto and Future of Women in Pakistan," *Asian Survey* 30, no. 5 (May 1990): 436.
3. Charles Kennedy, "Islamization and Legal Reform in Pakistan, 1979–89," *Pacific Affairs* 63, no. 1 (1990): 76.
4. Barbara Crossette, "Attack on US Site in Pakistan Growing into Crisis for Bhutto," *New York Times*, February 13, 1989.
5. Ibid.
6. "Pakistan: Violation of Human Rights of Ahmadis" (London: Amnesty International, September 1991).
7. Barbara Crossette, "Bhutto Must Now Confront Foes on Volatile Issue of Religion," *New York Times*, August 3, 1990.
8. Ibid.
9. "Minorities Urge NA, PA Seats," *Dawn*, August 31, 1990.
10. Barbara Crossette, "Pakistan's Minorities Face Voting Restrictions," *New York Times*, October 23, 1990.
11. Barbara Crossette, "In Pakistan, War Stirs Emotions and Politics," *New York Times*, February 1, 1991.
12. Rais Khan, "Pakistan in 1991: Lights and Shadow," *Asian Survey* 32, no. 2 (February 1992): 199.
13. Rais Khan, "Pakistan in 1992: Waiting for Change," *Asian Survey* 33, no. 2 (February 1993): 130–131.
14. "Pakistan: Blasphemy Charges against Ahmadis" (London: Amnesty International, April 1994).
15. Ibid.
16. "Pakistan: Violation of Human Rights of Ahmadis."
17. Ibid.

18. Khan, "Pakistan in 1992," 132.

19. Ibid.

20. Lawrence Ziring, *Pakistan: At the Crosscurrent of History* (Oxford: Oneworld, 2003), 235.

21. "Pakistan: Political Killing/Fear for Safety" (London: Amnesty International, April 6, 1994).

22. Paul Marshall and Nina Shea, *Silenced: How Apostasy and Blasphemy Codes Are Choking Freedom Worldwide* (New York: Oxford University Press, 2011), 88.

23. "Pakistan: Use and Abuse of the Blasphemy Laws" (London: Amnesty International, July 1994).

24. Ibid.

25. Ahmed Rashid, "The Taliban: Exporting Extremism," *Foreign Affairs* (November–December 1999).

26. Ibid.

27. Tahir Amin, "Pakistan in 1994: The Politics of Confrontation," *Asian Survey* 35, no. 2 (February 1995): 143–144.

28. Robert LaPorte Jr., "Pakistan in 1995: The Continuing Crises," *Asian Survey* 36, no. 2 (February 1996): 184–185.

29. Rashid, "Taliban."

30. S. V. R. Nasr, "The Rise of Sunni Militancy in Pakistan: The Changing Role of Islamism and the Ulema in Society and Politics," *Modern Asian Studies* 34, no. 1 (February 2000): 143.

31. Khaled Ahmed, *Sectarian War: Pakistan's Sunni–Shia Violence and Its Links to the Middle East* (Karachi: Oxford University Press, 2012), 133.

32. Benazir Bhutto, *Daughter of the East: An Autobiography* (London: Simon and Schuster, 2007), 416–418.

33. Nasr, "Rise of Sunni Militancy in Pakistan," 140–141.

34. "7 Die in City Violence," *Dawn*, February 24, 1995.

35. "Blast Kills 12 Outside Malir Mosque," *Dawn*, March 10, 1995.

36. "Pakistan: Another Ahmadi Deliberately Killed by Islamists" (London: Amnesty International, April 18, 1995).

37. Cited in LaPorte Jr., "Pakistan in 1995," 185.

38. Nasr, "Rise of Sunni Militancy in Pakistan," 140–141.

39. Ibid.

40. Marshall and Shea, *Silenced*, 93.

41. "Bill Tabled in NA: Quran and Sunnat Declared Supreme Law," *Dawn*, August 28, 1998.

42. "HRCP Criticizes Bill," *Dawn*, August 28, 1998.

43. "Bill Tabled in NA."

44. Ibid.

45. Barry Bearak, "After Dispute in Pakistan, Leader Leaves for US Visit," *New York Times*, September 20, 1998.

46. Ziring, *Pakistan*, 247.

47. Hasan-Askari Rizvi, "Pakistan in 1998: The Polity under Pressure," *Asian Survey* 39, no. 2 (February 1999): 179–180.

48. "Peace to Be Maintained during Muharram," Associated Press of Pakistan, *Business Recorder*, April 18, 1998.

49. Anwar H. Syed, "Pakistan in 1997: Nawaz Sharif's Second Chance to Govern," *Asian Survey* 38, no. 2 (February 1998): 120.

50. Nasr, "Rise of Sunni Militancy in Pakistan," 140–141.

51. "Pakistan: Persecution of Ahmadis Continues" (London: Amnesty International, July 24, 1997).

52. Ibid.

53. Rizvi, "Pakistan in 1998," 179–180.

54. Ziring, *Pakistan*, 247.

55. Ibid.

Chapter 7

1. "Text of the COAS Speech," *Dawn*, October 12, 1999.

2. "Text of Musharraf Speech," *Dawn*, October 17, 1999.

3. "Church Expects Musharraf to Honor Promises to Religious Minorities," February 24, 2000, http://www.ucanews.com/story-archive/?post_name=/2000/02/24/church-expects-musharraf-to-honor-promises-to-religious-minorities&post_id=15486, accessed September 26, 2015.

4. "I Want a True Democracy," Musharraf interview in *Time*, November 24, 1999.

5. Iftikhar A. Malik, "Pakistan in 2000: Starting Anew or Stalemate," *Asian Survey* 41, no. 2 (February 2001): 111.

6. "Pakistan: Insufficient Protection of Religious Minorities" (London: Amnesty International, May 2001).

7. "Pakistan: Ahmadiya Community: Fear for Safety" (London: Amnesty International, November 14, 2000).

8. Paul Marshall and Nina Shea, *Silenced: How Apostasy and Blasphemy Codes Are Choking Freedom Worldwide* (New York: Oxford University Press, 2011), 86.

9. Ibid., 95–96.

10. "Pakistan: Blasphemy Laws Should Be Abolished" (London: Amnesty International, August 21, 2001).

11. Khaled Ahmed, *Sectarian War: Pakistan's Sunni-Shia Violence and Its Links to the Middle East* (Karachi: Oxford University Press, 2012), 136.

12. "General Musharraf Says He Can Keep a Lid on Protests," BBC News, October 8, 2001.

13. Faraz Hashmi, "Musharraf's Speech Gets Mixed Reaction," *Dawn*, January 12, 2002.

14. Jon Boone, "Musharraf: Pakistan and India's Backing for 'Proxies' in Afghanistan Must Stop," *Guardian*, February 13, 2015, http://www.theguardian.com/world/2015/feb/13/pervez-musharraf-pakistan-india-proxies-afghanistan-ghani-taliban, accessed September 26, 2015.

15. Iktikhar A. Malik, "Pakistan in 2001: The Afghanistan Crisis and the Rediscovery of the Frontline State," *Asian Survey* 42, no. 1 (February 2002): 207–208.

16. Pervez Musharraf, *In the Line of Fire: A Memoir* (New York: Free Press, 2008), 203.

17. "Bahawalpur Carnage Leaves 16 Dead,' *Dawn*, October 28, 2001.

18. Ali Chisthi, "Madrassa Menace," *Friday Times*, January 21–27, 2011, www.thefridaytimes.com/21012011/page4.shtml.

19. Ahmed, *Sectarian War*, 128.

20. "Villager Stoned to Death on Imam's Call," *Dawn*, July 5, 2002.

21. "Man 'Declared Infidel' Killed by Mob," *Dawn*, April 20, 2005.

22. "Pakistan: Under-trial Prisoner Killed Following Fabricated Blasphemy Charges Having Been Laid against Him" (Hong Kong: Asian Human Rights Commission, June 21, 2006).

23. Marshall and Shea, *Silenced*, 90.

24. Ibid.

25. Ibid.

26. "Shias Killed in Pakistan Since 2001," South Asia Terrorism Portal, http://www.satp.org/satporgtp/countries/pakistan/database/Shias_killed_Pakistan.htm, accessed September 26, 2015.

27. Husain Haqqani, "Bhutto's Legacy," *Wall Street Journal*, December 28, 2007.

28. Ibid.

29. Abdul Qadoos, "31 Killed in Suicide Attack at Dera Ismail Khan Funeral," *Business Recorder* (Pakistan), February 21, 2009.

30. "26 Injured in Karachi Blast near Muharram Procession," *Daily Times* (Pakistan), December 27, 2009.

31. Riaz Khan, "After Twin Suicide Bombs Kill 42 at a Sufi Shrine, Some Pakistanis Blame United States," Associated Press, July 1, 2010.

32. Ali Syed, "Suicide Attack in Quetta Kills 55," *Express Tribune*, September 3, 2010.

33. Nauman Tasleem, "Death Toll from Lahore Attacks Rises to 35," *Express Tribune*, September 2, 2010.

34. "Failure to Protect Shi'a Muslims in Pakistan Leaves Many at Risk," Amnesty press release, September 21, 2011, http://www.amnesty.org/en/news-and-updates/failure-protect-shia-muslims-pakistan-leaves-many-risk-2011-09-21, accessed September 26, 2015.

35. "Shias Killed in Pakistan Since 2001."

36. "Shia Pilgrims' Killing Exposes State's Criminal Negligence," Human Rights Commission of Pakistan, June 29, 2012, http://hrcp-web.org/hrcpweb/shia-pilgrims-killing-exposes-states-criminal-negligence/, accessed September 26, 2015.

37. "HRCP Outrage at Minorities Flight," Human Rights Commission of Pakistan, August 10, 2012, http://hrcp-web.org/hrcpweb/hrcps-outrage-at-minorities-flight/, accessed September 26, 2015.

38. Rana Tanveer and Abdul Manan, "Over 88 Killed in Twin Gun and Bomb Attacks," *Express Tribune*, May 29, 2010.
39. Waqar Gillani and Jane Perlez, "Attackers Hit Mosques of Islamic Sect in Pakistan," *New York Times*, May 28, 2010.
40. Marshall and Shea, *Silenced*, 94.
41. Ibid.
42. Ibid.
43. "Pakistani Christian Woman Sentenced to Death" (London: Amnesty International, November 18, 2010).
44. "US Report Warns of Crisis for Pakistan's Minorities," *Express Tribune*, May 1, 2013.
45. Ibid.

ABOUT THE AUTHOR

Farahnaz Ispahani has been a leading voice for women and religious minorities in Pakistan for the past twenty-five years, first as a journalist, then as a member of Pakistan's National Assembly, and most recently as a scholar based in the United States. As advocate of Pakistan's return to democracy during the military regime of Pervez Musharraf, she served as a spokesperson and international media coordinator for the Pakistan Peoples Party, working alongside the late Benazir Bhutto. During her tenure in Parliament (2008–2012), she was a member of the Foreign Affairs and Human Rights Committees and of the Women's Parliamentary Caucus. In 2013–2014, she served as a Public Policy Scholar at the Woodrow Wilson International Center for Scholars. In 2012, she was listed among *Foreign Policy* magazine's Top 100 Global Thinkers, as well as *Newsweek* Pakistan's Top 100 Women Who Matter.

INDEX